Studies in Judaism

D1160759

STUDIES IN JUDAISM

ESSAYS ON PERSONS, CONCEPTS,
AND MOVEMENTS OF THOUGHT
IN JEWISH TRADITION

by SOLOMON SCHECHTER

A TEMPLE BOOK

ATHENEUM, NEW YORK, 1970

Published by Atheneum
Reprinted by arrangement with
The Jewish Publication Society of America
Copyright © 1958 by
The Jewish Publication Society of America
Studies in Judaism: First Series was reprinted in 1945
Studies in Judaism: Second Series copyright by
The Jewish Publication Society of America 1908
All rights reserved
Library of Congress catalog card number 58-11934
Manufactured in the United States of America by
The Murray Printing Company,
Forge Village, Massachusetts
Published in Canada by McClelland and Stewart Ltd.
First Atheneum Edition

PREFATORY NOTE

The essays presented in this volume do not presume to be a comprehensive survey of the range and interests of their author. They are, the publishers believe, among the most suggestive and enduring of the studies contained in the three volumes of Dr. Schechter's *Studies in Judaism*. The reader is referred, however, to the complete volumes published by The Jewish Publication Society of America.

"The History of Jewish Tradition," "The Dogmas of Judaism," "The Doctrine of Divine Retribution in Rabbinical Literature," "The Chassidim," "Nachmanides," "Rabbi Elijah Wilna, Gaon," and "Nachman Krochmal and the 'Perplexities of the Time'," are drawn from *Studies in Judaism: First Series*. "On the Study of the Talmud," "Saints and Saintliness," and "Safed in the Sixteenth Century" are drawn from *Studies in Judaism: Second Series*. None of the essays from *Studies in Judaism: Third Series*, published after their author's death, have been included.

All of the footnotes to the essays included in this volume are retained; however the appendices to "Safed" have been omitted. In all cases the author's spelling of Hebrew names and terms has been retained, although many of his spellings have been modified in the subsequent literature.

THE JEWISH PUBLICATION SOCIETY OF AMERICA

Solomon Schechter

Solomon Schechter, one of the most penetrating and influential Jewish thinkers of modern times, was born in Romania in 1849. After receiving a traditional Jewish education in Romania and Poland, he continued his Jewish studies at Vienna under three outstanding teachers, Isaac Hirsch Weiss, Meir Friedmann and Adolph Jellinek. At the importuning of Claude Montefiore, Schechter came to England in 1882 and was University Lecturer, and afterwards Reader, in Talmudics at Cambridge University from 1890-1902. The major scholarly discovery of his career was his rediscovery and manuscript identification of fragments found in the Cairo Genizah. In 1901 Schechter was invited to become the President of the Jewish Theological Seminary of America in New York. He accepted and formally assumed his office in 1902. More than any other figure of modern American Judaism the Conservative Movement in American Judaism is the extension and figuration of his basic conception of Judaism. Among his works are: *Some Aspects of Rabbinic Theology, Documents of Jewish Sectaries,* and the three volumes of *Studies in Judaism* from which the present volume is drawn. Solomon Schechter died on November 20, 1915 on the eve of Sabbath.

CONTENTS

INTRODUCTION to *Studies in Judaism: First Series*

THE essays published in this volume under the title of *Studies in Judaism* have been written on various occasions and at long intervals. There is thus no necessary connection between them. If some sort of unity may be detected in the book, it can only be between the first three essays—on the Chassidim, Krochmal, and the Gaon—in which there is a certain unity of purpose. The purpose in view was, as may easily be gathered from the essays themselves, to bring under the notice of the English public a type of men produced by the Synagogue of the Eastern Jews. That Synagogue is widely different from ours. Its places of worship have no claims to "beauty of holiness," being in their outward appearance rather bare and bald, if not repulsive; whilst whose who frequent them are a noisy, excitable people, who actually dance on the "Season of Rejoicing" and cry bitterly on the "Days of Mourning." But among all these vagaries—or perhaps because of them—this Synagogue has had its moments of grace, when enthusiasm wedded to inspiration gave birth to such beautiful souls as Baalshem, such fine sceptics as Krochmal, and such saintly scholars as Elijah Wilna. The Synagogue of the West is certainly of a more presentable character, and free from excesses; though it is not devoid of an enthusiasm of its own which finds its outlet in an ardent and self-sacrificing philanthropic activity. But owing to its practical tendency there is too little room in it for that play of intellectual forces which finds its extravagant expression in the saint on the one hand, and the learned heretic on the other.

These essays are more or less of a theological nature. But in reading the proofs I have been struck by the fact that there is assumed in them a certain conception of the Synagogue which, familiar though it be to the Jewish student, may appear obscure and even strange to the general English reader. For brevity's sake I will call it the High Synagogue, though it does not correspond in all details to what one is accustomed to understand under the term of High Church. The High Synagogue has a history which is not altogether without its points of interest.

Some years ago when the waves of the Higher Criticism of the Old Testament reached the shores of this country, and such questions as the heterogeneous composition of the Pentateuch, the comparatively late date of the Levitical Legislation, and the post-exilic origin of certain Prophecies as well as of the Psalms began to be freely discussed by the press and even in the pulpit, the invidious remark was often made: What will now become of Judaism when its last stronghold, the Law, is being shaken to its very foundations?

Such a remark shows a very superficial acquaintance with the nature of an old historical religion like Judaism, and the richness of the resources it has to fall back upon in cases of emergency.

As a fact, the emergency did not quite surprise Judaism. The alarm signal was given some one hundred and fifty years ago by an Italian Rabbi, Abiad Sar Shalom Bazilai, in his pamphlet *The Faith of the Sages*. The pamphlet is, as the title indicates, of a polemical character, reviewing the work of the Jewish rationalistic schools; and after warming up in his attacks against their heterodox views, Bazilai exclaims: "Nature and simple meaning, they are our misfortune." By "nature and simple meaning" Bazilai, who wrote in Hebrew, understood what we would call Natural Science and Philology. With the right instinct of faith, Bazilai hit on the real sore points. For though he mostly argues against the philosophical systems of Aristotle and his commentators, he felt that it is not speculation that will ever seriously endanger religion. There is hardly any metaphysical system, old or new, which has not in course of time been adapted by able dialecticians to the creed which they happened to hold. In our own time we have seen the glorious, though not entirely novel spectacle, of Agnosticism itself becoming the rightful handmaid of Queen Theology. The real danger lies in "nature" (or Natural Science) with its stern demand of law and regularity in all phenomena, and in the "simple meaning" (or Philology) with its inconsiderate insistence on truth. Of the two, the "simple meaning" is the more objectionable. Not only is it very often at variance with Tradition, which has its own code of interpretation, but it is constantly increasing the difficulties raised by science. For if words could only have more than one meaning, there would be no objection to reading the first words of Genesis, "In *a* beginning God *evolved*." The difficulties of science would then be disposed of easily enough. Maimonides, who was as bold an interpreter as he was a deep metaphysician, hinted plainly enough that were he as convinced of the eternity of matter as he was satisfied of the impossibility of any corporeal quality in the deity, he would feel as little compunction in explaining (figuratively) the contents of the first chapter of Genesis as he did in allegorising the anthropomorphic passages of the Bible. Thus in the end all the difficulties resolve themselves into the one great difficulty of the "simple meaning." The best way to meet this difficulty was found to be to shift the centre of gravity in Judaism and to place it in the secondary meaning, thus making religion independent of philology and all its dangerous consequences.

This shifting work was chiefly done, perhaps not quite consciously, by the historical school which followed upon that of Mendelssohn and his first successors. The historical school, which is still in the ascendant, comprises many of the best Jewish writers who either by their learning or by their ecclesiastical profession as Rabbis and preachers in great communities have acquired some important position among their brethren. The men who have inaugurated this movement were Krochmal (1785-1841), Rapoport (1790-1867), and Zunc (1794-1886).

It is not a mere coincidence that the first representatives of the historical school were also the first Jewish scholars who proved themselves more or less ready to join the modern school of Bible Criticism, and even to contribute their share to it. The first two, Krochmal and Rapoport, early in the second quarter of this century accepted and defended the modern view about a second Isaiah, the post-exilic origin of many Psalms, and the late date of Ecclesiastes; whilst Zunz, who began (in 1832) with denying the authenticity of Ezekiel; concluded his literary career (1873) with a study on the Bible (*Gesammelte Schriften*, i. pp. 217-290), in which he expressed his view "that the Book of Leviticus dates from a later period than the Book of Deuteronomy, later even than Ezekiel, having been composed during the age of the Second Temple, when there already existed a well-established priesthood which superintended the sacrificial worship." But when Revelation or the Written Word is reduced to the level of history, there is no difficulty in elevating history in its aspect of Tradition to the rank of Scripture, for both have then the same human or divine origin (according to the student's predilection for the one or the other adjective), and emanate from the same authority. Tradition becomes thus the means whereby the modern divine seeks to compensate himself for the loss of the Bible, and the theological balance is to the satisfaction of all parties happily readjusted.

Jewish Tradition, or, as it is commonly called, the Oral Law, or, as we may term it (in consideration of its claims to represent an interpretation of the Bible), the Secondary Meaning of the Scriptures, is mainly embodied in the works of the Rabbis and their subsequent followers during the Middle Ages. Hence the zeal and energy with which the historical school applied itself to the Jewish post-biblical literature, not only elucidating its texts by means of new critical editions, dictionaries, and commentaries, but also trying to trace its origins and to pursue its history through its gradual development. To the work of Krochmal in this direction a special essay is devoted in this volume. The labours of Rapoport are more of a biographical and bibliographical nature, being occupied mostly with the minor details in the lives and writings of various famous Jewish Rabbis in the Middle Ages; thus they offer but little opportunity for general theological comment. Of more importance in this respect are the hints thrown out in his various works by Zunz, who was just as emphatic in asserting the claims of Tradition as he was advanced in his views on Bible criticism. Zunz's greatest work is *Die Gottesdienstliche Vorträge*—an awkward title, which in fact means "The History of the Interpretation of the Scriptures as forming a part of the divine service." Now if a work displaying such wide learning and critical acumen and written in such an impartial spirit can be said to have a bias, it was towards bridging over the seemingly wide gap between the Written Word (the Scriptures) and the Spoken Word (the Oral Law or Tradition), which was the more deeply felt, as most of Zunz's older contemporaries were men, grown up in the habits of thought of the eighteenth century—a century distinguished both for its ignorance of, and its power of ignoring, the teachings of history. Indeed it would seem that ages employed in making history have no time for studying it.

Zunz accomplished the task he set himself, by showing, as already indicated, the late date of certain portions of the Bible, which by setting the early history of Israel in an ideal light betray the moralising tendency of their authors, and are, in fact, little more than a traditional interpretation of older portions of Scripture, adapted to the religious needs of the time. Placing thus the origin of Tradition in the Bible itself, it was a comparatively easy matter for Zunz to prove its further continuity. Prophecy and Interpretation are with him the natural expressions of the religious life of the nation; and though by the loss of Israel's political independence the voice of the prophets gradually died away, the voice of God was still heard. Israel continues to consult God through the medium of the Scriptures, and He answers His people by the mouth of the Scribes, the Sages, the Interpreters of the Law; whilst the liturgy of the Synagogue, springing up at the time when Psalms were still being composed, expands in its later stages through the work of the Poets of the Synagogue into such a rich luxuriance "that it forms in itself a treasure of history, poetry, philosophy; and prophecy and psalms are again revived in the hymnology of the Middle Ages." This is in brief the lesson to be learned from Zunz's *Gottesdienstliche Vorträge* as far as it deals with the significance of Tradition; and it is in the introduction to this work that Zunz expresses himself to the following effect: Indispensable is the free Spoken Word. Mankind has acquired all its ideal treasures only by Word of Mouth; an education continuing through all stages of life. In Israel, too, the Word of

Instruction transmitted from mouth to mouth was never silenced.

The historical school has never, to my knowledge, offered to the world a theological programme of its own. By the nature of its task, its labours are mostly conducted in the field of philology and archæology, and it pays but little attention to purely dogmatic questions. On the whole, its attitude towards religion may be defined as an enlightened Scepticism combined with a staunch conservatism which is not even wholly devoid of a certain mystical touch. As far as we may gather from vague remarks and hints thrown out now and then, its theological position may perhaps be thus defined:— It is not the mere revealed Bible that is of first importance to the Jew, but the Bible as it repeats itself in history, in other words, as it is interpreted by Tradition. The Talmud, that wonderful mine of religious ideas from which it would be just as easy to draw up a manual for the most orthodox as to extract a vade-mecum for the most sceptical, lends some countenance to this view by certain controversial passages— not to be taken seriously—in which "the words of the scribes" are placed almost above the words of the Torah. Since then the interpretation of Scripture or the Secondary Meaning is mainly a product of changing historical influences, it follows that the centre of authority is actually removed from the Bible and placed in some *living body*, which, by reason of its being in touch with the ideal aspirations and the religious needs of the age, is best able to determine the nature of the Secondary Meaning. This living body, however, is not represented by any section of the nation, or any corporate priesthood, or Rabbihood, but by the collective conscience of Catholic Israel as embodied in the Universal Synagogue. The Synagogue "with its long, continuous cry after God for more than twenty-three centuries," with its unremittent activity in teaching and developing the Word of God, with its uninterrupted succession of prophets, Psalmists, Scribes, Assideans, Rabbis, Patriarchs, Interpreters, Elucidators, Eminences, and Teachers, with its glorious record of Saints, martyrs, sages, philosophers, scholars, and mystics; this Synagogue, the only true witness to the past, and forming in all ages the sublimest expression of Israel's religious life, must also retain its authority as the sole true guide for the present and the future. And being in communion with this Synagogue, we may also look hopefully for a safe and rational solution of our present theological troubles. For was it not the Synagogue which even in antiquity determined the fate of Scripture? On the one hand, for example, books like Ezekiel, the Song of Songs, and Ecclesiastes, were only declared to be Holy Writ in virtue of the interpretation put upon them by the Rabbis: and, on the other hand, it was the veto of the Rabbis which excluded from the canon the works that now pass under the name of Apocrypha. We may, therefore, safely trust that the Synagogue will again assert its divine right in passing judgment upon the Bible when it feels called upon to exercise that holy office. It is "God who has chosen the Torah, and Moses His servant, and Israel His people." But indeed God's choice invariably coincides with the wishes of Israel; He "performeth all things" upon which the councils of Israel, meeting under promise of the Divine presence and communion, have previously agreed. As the Talmud somewhere expresses itself with regard to the Book of Esther, "They have confirmed above what Israel has accepted below."

Another consequence of this conception of Tradition is that it is neither Scripture nor primitive Judaism, but general custom which forms the real rule of practice. Holy Writ as well as history, Zunz tells us, teaches that the law of Moses was never fully and absolutely put in practice. Liberty was always given to the great teachers of every generation to make

modifications and innovations in harmony with the spirit
of existing institutions. Hence a return to Mosaism would be
illegal, pernicious, and indeed impossible. The norm as well
as the sanction of Judaism is the practice actually in vogue.
Its consecration is the consecration of general use—or, in
other words, of Catholic Israel. It was probably with a view
to this communion that the later mystics introduced a short
prayer to be said before the performance of any religious
ceremony, in which, among other things, the speaker pro-
fesses his readiness to act "in the name of all Israel."

It would be out of place in an introductory essay to pursue
any further this interesting subject with its far-reaching consequences upon Jewish life and Jewish thought. But the foregoing remarks may suffice to show that Judaism did not
remain quite inactive at the approach of the great religious
crisis which our generation has witnessed. Like so many other
religious communities, it reviewed its forces, entrenched
itself on the field of history, and what it lost of its old devotion to the Bible, it has sought to make up by a renewed
reverence for institutions.

In this connection, a mere mention may suffice of the ultra-
Orthodox party, led by the late Dr. S. R. Hirsch of Frankfort
(1808-1889) whose defiance of reason and criticism even a
Ward might have envied, and whose saintliness and sublimity
even a Keble might have admired. And, to take an example
from the opposite school, we must at least record the name
of that devout Jew, Osias Schorr (1816-1895), in whom we
have profound learning combined with an uncompromising
disposition of mind productive of a typical champion of
Radicalism in things religious. These men are, however,
representative of two extremes, and their followers constitute
mere minorities; the majority is with the historical school.

How long the position of this school will prove tenable is
another question. Being brought up in the old Low Syna-

gogue, where, with all attachment to tradition, the Bible was looked upon as the crown and the climax of Judaism, the old Adam still asserts itself in me, and in unguarded moments makes me rebel against this new rival of revelation in the shape of history. At times this now fashionable exaltation of Tradition at the expense of Scripture even impresses me as a sort of religious bimetallism in which bold speculators in theology try to keep up the market value of an inferior currency by denouncing loudly the bright shining gold which, they would have us believe, is less fitted to circulate in the vulgar use of daily life than the small cash of historical interpretation. Nor can I quite reconcile myself to this alliance of religion with history, which seems to me both unworthy and unnatural. The Jew, some writer aptly remarked, was the first and the fiercest Nonconformist of the East, and so Judaism was always a protesting religion. To break the idols, whether of the past or of the present, has always been a sacred mission of Judaism, and has indeed been esteemed by it as a necessary preliminary to the advent of the kingdom of God on earth. One of its daily prayers was and still is: "We therefore hope in Thee, O Lord our God, that we may speedily behold the glory of Thy might, when . . . the idols will be cut off, when the world will be perfected under the kingdom of the Almighty." It bowed before truth, but it had never made a covenant with facts only because they were facts. History had to be remade and to sanctify itself before it found its way into its sacred annals. Nor did Judaism make a virtue of swallowing down institutions. Such institutions as crept into it in course of time had, when the Synagogue was conscious of their claims to form part of religion, to submit to the laborious process of a thorough adaptation to prophetic notions before they were formally sanctioned. But when this process was deemed impossible or impracticable, Judaism boldly denounced the past in such fierce language as the prophets used and as still finds its echo in such passages of the liturgy as "First our ancestors were worshippers of idols and now God has brought us near to His service"; or "But of a truth, we and our ancestors have sinned."

However, it would be unfair to argue any further against a theological system which, as already said, was never avowed distinctly by the historical school—a school, moreover, with which speculation is a matter of minor importance. The main strength of this school lies in its scientific work, for which Judaism will always be under a sense of deep gratitude. And living as we do in an age in which history reigns supreme in all departments of human thought, we may hope that even its theology, as far as it goes, will "do" for us, though I neither hope nor believe that it will do for those who come after us. I may, however, humbly confess that the essay on "The Dogmas of Judaism" in this volume was written in a spirit of rebellion against this all-absorbing Catholic Israel, with its decently veiled scepticism on the one hand, and its unfortunate tendency with many people to degenerate into a soulless conformity on the other hand. There is, I am afraid, not much to be said in favour of this essay. It is deficient both in matter and in style. It proved to be a futile attempt to bring within the compass of an essay what a whole book could hardly do justice to. The Hebrew documents bearing upon the question of dogma which I have collected from various manuscripts and rare printed books, would alone make a fair-sized volume. I only venture to offer it to the public in the absence of anything better; since, so far as I know, no other attempt has ever been made to treat the subject even in its meagrest outlines. I even venture to hope that, with all its shortcomings, it will contribute something towards destroying the illusion, in which so many theologians indulge, that Judaism is a religion without dogmas. To declare that a religion has no dogmas is tantamount to saying that it was wise enough not to commit itself to any vital principles. But prudence, useful as it may be in worldly affairs, is quite unworthy of a great spiritual power.

Jewish mysticism in the Middle Ages and in modern times is represented in this volume by two essays ("The Chassidim" and "Nachmanides"). But in order to avoid mistakes which might be implied by my silence, I think it desirable to state that there are also to be found many mystical elements in the old Rabbinic literature. Mysticism, not as a theosophic system or as an occult science, but as a manifestation of the spiritual and as an expression of man's agonies in his struggle after communion with God, as well as of his ineffable joy when he receives the assurance that he has found it, is not, as some maintain, foreign to the spirit of old Rabbinic Judaism. There was no need for the mediæval Rabbi to borrow the elements of such a mysticism from non-Jewish sources. The perusal of the old Homilies on the Song of Songs, and on the Lessons from the Prophets, or even a fair acquaintance with the Jewish liturgy would, in itself, suffice to refute such baseless assertions. Those who are at all familiar with old Rabbinic literature hardly need to be told that "the sea of the Talmud" has also its gulf stream of mysticism which, taking its origin in the moralising portions of the Bible, runs through the wide ocean of Jewish thought, constantly commingling with the icy waters of legalism, and unceasingly washing the desolate shores of an apparently meaningless ceremonialism, communicating to it life, warmth, and spirituality.

I shall be pleased if the more serious side of this volume —Jewish mysticism and Rabbinic theology—should attract the attention of students, and so draw some fellow-workers into a field which is utterly neglected. Notwithstanding the numerous Manuals and Introductions which all more or less touch on the subject of Rabbinic theology, there is, after nearly two hundred and fifty years, not a single work among them which, either in knowledge of facts or in their interpretation, is a single step in advance of the Cambridge Platonist, John Smith, in his *Select Discourses*. But those who try so hard to determine the miraculous distance of Christianity by the eclipses in Rabbinism, should, if they wish to be just or prove themselves worthy scholars, also endeavour to make themselves acquainted with the numberless bright stars that move in the wide universe of Jewish thought. We are often told that no creed or theological system which has come down to us from antiquity can afford to be judged by any other standard than by its spiritual and poetic *possibilities:* this indulgence Judaism is as justly entitled to claim as any other religion. The great and saintly Franz Delitzsch who, born with an intellect of admirable temper, was also endowed by Heaven with a soul—and a beautiful soul it was —was one of the few theologians who, partly at least, admitted this claim, and sought earnestly and diligently after these spiritual and poetic possibilities, and was amply rewarded for his labours.

PART ONE: *Movements and Ideas*

THE HISTORY OF JEWISH TRADITION

THERE is an anecdote about a famous theologian to the effect that he used to tell his pupils, "Should I ever grow old and weak—which usually drives people to embrace the safer side —and alter my opinions, then pray do not believe me." The concluding volume of Weiss's *History of Jewish Tradition*[1] shows that there was no need for our author to warn his pupils against the dangers accompanying old age. For though Weiss had, when he began to write this last volume, already exceeded his three-score and ten, and, as we read in the preface, had some misgivings as to whether he should continue his work, there is no trace in it of any abatement of the great powers of the author. It is marked by the same freshness in diction, the same marvellous scholarship, the same display of astonishing critical powers, and the same impartial and straightforward way of judging persons and things, for which the preceding volumes were so much distinguished and admired.

This book, which is recognized as a standard work abroad, is, I fear, owing to the fact of its being written in the Hebrew language, not sufficiently known in this country. Weiss does not want *our* recognition; we are rather in need of his

instruction. Some general view of his estimate of Jewish
Tradition may, therefore, be of service to the student. It is,
indeed, the only work of its kind. Zunz has confined himself
to the history of the Agadah. Graetz gave most of his attention to the political side of Jewish history. But comparatively
little has been done for the Halachah, though Frankel,
Geiger, Herzfeld, and others have treated some single points
in various monographs. Thus it was left for Weiss to write
the *History of Tradition,* which includes both the Agadah
and the Halachah. The treatment of this latter must have
proved, in consequence of the intricate and intractable
nature of its materials, by far the more difficult portion of his
task.

In speaking of the *History* of Tradition, a term which
suggests the fluctuating character of a thing, its origin,
development, progress, and retrogression, we have already
indicated that Weiss does not consider even the Halachah as
having come down from heaven, ready-made, and definitely
fixed for all time. To define it more clearly, Tradition is,
apart from the few ordinances and certain usages for which
there is no precedent in the Bible, the history of interpretation of the Scriptures, which was constantly liable to
variation, not on grounds of philology, but through the subjective notions of successive generations regarding religion
and the method and scope of its application.

Weiss's standpoint with reference to the Pentateuch is the
conservative one, maintaining both its unity and its Mosaic
authorship. Those passages and accounts in the Bible in
which the modern critic discerns traces of different traditional sources, are for Weiss only indicative of the various
stages of interpretation through which the Pentateuch had to
pass. The earliest stage was a very crude one, as may be seen
from the case of Jephthah's vow, for which only a misinter-
pretation of certain passages in the Pentateuch (Gen. xxii. 2;

Num. xxv. 4) could be made responsible. Nor was Jephthah, who felt himself bound to carry out his vow, acquainted with the provision for dissolving vows[2] that was sufficiently familiar to later ages. When, on the other hand, Jeremiah declared sacrifices to be altogether superfluous, and said that God did not command Israel, when he brought them from the land of Egypt, concerning burnt offerings or sacrifices (vii. 22), he was not in contradiction with Leviticus, but interpreted the laws contained in this book as a concession to popular custom, though not desirable on their own account. This concession, whenever it was of a harmless nature, the prophets carried so far as to permit altars outside the Tabernacle or Temple, though this was against the plain sense of Deuteronomy. Elijah even bewailed their destruction (1 Kings xix. 10). He and other prophets probably interpreted the law in question as directed against the construction and maintenance of several chief sanctuaries, but not against sacrificing in different places on minor occasions. This is evidently a free interpretation, or rather application, of the Law. Occasionally the conception as to when and how a law should be applied took a completely negative form. In this manner is to be explained the action of Solomon in suspending the Fast of the Day of Atonement before the festival he was going to celebrate in honour of the consecration of the Temple (1 Kings viii. 65), the king being convinced that on this unique occasion the latter was of more religious importance than the former. Weiss thinks that the later custom of holding public dances in the vineyards on the 10th of Tishri might have had its origin in this solemn, but also joyful, festival. Ezekiel, again, though alluding more frequently than any other prophet to the laws in the Pentateuch, is exceedingly bold in his interpretation of them, as, for instance, when he says that *priests* shall not eat anything that is dead or torn (xliv. 31), which shows that he took the verses in Exod. xxii. 30, and Deut. xiv. 20, to have been meant only as a good advice to the laymen to refrain from eating these unclean things, but not as having for them the force of a real commandment.

Starting from this proposition, that there existed always some sort of interpretation running side by side with the recognised Scriptures, which from the very looseness of its connection with the letter of the Scripture could claim to be considered a thing independent in itself, and might therefore be regarded as the *Oral Law,* in contradistinction to the *Written Law,* the author passes to the age of the Second Temple, the period to which the rest of the first volume is devoted. In these pages Weiss reviews the activity of Ezra and Nehemiah, the ordinances of the Men of the Great Synagogue, the institutions of the Scribes, the Lives of the so-called Pairs,[3] the characteristics of the three sects, the Sadducees, Pharisees, and Essenes, and the differences between the schools of Shammai and Hillel. To each of these subjects Weiss gives his fullest attention, and his discussions of them would form perfect monographs in themselves. To reproduce all the interesting matter would mean to translate the whole of this portion of his work into English. I shall only draw attention to one or two points.

First, this liberal interpretation was active during the whole period referred to. Otherwise no authority could have abolished the *lex talionis,* or have permitted war on Sabbath, or made the condition that no crime should be punished without a preceding warning (which was chiefly owing to the aversion of the Rabbis to the infliction of capital punishment), or have sanctioned the sacrificing of the Passover when the 14th of Nisan fell on Sabbath. Indeed Shemaiah and Abtalyon, in whose name Hillel communicated this last law, were called the Great Interpreters.[4]

Secondly, as to the so-called *laws given to Moses on Sinai.*[5]

Much has been said about these. The distinction claimed for them by some scholars, *viz.* that they were never contested, is not tenable, considering that there prevailed much difference of opinion about some of them. Nor is the theory that they were ancient religious usages, dating from time immemorial, entirely satisfactory. For though the fact may be true in itself, this could not have justified the Rabbis in calling them all Sinaitic laws, especially when they were aware that not a few of them were contested by certain of their colleagues, a thing that would have been quite impossible if they had a genuine claim to Mosaic authority. But if we understand Weiss rightly these laws are only to be considered as a specimen of the whole of the Oral Law, which was believed to emanate, both in its institutional and in its expository part, from the same authority. The conviction was firmly held that everything wise and good, be it ethical or ceremonial in its character, whose effect would be to strengthen the cause of religion, was at least potentially contained in the Torah, and that it only required an earnest religious mind to find it there. Hence the famous adage that "everything which any student will teach at any future time was already communicated to Moses on Mount Sinai"; or the injunction that any acceptable truth, even if discovered by an insignificant man in Israel, should be considered as having the authority of a great sage or prophet, or even of Moses himself. The principle was that the words of the Torah are "fruitful and multiply."

It will probably be said that the laws of clean and unclean, and such like, have proved rather too prolific; but if we read Weiss carefully, we shall be reminded that it was by the same process of propagation that the Rabbis developed from Deut. xxii. 8, a whole code of sanitary and police-laws which could even now be studied with profit; from the few scanty civil laws in Exod. xxi., a whole *corpus juris,* which might well excite the interest and the admiration of any lawyer; and from the words "And thou shalt teach them diligently unto thy children," a complete school-system on the one hand, and on the other the *résumé* of a liturgy that appears to have sufficed for the spiritual needs of more than fifty generations of Israelites.

Before we pass to the age of the Tannaim,[6] the subject of Weiss's second volume, we must take account of two important events which have greatly influenced the further development of Tradition. I refer to the destruction of the Temple and the rise of Christianity. With the former event Judaism ceased to be a political commonwealth, and if "the nation was already in the times of Ezra converted into a church"—an assertion, by the way, which has not the least basis in fact—it became the more so after it had lost the last remains of its independence. But it was a church without priests, or, since such a thing, as far as history teaches us, has never existed, let us rather call it a Synagogue.

From this fact diverse results flowed. A synagogue can exist not only without priests, but also without sacrifices, for which prayer and charity were a sufficient substitute. With the progress of time also many agricultural laws, as well as others relating to sacerdotal purity, gradually became obsolete, though they lingered on for some generations, and, as a venerable reminiscence of a glorious time, entered largely into Jewish literature. This disappearance of so many laws and the weakening of the national element, however, required, if Judaism was to continue to exist, the strengthening of religion from another side. The first thing needed was the creation of a new religious centre which would not only replace the Temple to a certain degree, but also bring about a greater solidarity of views, such as would render impossible the ancient differences that divided the schools of Hillel and Shammai. The creator of this centre was R.

Johanan ben Zaccai, who founded the school of Jamnia, and invested it with the same authority and importance as the Sanhedrin had enjoyed during Temple times. The consciousness that they were standing before a new starting-point in history, with a large religious inheritance from the past, actuated them not only to collect the old traditional laws and to take stock of their religious institutions, but also to give them more definite shape and greater stability. As many of these traditions were by no means undisputed, the best thing was to bring them under one or other heading of the Scriptures. This desire gave the impulse to the famous hermeneutic schools of R. Akiba and R. Ishmael.

The next cause that contributed to give a more determinate expression to the Law was the rise of Christianity. This is not the place to give an account of the views which the Rabbis entertained of Christianity. Suffice it to say they could not see in the destruction of the Law its fulfilment. They also thought that under certain conditions it is not only the letter that killeth, but also the spirit, or rather that the spirit may sometimes be clothed in a letter, which, in its turn, will slay more victims than the letter against which the loudest denunciations have been levelled. Spirit without letter, let theologians say what they will, is a mere phantasm. However, the new sect made claims to the gift of prophecy, which, as they thought, placed them above the Law. It would seem that this was a time of special excitement. The student of the Talmud finds that such marvels as predicting the future, reviving the dead, casting out demons, crossing rivers dry-shod, curing the sick by a touch of prayer, were the order of the day, and performed by scores of Rabbis. Voices from heaven were often heard, and strange visions were frequently beheld. Napoleon I is said to have forbidden the holy coat of Treves to work miracles. The Jewish legislature, however, had no means of preventing these supernatural workings; but when the Rabbis saw their dangerous consequences, they insisted that miracles should have no influence on the interpretation and development of the Law. Hence the saying with regard to Lev. xxvii. 34, that no prophet is authorised to add a new law. And when R. Eliezer b. Hyrkanos (about 120 A.C.) thought to prove the justice of his case by the intervention of miracles, the majority answered that the fact of this or that variation, effected at his bidding, in the established order of nature, proved nothing for the soundness of his argument. Nay, they even ignored the *Bath-Kol* [7] (the celestial voice), which declared itself in favour of R. Eliezer, maintaining that the Torah having once been given to mankind, it is only the opinion of the majority that should decide on its interpretation and application. Very characteristic is the legend connected with this fact. When one of the Rabbis afterwards met Elijah and asked him what they thought in heaven of the audacity of his colleagues, the prophet answered, "God rejoiced and said, my children have conquered me."

Into such discredit did miracles fall at that period, whilst the opinion of the interpreting body, or the Sanhedrin, became more powerful than ever. These were merely dogmatical consequences. But new laws were enacted and old ones revived, with the object of resisting Christian influences over the Jews. To expand the Oral Law, and give it a firm basis in the Scriptures, were considered the best means of preserving Judaism intact. "Moses desired," an old legend narrates, "that the Mishnah also (that is Tradition) should be written down"; but foreseeing the time when the nations of the world would translate the Torah into Greek, and would assert their title to rank as the Children of God, the Lord refused to permit tradition to be recorded otherwise than by word of mouth. The claim of the Gentiles might then be refuted by asking them whether they were also in possession of "the Mystery." The Rabbis therefore concentrated their attention upon "the Mystery," and this contributed largely towards making the expository methods of R. Akiba and R. Ishmael, to which I have above referred, the main object of their study in the schools.

It would, however, be a mistake to think that the Sanhedrin now spent their powers in "enforcing retrograde measures and creating a strange exegesis." I especially advise the student to read carefully that admirable chapter (VII, of Vol. II) in which Weiss classifies all the Ordinances, "Fences," Decrees, and Institutions, dating both from this and from earlier ages, under ten headings, and also shows their underlying principles. The main object was to preserve the Jewish religion by strengthening the principle of Jewish nationality, and to preserve the nationality by the aid of religion. But sometimes the Rabbis also considered it necessary to preserve religion against itself, so to speak, or, as they expressed it, "When there is time to work for the Lord, they make void thy Torah." This authorised the *Beth Din*[8] to act in certain cases against the letter of the Torah. "The welfare of the World" was another great consideration. By "World" they understood both the religious and the secular world. From a regard to the former resulted such "Fences" and Ordinances as were directed against "the transgressors," as well as the general injunction to "keep aloof from what is morally unseemly, and from whatever bears any likeness thereto." In the interests of the latter—the welfare of the secular world—they enacted such laws as either tended to elevate the position of women, or to promote the peace and welfare of members of their own community, or to improve the relations between Jews and their Gentile neighbours. They also held the great principle that nothing is so injurious to the cause of religion as increasing the number of sinners by needless severity. Hence the introduction of many laws "for the benefit of penitents," and the maxim not to issue any decree which may prove too heavy a burden to the majority of the community. The relaxation of certain traditional laws was also permitted when they involved a serious loss of property, or the sacrifice of a man's dignity. Some old decrees were even permitted to fall into oblivion when public opinion was too strong against them, the Rabbis holding that it was often better for Israelites to be unconscious sinners than wilful transgressors. The *Minhag*, or religious custom, also played an important part, it being assumed that it must have been first introduced by some eminent authority; but, if there was reason to believe that the custom owed its origin to some fancy of the populace, and that it had a pernicious effect on the multitude, no compunction was felt in abolishing it.

Very important it is to note that the Oral Law had not at this period assumed a character of such rigidity that all its ordinances, etc., had to be looked upon as irremovable for all times. With those who think otherwise, a favourite quotation is the administratory measure laid down in Tractate *Evidences*,[9] I. 5, where we read that no *Beth Din* has the right of annulling the dicta of another *Beth Din,* unless it is stronger in numbers (having a larger majority) and greater in wisdom than its fellow tribunal. Confess with becoming modesty that the world is always going downhill, decreasing both in numbers and in wisdom, and the result follows that any decision by the earlier Rabbis is fixed law for all eternity. Weiss refutes such an idea not only as inconsistent with the nature of Tradition, but also as contradictory to the facts. He proves by numerous instances that the Rabbis did abolish ordinances and decrees introduced by preceding authorities, and that the whole conception is based on a misunderstanding. For the rule in question, as Weiss clearly points out, originally only meant that a *Beth Din* has no right to undo the decrees of another *contemporary Beth Din,* unless it was justified in doing so by the weight of its greater authority. This was necessary if a central authority was to exist at all. Weiss is indeed of the opinion that the whole passage is a later interpolation from the age of R. Simeon b. Gamaliel II, when certain Rabbis tried to emancipate themselves from the authority of the Patriarch. But it was not meant that the decision of a *Beth Din* should have perpetual binding power for all posterity. This was left to the discretion of the legislature of each generation, who had to examine whether the original cause for maintaining such decision still existed.

The rest of this volume is for the greater part taken up with complete monographs of the Patriarchs and the heads of the schools of that age, whilst the concluding chapters give us the history of the literature, the Midrash, Mechilta, Siphra, Siphré, Mishnah, etc., which contain both the Halachic and the Agadic sayings emanating from these authorities.

With regard to these Patriarchs, I should like only to remark that Weiss defends them against the charge made by Schorr and others, who accuse them of having assumed too much authority on account of their noble descent, and who describe their opponents as the true friends of the people. Weiss is no lover of such specious phrases. The qualifications required for the leadership of the people were a right instinct for the necessities of their time, a fair amount of secular knowledge, and, what is of chief importance, an unbounded love and devotion to those over whose interests they were called to watch. These distinctions, as Weiss proves, the descendants of Hillel possessed in the highest degree. It is true that occasionally, as for instance in the famous controversy of R. Gamaliel II with R. Joshua b. Hananiah, or that of R. Simeon b. Gamaliel II with R. Nathan and R. Meir, they made their authority too heavily felt;[10] but this was again another necessity of those troubled times, when only real unity could save Israel.

However, Weiss is no partisan, and the love he lavishes on his favourite heroes does not exhaust his resources of sympathy and appreciation for members of the other schools. Weiss is no apologist either, and does not make the slightest attempt towards explaining away even the defects of R. Akiba in his somewhat arbitrary method of interpretation, which our author thinks much inferior to the expository rules of R. Ishmael; but this does not prevent him from admiring his excellences.

Altogether it would seem that Weiss thinks R. Akiba more happy in his quality as a great saint than in that of a great exegete. What is most admirable is the instinct with which Weiss understands how to emphasise the right thing in its right place. As an indication of the literary honesty and marvellous industry of our author, I would draw attention to the fact that the sketch of R. Akiba and his school alone is based on more than two thousand quotations scattered over the whole area of the Rabbinic literature; but he points in a special note to a sentence attributed to R. Akiba, which presents the whole man and his generation in a single stroke. I refer to that passage in Tractate *Joys*,[11] in which R. Akiba speaks of the four types of sufferers. He draws the comparison of a king chastising his children; the first son maintains stubborn silence, the second simply rebels, the third supplicates for mercy, and the fourth (the best of sons) says: "Father, proceed with thy chastisement, as David said, Wash me thoroughly from mine iniquity and cleanse me from my sin" (Ps. li. 4). This absolute submission to the will of God, which perceives in suffering only an expression of His fatherly love and mercy, was the ideal of R. Akiba.

The great literary production of this period was the Mishnah, which, through the high authority of its compiler, R. Judah the Patriarch, his saintliness and popularity, soon superseded all the collections of a similar kind, and became the official text-book of the Oral Law. But a text requires interpretation, whilst other collections also demanded some attention. This brings us to the two *Talmuds,* namely, the Talmud of Jerusalem and the Talmud of Babylon, the origin and history of which form the subject of Weiss's third volume.

Here again the first chapters are more of a preliminary character, giving the student some insight into the labyrinth of the Talmud. The two chapters entitled "The instruments employed in erecting the great Edifice," and the "Workmanship displayed by the Builders," give evidence of almost unrivalled familiarity with the Rabbinical literature, and of critical powers of the rarest kind. Now these instruments were by no means new, for, as Weiss shows, the Amoraim employed in interpreting the Mishnah the same explanatory rules that are known to us from the School of R. Ishmael as "the Thirteen Rules by which the Torah is explained," though they appear in the Talmud under other names, and are in reality only a species of Midrash. Besides this there comes another element into play. It was the exaggerated awe of all earlier authorities that endeavoured to reconcile the most contradictory statements by means of a subtle dialectic for which the schools in Babylon were especially famous. There were certainly many opponents of this system, and from the monographs which Weiss gives on the various heads of the western and eastern schools we see that not all followed this method, and some among them even condemned it in the strongest words. However, it cannot be denied that there is a strong scholastic feature in the Talmud, which is very far from what we should look for in a trustworthy exegesis. Thus we must not always expect to find in the Talmud the true meaning of the sayings of their predecessors, and it is certain that a more scientific method in many cases has led to results the very opposite of those at which the later Rabbis have arrived. This fact was already recognised in the sixteenth century, though only in part, by R. Yom-Tob Heller and others. Only he insisted that in this matter a line must be drawn between theory and practice. But Weiss gives irrefragable proofs that even this line was often overstepped by the greatest authorities, though they remained always within the limits of Tradition. Indeed, as Weiss points out, not every saying to be found in the Talmud is to be looked upon as representing Tradition; for there is much in it which only gives the individual opinion or is merely an interpolation of later hands; nor does the Talmud contain the *whole* of Tradition, this latter proceeding and advancing with the time, and corresponding to its conditions and notions. As we read Weiss, the conviction is borne in upon us that there was a Talmud before, and another after *The Talmud*.

Much space in this volume is given to the Agadah and the so-called "Teachers of the Agadah." Weiss makes no attempt at apology for that which seems to us strange, or even repugnant in this part of the Rabbinic literature. The greatest fault to be found with those who wrote down such passages as appear objectionable to us is, perhaps, that they did not observe the wise rule of Johnson, who said to Boswell on a certain occasion, "Let us get serious, for there comes a fool." And the fools unfortunately did come in the shape of certain Jewish commentators and Christian controversialists, who took as serious things which were only the expression of a momentary impulse, or represented the opinion of some isolated individual, or were meant simply as a piece of humorous by-play, calculated to enliven the interest of a languid audience. But on the other hand, as Weiss proves, the Agadah contains also many elements of real edification and eternal truths as well as abundant material for building up the edifice of dogmatic Judaism. Talmudical quotations of such a nature are scattered by thousands over Weiss's work, particularly in those chapters in which he describes the lives of the greatest Rabbinical heroes. But the author lays the student under special obligations by putting together in the concluding pages of this volume some of these sentences, and classifying them under various headings. I give here a few extracts. For the references to authorities I must direct the reader to the original:

"The unity of God is the keystone of dogmatic Judaism. The Rabbis give Israel the credit of having proclaimed to the world the unity of God. They also say that Israel took an oath never to change Him for another God. This only God is eternal, incorporeal, and immutable. And though the prophets saw Him in different aspects, He warned them that they must not infer from the visions vouchsafed to them that there are different Gods. 'I am the first,' He tells them, which implies that he had no father, and the words, 'There is no God besides me,' mean that he has no son. Now, this God, the God of Israel, is holy in every thinkable way of holiness. He is merciful and gracious, as it is said, 'And I will be gracious to whom I will be gracious,' even though he who is the recipient of God's grace has no merit of his own. 'And I will show mercy to whom I will show mercy,' that is, even to those who do not deserve it. His attributes are righteousness, loving-kindness, and truth. God speaks words of eternal truth, even as He himself is the eternal life. All that the Merciful One does is only for good, and even in the time of His anger He remembers His graciousness, and often suppresses His attribute of judgment before His attribute of mercy. But with the righteous God is more severe than with the rest of the world, and when His hand falls in chastening on His saints His name becomes awful, revered, and exalted. This God of Israel, again, extends His providence over all mankind, and especially over Israel. By His eye everything is foreseen, yet freedom of choice is given, and the world is judged by grace, yet all according to the works wrought. Hence, know what is above thee, a seeing eye and a hearing ear, and that all thy deeds are written in a book.

"They [the Rabbis] believed that God created the world out of nothing, without toil and without weariness. This world was created by the combination of His two attributes, mercy and justice. He rejoices in His creation, and if the Maker praises it, who dares to blame it? And if He exults in it, who shall find a blemish in it? Nay, it is a glorious and a beautiful world. It is created for man, and its other denizens were all meant but to serve him. Though all mankind are formed after the type of Adam, no one is like his fellowman (each one having an individuality of his own). Thus he is able to say, 'For my sake, also, was the world created'; and with this thought his responsibilities increase. But the greatest love shown to man is that he was created in the image of God. Man is a being possessed of free will, and, though everything is given on pledge, whosoever wishes to borrow may come and borrow. Everything is in the gift of Heaven except the fear of God. In man's heart abide both the evil inclination and the good inclination; and the words of Scripture, 'Thou shalt not bow down before a strange god,' point to the strange god who is within man himself, who entices him to sin in this world, and gives evidence against him in the next. But the Holy One—blessed be He!—said, 'I have created the evil inclination, but I have also created its antidote, the Torah.' And when man is occupied with the Torah and in works of charity, he becomes the master of the evil inclination; otherwise, he is its slave. When man reflects the image of God, he is the lord of creation, and is feared by all creatures; but this image is defaced by sin, and then he has no power over the universe, and is in fear of all things.

"Another principle of Judaism is the belief in reward and punishment. 'I am the Lord, your God,' means, 'it is I who am prepared to recompense you for your good actions, and to bring retribution upon you for your evil deeds.' God does not allow to pass unrewarded even the merit of a kind and considerate word. By the same measure which man metes out, it shall be meted out to him. Because thou drownedst others, they have drowned thee, and at the last they who drowned thee shall themselves be drowned. Though it is not in our power to explain either the prosperity of the wicked or the affliction of the righteous, nevertheless know before whom thou toilest, and who thy employer is, who will pay thee the reward of thy labour. Here at thy door is a poor man standing, and at his right hand standeth God. If thou grantest his request, be certain of thy reward; but if thou refusest, think of Him who is by the side of the poor, and will avenge it on thee. 'God seeketh the persecuted' to defend him, even though it be the wicked who is persecuted by the righteous. The soul of man is immortal, the souls of the righteous being treasured up under the throne of God. Know that everything is according to the reckoning, and let not thy imagination give thee hope that the grave will be a place of refuge for thee, for perforce thou wast formed, and perforce thou wast born, and thou livest perforce, and perforce thou wilt die, and perforce thou wilt in the future have to give account and reckoning before the Supreme King of kings, the Holy One, blessed be He.

"The advent of the Messiah is another article of the belief of the Rabbis. But if a man tell thee that he knows when the redemption of Israel will take place, believe him not, for this is one of the unrevealed secrets of the Almighty. The mission of Elijah is to bring peace into the world, while the Messiah, in whose days Israel will regain his national independence, will lead the whole world in repentance to God. On this, it is believed, will follow the resurrection of the dead.

"Another main principle in the belief of the Rabbis is the election of Israel, which imposes on them special duties, and gives them a peculiar mission. Beloved are Israel, for they are called the children of God, and His firstborn. 'They shall endure for ever' through the merit of their fathers. There is an especial covenant established between God and the tribes of Israel. God is their father, and He said to them, My children, even as I have no contact with the profanity of the world, so also withdraw yourselves from it. And as I am holy, be ye also holy. Nay, sanctify thyself by refraining even from that which is not forbidden thee. There is no holiness without chastity.

"The main duty of Israel is to sanctify the name of God, for the Torah was only given that His great name might be glorified. Better is it that a single letter of the law be cast out than that the name of Heaven be profaned. And this also is the mission of Israel in this world: to sanctify the name of God, as it is written, 'This people have I formed for myself, that they may show forth my praise.' Or, 'And thou shalt love the Lord thy God,' which means, Thou shalt make God beloved by all creatures, even as Abraham did. Israel is the light of the world; as it is said, 'And nations shall walk by thy light.' But he who profanes the name of Heaven in secret will suffer the penalty thereof in public; and this whether the Heavenly Name be profaned in ignorance or in wilfulness.

"Another duty towards God is to love Him and to fear Him. God's only representative on earth is the God-fearing man. Woe unto those who are occupied in the study of the

Torah, but who have no fear of God. But a still higher duty it is to perform the commandments of God from love. For greater is he who submits to the will of God from love than he who does so from fear.

"Now, how shall man love God? This is answered in the words of Scripture, 'And these words shall be upon thy heart.' For by them thou wilt recognise Him whose word called the world into existence, and follow His divine attributes.

"God is righteous; be ye also righteous, O Israel. By righteousness the Rabbis understand love of truth, hatred of lying and backbiting. The seal of the Holy One, blessed be He, is Truth, of which the actions of man should also bear the impress. Hence, let thy yea be yea, and thy nay, nay. He who is honest in money transactions, unto him this is reckoned as if he had fulfilled the whole of the Torah. Greater is he who earns his livelihood by the labour of his hands than even the God-fearing man; whilst the righteous judge is, as it were, the companion of God in the government of the world. For upon three things the world stands: upon truth, upon judgment, upon peace; as it is said, 'Judge ye the truth and the judgment of peace in your gates.' But he who breaks his word, his sin is as great as if he worshipped idols; and God, who punished the people of the time of the Flood, will also punish him who does not stand by his word. Such a one belongs to one of the four classes who are not admitted into the presence of the Shechinah; there are the scoffers, the hypocrites (who bring the wrath of God into the world), the liars, and the slanderers. The sin of the slanderer is like that of one who would deny the root (the root of all religion, *i.e.*, the existence of God). The greatest of liars, however, is he who perjures himself, which also involves the sin of profanation of the name of God. The hypocrite, who insinuates himself into people's good opinions, who wears his phylacteries and is enwrapped in his gown with the fringes, and secretly commits sins, equally transgresses the command, 'Thou shalt not take the name of the Lord thy God in vain.'

"God is gracious and merciful; therefore man also should be gracious and merciful. Hence, 'Thou shalt love thy neighbour as thyself,' which is a main principle in the Torah. What is unpleasant to thyself, do not unto thy neighbour. This is the whole Torah, to which the rest is only to be considered as a commentary. And this love is also extended to the stranger, for as it is said with regard to Israel, 'And thou shalt love thy neighbour as thyself,' so it is also said, 'And thou shalt love him (the stranger) as thyself.' And thus said God to Israel, 'My beloved children, Am I in want of anything that I should request it of you? But what I ask of you is that you should love, honour, and respect one another.' Therefore, love mankind, and bring them near to the Torah. Let the honour of thy friend be as dear to thee as thine own. Condemn not thy fellow-man until thou art come into his place, and judge all men in the scale of merit. Say not 'I will love scholars, but hate their disciples'; or even, 'I will love the disciples, but hate the ignorant,' but love all, for he who hates his neighbour is as bad as a murderer. Indeed, during the age of the second Temple, men studied the Torah and the commandments, and performed works of charity, but they hated each other, a sin that outweighs all other sins, and for which the holy Temple was destroyed. Be careful not to withdraw thy mercy from any man, for he who does so rebels against the kingdom of God on earth. Walk in the ways of God, who is merciful even to the wicked, and as He is gracious alike to those who know Him, and to those who know Him not, so be thou. Indeed, charity is one of the three pillars on which the world is based. It is more precious than all other virtues. The man who gives charity in secret is greater even than Moses our teacher. An act of charity and love it is to pray for our fellow-man, and to admonish him. 'Thou shalt in any wise rebuke thy neighbour, and not suffer sin upon him' (Lev. xix. 18), means it is thy duty to admonish him a hundred times if need be, even if he be thy superior; for Jerusalem was only destroyed for the sin of its people in not admonishing one another. The man whose protest would be of any weight, and who does not exercise his authority (when any wrong is about to be committed), is held responsible for the whole world.

"Peacefulness and humility are also the fruit of love. Be of the disciples of Aaron, loving peace, and pursuing peace. Let every man be cautious in the fear of God; let him ever give the soft answer that turneth away wrath; let him promote peace, not only among his own relatives and acquaintances, but also among the Gentiles. For (the labour of) all the prophets was to plant peace in the world. Be exceeding lowly of spirit, since the hope of man is but the worm. Be humble as Hillel, for he who is humble causes the Divine presence to dwell with man. But the proud man makes God say, 'I and he cannot dwell in the same place.' He who runs after glory, glory flees from him, and he who flees from glory, glory shall pursue him. Be of those who are despised rather than of those who despise; of the persecuted rather than of the persecutors; be of those who bear their reproach in silence and answer not.

"Another distinctive mark of Judaism is faith in God, and perfect confidence in Him. Which is the right course for a man to choose for himself? Let him have a strong faith in God, as it is said, 'Mine eye shall be upon the faithful (meaning those possessing faith in God) of the land.' And so also Habakkuk based the whole Torah on the principle of faith, as it is said, 'And the just shall live by his faith' (ii. 4). He who but fulfils a single commandment in absolute faith in God deserves that the Holy Spirit should rest on him. Blessed is the man who fears God in private, and trusts in Him with all his heart, for such fear and trust arms him against every misfortune. He who puts his trust in the Holy One, blessed be He, God becomes his shield and protection in this world and in the next. He who has bread in his basket for to-day, and says, 'What shall I have to eat to-morrow?' is a man of little faith. One consequence of real faith is always to believe in the justice of God's judgments. It is the duty of man to thank God when he is visited with misfortune as he does in the time of prosperity. Therefore, blessed is the man who, when visited by suffering, questions not God's justice. But what shall he do? Let him examine his conduct and repent.

"For repentance is the greatest prerogative of man. Better is one hour of repentance and good deeds in this world than the whole life of the world to come. The aim of all wisdom is repentance and good deeds. The place where the truly penitent shall stand is higher than that of the righteous. Repentance finds its special expression in prayer; and when it is said in Scripture, 'Serve God with all thy heart,' by this is meant, serve Him by prayer, which is even greater than worship by means of sacrifices. Never is a prayer entirely unanswered by God. Therefore, even though the sword be on a man's neck, let him not cease to supplicate God's mercy. But regard not thy prayer as a fixed mechanical task, but as an appeal for mercy and grace before the All-Present; as it is said, 'For He is gracious and full of mercy, slow to anger, abounding in loving-kindness, and repenteth him of the evil.' "

The last two volumes of Weiss's work deal with the history of Tradition during the Middle Ages, that is, from the conclusion of the Talmud to the compilation of the Code of the Law by R. Joseph Caro. I have already indicated that with Weiss Tradition did not terminate with the conclusion of the Talmud. It only means that a certain undefinable kind of literature, mostly held in dialogue form and containing many elements of Tradition, was at last brought to an end. The authorities who did this editorial work were the so-called *Rabbanan Saburai*[12] and the *Gaonim,* whose lives and literary activity are fully described by Weiss. But, while thus engaged in preserving their inheritance from the past, they were also enriching Tradition by new contributions, both the Saburai and the Gaonim having not only added to and diminished from the Talmud, but having also introduced avowedly new ordinances and decrees, and created new institutions.

Now, it cannot be denied that a few of these ordinances and decrees had a reforming tendency (see the second and twentieth chapters of vol. iv.); in general, however, they took a more conservative turn than was the case in the previous ages. This must be ascribed to the event of the great schism within the Rabbinical camp itself. I refer to the rise of Caraism, which took place during the first half of the eighth century.

There is probably no work in which the Halachic or legalistic side of this sect is better described than in this volume of Weiss. I regret that I am unable to enter into its details. But I cannot refrain from pointing to one of the main principles of the Caraites. This was "Search the Scriptures." Now this does not look very dissimilar from the principle held by the Rabbis. For what else is the Talmud, but a thorough searching through the Bible for whatever was suggestive by time and circumstances? The light which the Caraites applied to the searching of the Scriptures was the same which illumined the paths of the Rabbis' investigations. They employed most of the expository rules of the Tannaite schools. The fact is that they were only determined to find something different from what the Rabbis found in the Scriptures. They wanted to have gloomy Sabbaths and Festivals, and discovered authority for it in the Bible; they wanted to retain most of the dietary laws which had their root only in Tradition, but insisted on petty differences which they thought might be inferred from the Scriptures, and they created a new "order of inheritance," and varied the forbidden degrees in marriage, in all of which the only merit was that they were in contradiction to the interpretation of the Rabbis. They also refused to accept the Liturgy of Rabbinical Judaism, but never succeeded in producing more than a patchwork from verses of the Bible, which, thus recast, they called a prayer-book. There were undoubtedly among their leaders many serious and sincere men, but they give us the impression of prigs, as for instance, Moses Darai, when he reproaches the Rabbinical Jews for having an "easy religion," or Israel Hammaarabi, when he recommended his book on the laws regarding the slaughtering of animals, as having the special advantage that his decisions were always on the more stringent side. Those who made a pilgrimage to the Holy Land were by the Caraites canonised as "mourners." The Rabbanite R. Judah Hallevi also visited the ruins of Jerusalem, but he did something more than "mourn and sigh and cry," he became a God-intoxicated singer, and wrote the "Zion-Elegy." The novel terminology which they use in their exegetical and theological works, was only invented to spite the Rabbanites, and marks its authors as pedants. On the other hand, it is not to be denied that their opponents did not employ the best means to conciliate them. The Middle Ages knew no other remedy against schism than excommunication, and the Gaonim were the children of their time. Nor were the arguments which the latter brought forward in defence of Tradition always calculated to convince the Caraites of their error. When R. Saadiah, in his apology for the institution of the Second Day of the Festival,[13] went the length of assigning to it a Sinaitic origin, he could only succeed in making the Caraites more suspicious of the claims of Tradition than before. In a later generation one of his own party, R. Hai Gaon, had to declare his predecessor's words a "controversial exaggeration." The zeal which some of the Gaonim showed in their defence of such works as the *Chambers* and the *Measure of the Stature*[14] was a not less unfortunate thing, for it involved the Rabbanites in unnecessary responsibilities for a new class of literature of doubtful origin, which in succeeding centuries was disowned by the best minds in Judaism.

The Gaonic period, to which we also owe the rise of the Massorah and the introduction of points in the text of the Bible—of which Weiss treats fully in the twenty-third and twenty-fourth chapters of vol. iv—comes to an end with the death of R. Hai. The famous schools of Sura and Pumbeditha, over which these two Gaonim presided, fell into decay, and Babylon ceased to be the centre of Judaism. To be more exact, we should say that Judaism had no longer any real centre. Instead of dwelling in one place for centuries, we now have to be perpetually on our journey, accompanying our authors through all the inhabited parts of the world— France, Italy, Spain, Germany, with an occasional trip to Africa and Russia. There we shall meet with the new schools, each of which, though interpreting the same Torah, occupied with the study of the same Talmud, and even conforming more or less to the same mode of life, has an individuality and character of its own, reflecting the thought and habits of the country which it represents. Thus "geographical Judaism" becomes a factor in history which no scholar can afford to neglect. It is true that Judaism never remained entirely unbiased by foreign ideas, and our author points in many a place to Persian, Greek, and Roman influences on Tradition; still, these influences seem to have undergone such a thorough "Judaization" that it is only the practised eye of the scholar that is able to see through the transformation. But it requires no great skill to discriminate between the work produced by a Spanish and that of a French Rabbi. Though both would write in Hebrew, they betray themselves very soon by the style, diction, and train of thought peculiar to each country. The Spaniard is always logical, clear, and systematising, whilst the French Rabbi has very little sense of order, is always writing occasional notes, has a great tendency to be obscure, but is mostly profound and critical. Hence the fact that whilst Spain produced the greatest codifiers of the law, we owe to France and Germany the best commentaries on the Talmud. What these codes and commentaries meant for Judaism the student will find in Weiss's book, and still more fully in his admirable essays on Rashi (Solomon b. Isaac), Maimonides, and R. Jacob Tam (published in his periodical, *Beth Talmud,* and also separately). It is enough for us here only to notice the fact of the breadth of Tradition, which could include within its folds men of such different types as the sceptics, Maimonides, Solomon b. Gabirol, and Ibn Ezra on one side, and the simple "non-questioning" Rabbenu Gershom, Rashi, and Jacob Tam on the other.

The last three centuries, which occupy our author's attention in the fifth volume, are not remarkable for their progress. The world lives on the past. The rationalists write treatises on Maimonides' philosophical works, whilst the German Talmudists add commentary to commentary. It is, indeed, the reign of authority, "modified by accidents." Such an accident was the struggle between the Maimonists and Anti-Maimonists, or the rise of the Cabbalah, or the frequent controversies with Christians, all of which tended to direct the minds of people into new channels of thought. But though this period is less original in its work, it is not on that account less sympathetic. One cannot read those beautiful descriptions which Weiss gives of R. Meir of Rothenburg and his school, or of R. Asher and his descendants, without feel-ing that one is in an atmosphere of saints, who are the more attractive the less they were conscious of their own saintli-ness. The only mistake, perhaps, was that the successors of these "Chassidim or pious men of Germany" looked on many of the religious customs that were merely the voluntary ex-pression of particularly devout souls as worthy of imitation by the whole community, and made them obligatory upon all.

This brings us to the question of the Code already men-tioned (by R. Joseph Caro), with which Weiss's work con-cludes. I have already transgressed the limits of an essay, without flattering myself that I have done anything like justice to the greatest work on Jewish Tradition which modern Jewish genius has produced. But I should not like the reader to carry away with him the false impression that our author shares in the general cry, "Save us from the codifiers." Weiss, himself a Rabbi, and the disciple of the greatest Rabbis of the first half of this century, is quite aware of the impossibility of having a law without a kind of manual to it, which brings the fluid matter into some fixed form, classifying it under its proper headings, and this is what we call codifying the law. And thus he never passes any attempt made in this direction without paying due tribute to its author—be it Maimonides or Caro. But however great the literary value of a code may be, it does not invest it with the attribute of infallibility, nor does it exempt the student or the Rabbi who makes use of it from the duty of examining each paragraph on its own merits, and subjecting it to the same rules of interpretation that were always applied to Tradition. Indeed, Weiss shows that Maimonides deviated in some cases from his own code, when it was required by circumstances.

Nor do I know any modern author who is more in favour

of strong authority than Weiss. His treatment of the struggle between the Patriarch R. Gamaliel and his adversaries, which I have touched on above, proves this sufficiently. What Weiss really objects to, is a *weak* authority—I mean that phonograph-like authority which is always busy in reproducing the voice of others without an opinion of its own, without originality, without initiative and discretion. The real authorities are those who, drawing their inspiration from the past, also understand how to reconcile us with the present and to prepare us for the future.

2

ON THE STUDY OF THE TALMUD [1]

IT IS now more than half a century since Renan put the question, "Has Jewish tradition anything to teach us concerning Jesus?" This question must be answered in the negative. As far as the contemporaneous Jewish literature goes, it does not contain a single reference to the founder of Christianity. All the so-called Anti-Christiana collected by mediæval fanatics, and freshened up again by modern ignoramuses, belong to the later centuries, when history and biography had given way to myth and speculation. Almost every Christian sect, every Christian community, created a Christ after its own image or dogma. The Jewish legend—a growth of those later centuries—gave him an aspect of its own, purely apocryphal in its character, neither meant nor ever taken by the Jews as real history.

But if the Rabbis have nothing to tell us about the personality of Jesus, Rabbinic literature has a good deal to teach us about the times in which he lived and laboured. And what is more important is that a thorough study of this literature might, with due discretion, help us to a better understanding of the writings attributed to Jesus and his disciples. To prove this by a few instances will be the aim of my present lecture.

It is intended as an invitation to fellow-students to devote more attention to a branch of literature, from the study of which the Christian divine might derive as much profit as the Jewish Rabbi.

In justice to by-gone times, it should be pointed out that this fact had by no means escaped the searching eyes of Christian scholars of previous generations. They both recognised the importance of the Talmud for a better knowledge of the two Testaments, and applied themselves to an honest study of its contents. As the fruits of these studies, it is sufficient to mention here the *Porta Mosis* of Pocock, the *De Synedriis* of Selden, the *Horae Rabbinicae* of Lightfoot. The Cambridge Platonists also deserve honourable mention. These great and hospitable minds extended the range of their literary acquaintances also to the Rabbis, and the *Select Discourses* of John Smith, and the *Discourse on the Lord's Supper* by Cudworth,[2] show that this acquaintance was by no means a passing one.

All the names just given belong to England, but the Continent in no way remained behind. The names of the Continental students of Rabbinism are duly recorded in Zunz's *Zur Literatur und Geschichte,* and in other bibliographical works. It is sufficient to mention the name of Reuchlin, who saved the Talmud from the torch which a converted Jew was about to apply to it; the two Buxtorfs, whose works bearing on Rabbinic literature fill pages in the catalogues of the British Museum; and Vitringa, whose books on Rabbinic topics are considered by the best scholars as classical pieces of work.

However, these good things are (as already indicated) a matter of the past. The present shows a decided deterioration. Not only has the number of students devoting themselves to Rabbinic literature shrunk to a miserable minimum, but the quality of the work produced by these latter-day students is such as to show a distinct decay, among the very few praise-worthy exceptions being, for instance, the theological works of Dr. C. Taylor. No student who is interested in the constitution of the ancient Synagogue dare neglect Vitringa's *De Synagoga vetere,* which appeared in the year 1696; but he would certainly lose nothing by omitting to read most of the productions of our own century on the same subject.

The causes of this decay are not to be sought for far off. There was first the influence of Schleiermacher, whose interpretation of Christianity formed, as far as its negative side is concerned, one long strained effort to divorce it from Judaism. "I hate historic relations of this sort," he exclaims in one place; and proceeds to say, "every religion is conditioned by itself, and forms an eternal necessity." Scheiermacher's theory of the origin of Christianity was, as is well known, mainly based on the Johannine Gospel, to the disparagement of the Synoptics. The German Marcion had thus every reason to hate history. But as the Talmud still reminded the world of these historical relations, Schleiermacher and his school adopted the course of vulgar *parvenus,* and cut the Rabbis and their literary remains. The second cause of this decay is the suspicion thrown on all Jewish tradition by the higher criticism. Anybody who has ever read any modern Introductions to the Old Testament will remember, that as a rule they open with a reference to the Rabbinic account of the rise of the Canon, followed by a lengthy exposition showing its utter untrustworthiness. To make matters more complete, efforts were made to disqualify the Rabbis from bearing witness even to events which took place when the Synagogue was a fully-established institution, administered by the ancestors of the Rabbis in their capacity as scribes and saints, or Chasidim. I am referring to the controversy as to the existence of the so-called Great Synagogue, commencing, according to tradition, with Ezra the Scribe, and succeeded by a permanent court, consisting of seventy-one members, called Sanhedrin; which court again was, according to tradition, presided over by two members, the one called Nasi, or Prince-President, whilst the other bore the title of Ab-Beth-Din, Father of the Court of Justice, or Vice-President, both of whom were recruited for the most part from Pharisaic circles. Modern criticism, mainly on the strength of certain passages in Josephus and in the New Testament, maintains a negative attitude toward these accounts. The questions involved are too important and too complicated to be entered upon in a casual way. We need notice only the following fact. This is that the doubts regarding the traditional account of the constitution of the Sanhedrin were first raised in this century by Krochmal in the "forties," taken up again by Kuenen in the "sixties," to be followed by Wellhausen in the "eighties." But when reading their works you will observe that, whilst Krochmal respectfully questions tradition, and Kuenen enters into elaborate examination of the documents, Wellhausen summarily dismisses them. Matters have now, indeed, come to such a pass that the principle has been laid down that it is not necessary to have a thorough knowledge of Rabbinic literature in order to express an opinion about its merits or demerits. It is probably thought that we may condemn it by mere intuition. It is impossible to argue with transcendental ignorance.

Trusting that none of those present have any reason to hate history, or to believe in the superior virtue of ignorance, I will now proceed to the subject of my lecture.

Let me first state the fact that the impression conveyed to the Rabbinic student by the perusal of the New Testament is in parts like that gained by reading certain Rabbinic homilies. On the very threshold of the New Testament he is confronted by a genealogical table,[3] a feature not uncommon in the later Rabbinic versions of the Old Testament, which are rather fond of providing Biblical heroes with long pedigrees. They are not always accurate, but have as a rule some edifying purpose in view. The Rabbis even declare that the Book of Chronicles, with its long series of names, has no other purpose than that of being interpreted,[4] that is to say, of enabling us to derive some lesson from them. In the fifth chapter of the Sayings of the Jewish Fathers, dealing mostly with round numbers, we read: "There were ten generations from Noah to Abraham to make known how long-suffering God is."

In the second chapter of Matthew the Rabbinic student meets with many features known to him from the Rabbinic narratives about the birth of Abraham; the story of the Magi in particular impresses him as a homiletical illustration of Num. 24: 17, "There shall come a star out of Jacob," which star the interpretation of the Synagogue referred to the star of the Messiah.[5] This impression grows stronger the more we advance with the reading of the Apostle's writings. Take, for instance, Matt. 3: 9, "Bring forth fruit worthy of repentance." This verse, like so many others in the New Testament in which fruits or harvest are used as metaphors or similes in parables, gains both in intensity and in freshness when studied in connexion with many allegorical interpretations of the Rabbis in which the produce of the field and the vineyard play a similar part. One or two instances will not be uninteresting. Thus, with reference to Song of Songs 2: 2, "As the lily among the thorns, so is my love among the daughters," a famous Rabbi says: There was a king who had a paradise (or garden), which he had laid out with rows of fig-trees, rows of vines, and rows of pomegranates. He put the paradise in the hands of a tenant, and left. In after days the king came to see what his tenant had accomplished. He found the garden neglected, and full of thorns and thistles. He then brought woodcutters to cut it down. Suddenly he perceived a lily. The king plucked it, and smelled it, and his soul returned upon him. He turned and said, "For the sake of the lily the garden shall be saved." The lily is the Congregation of Israel; intent on the strength of its devotion to the Torah, it saved the world from the destruction to which the generation of the deluge had condemned it by their wicked deeds.[6]

In another place, however, it is the individual who is compared to the lily. Thus, Song of Songs 6: 2, "My beloved went down to his garden to gather the lilies," is applied to the death of the righteous, whose departure from this world is a gathering of flowers undertaken by God himself, who is the beloved one.[7]

In connexion with this we may mention another Rabbinic parable, in which the wheat takes the place of the lily. It is given as an illustration of Song of Songs 7: 3, and Psalm 2: 12. The Scriptural words in the latter place are נשקו בר which the Rabbis explain to mean "kiss the wheat," illustrating it by the following parable: The straw and the chaff were arguing together. The straw maintained that it was for its sake that the field was sown and ploughed, whilst the stem insisted that it was on its account that the work was undertaken. Thereupon the wheat said, "Wait until the harvest comes, and we shall know with what purpose the field was sown." When the harvest came, and the work of threshing began, the chaff was scattered to the wind, the stem was given to the flames, whilst the wheat was carefully gathered on the floor. In a similar way the heathens say, "It is for our sake that the world was created," whilst Israel makes the same claim for itself. But wait for the Day of Judgment, when the chaff will be eliminated, and the wheat will be kissed. I need hardly remind you of the parable in Matt. 13.[8]

To return to Chapter 3. I will quote verse 11, in which
the Baptist in his testimony to Jesus says, "I, indeed, baptised
you with water unto repentance, but he that cometh after me
is mightier than I, whose shoes I am not worthy to bear; he
shall baptise you with the Holy Ghost and with fire." The
baptism, of course, represents the טבילה, or immersion, of the
Bible, enforced by the Rabbis in the case of proselytes. According to some authorities it was also customary with people entering on a course of repentance.[9] The expression,
"whose shoes I am not worthy to bear," reminds one of the
similar Talmudic phrase, running, "he who will explain to
me a certain word, I will carry his cloth after him to the
bath," [10] that is to say, he will show submission to his authority by performing menial work for him. As to the term,
"baptism by the Holy Ghost and fire," the latter has a parallel in the Talmudic dictum, that in the main טבילה, immersion, as a means of purification, is by fire.[11] The former term,
"baptism by the Holy Ghost," is certainly obscure, and has
given a good deal of trouble to the commentators; but it
must have been readily understood by the Jews, who even
spoke of drawing the Holy Spirit, שואבין רוה הקודש, a term
applied only to liquids.[12] Note also the following passage
from a sermon by R. Akiba: "Blessed are ye Israelites. Before whom are ye purified, and who is he who purifies you?
Ye are purified before your Father in Heaven, and it is he
who purifies you," as it is said, "The Lord is the *Mikweh* of
Israel." [13] The word מקוה is taken in the sense in which it
occurs several times in the Pentateuch, meaning "a gathering
of waters," or a ritual bath, taken after various kinds of
uncleanness. The Rabbi then derives from the words of
Jeremiah (17: 13) the lesson, that as the *Mikweh* is the means
of purification for defilement (in the sense of the Levitical
legislation), so God is the source of purity for Israel. It
should be borne in mind, that according to the Rabbinic

interpretation, the term טומאה, "defilement," applies to all kinds of sins, ritual as well as moral, especially the latter, whilst the process of purifying mostly concerns the heart. "Purify our hearts, that we serve thee in truth," is the constant prayer of the Synagogue.

טָהֳרָה, or "purification," is, according to the mystic R. Phinehas ben Jair, of the second century, one of the higher rungs on the ladder leading to the attainment of the holy spirit.[14] I do not know how far this conception may be connected with the gospel narrative, according to which the baptism of Jesus (or the Taharah of Jesus) was followed by the descent of the holy spirit. If R. Phinehas ben Jair could be taken, as some maintain, as one of the last representatives of the Essenes, there would, indeed, be no objection to see in the synoptic account an illustration of the principle laid down by these mystics. At any rate, it may serve as a transition to the verses I am about to quote from Matt. 3 (16, 17), running thus: "And Jesus, when he was baptised, went up straightway from the water: and, lo, the heavens were opened unto him, and he saw the Spirit of God descending as a dove, and coming upon him: and, lo, a voice out of the heavens saying, This is my beloved son in whom I am well pleased." The symbolism of the Holy Ghost by a dove is a common notion in Rabbinic literature. The dove is considered as the most chaste among the birds, never forsaking her mate. The congregation of Israel, which never betrays its God, is therefore compared to the dove.[15] "Once upon a time," so runs a Rabbinic legend, which I give here in substance, "King David went out on a hawking expedition. Whereupon Satan came and turned himself into a deer, which David tried to hit, but could not reach. Constantly pursuing the animal, David was thus carried from his suite, owing to the machinations of Satan, into the land of the Philistines, where he was suddenly confronted by the relatives of Goliath, who were all thirsting for his blood. Thereupon a dove descended before Abishai, who had remained behind in the king's camp, and began to emit wailing tones. Abishai at once understood its meaning, saying, 'The congregation of Israel is compared to a dove, as it is said, Wings of a dove covered with silver' (Ps. 68: 14), and thus interpreted the appearance of the dove as a sign that King David, the hope of Israel, was in danger of his life, and he set out to his rescue." [16]

A closer parallel, however, is the following passage attributed to the well-known mystic, Ben Soma, a younger contemporary of the Apostles. The passage runs thus: R. Joshua ben Hananiah was standing upon the terrace of the Temple mountain. Ben Soma saw him, but did not rise up before him (as he ought to have done, seeing that R. Joshua was his master). R. Joshua asked him, "Whence and whither, Ben Soma?" The answer Ben Soma gave him was, "I was looking at (or rather meditating upon) the upper waters (above the firmament) and the under waters (under the firmament). The space between the two waters is not broader than three fingers; as it is said, 'the Spirit of God was brooding upon the face of the waters,' like a dove brooding over her young, partly touching them and partly not touching them." [17]

I need hardly say that we have here to deal with a fragment of a Jewish Gnosis, and I must refer the reader to the works of Joel, Graetz, and Freudenthal, for more information upon this point, but it must be noted that some parallel passages read "eagle" instead of "dove." Deut. 32: 11 lends some countenance to this reading, but the parallels just quoted from the New Testament as well as the famous vision of R. Jose, in which the daughter-voice is complaining in a tender voice like a dove, saying "Woe unto the father, whose children were expelled from his table," [18] speak for the reading given first.

After the appearance of the Holy Ghost, Jesus is greeted, as we have seen, by a voice from the heavens, saying, "This is my beloved son, in whom I am well pleased." These words represent, as rightly remarked by the commentators, a combined paraphrase of Ps. 2: 7 and Isa. 41: 1. The voice from heaven, as is well known, corresponds with the Rabbinic "daughter of a voice" (בת קול), or daughter-voice, occupying the third place in the scale of revelation. I cannot enter here into the various aspects and functions of the daughter-voice, about which a good deal has been written, but I should like to note two peculiar features.[19]

The first is, that in many cases the daughter-voice, when employed as a means of revelation, finds its expression, not in a fresh message, but in reproducing some verse or sentence from the Hebrew Bible. Thus it is recorded by the Rabbis that when they (the authorities) intended to include King Solomon in the number of those who forfeited their salvation, the daughter-voice put in the protest of heaven, in the words of Job (34: 33), "Shall his recompense be as thou wilt, that thou refusest it?"[20] The great reconciliation, again, of God with the house of David, as represented by the exiled king Jeconiah, when the Babylonian captivity was nearing its end, was announced by the daughter-voice in the words of Jeremiah, "Return, ye backsliding children, and I will heal your backslidings. Behold, we come unto thee; for thou art the Lord our God" (3: 22).[21] It should be noted, however, that the daughter-voice is not confined in its quotations to the Canonical Scriptures. Sometimes the daughter-voice even quotes sentences from the Apocrypha. This was the case in Jabneh, where the Sanhedrin met after the destruction of the Temple. There a voice from heaven was heard reproducing a verse from the Wisdom of Ben Sira (3: 22), "Ye have no need of the things that are secret."[22] It is true that Ben Sira has "thou hast no need" (in the singular), but it would seem as if the voice from heaven is not always very exact in its quotations, adapting them in its own way to the message to be announced. Thus, for instance, on the occasion of Saul's disobeying the commandment of God regarding the extermination of the Amalekites, there came the daughter-voice and said unto him, "Be not more righteous than thy Maker," אל הצדק יתר מקונך.[23] We will easily recognise in this warning the words of Ecclesiastes (7: 16), "Be not righteous over-much," אל הצדק הרבה, only that הרבה was altered into יתר, required by the prefix of מקונך, which word was apparently added by the voice from heaven.

Another important feature of the daughter-voice is, that in some cases it is audible only to those who are prepared to hear it. "Every day," says the rather mystically inclined R. Joshua ben Levi, "goes forth a voice from Mount Sinai, and makes proclamation and says, 'Woe to the creatures for their contempt of the Torah.'" As rightly pointed out by the commentators, this voice is heard only by fine, sensitive natures that are susceptible to Divine messages even after the discontinuance of prophecy.[24] In this case the daughter-voice becomes something quite subjective, and loses a great deal of its authoritative character. The renegade Elisha ben Abuyah, or, as he is commonly called, אחר the "other one," in his despair of "doing repentance," heard a voice coming straight from behind the throne of God, saying unto him, "Come back, ye backsliding children, except thou 'other one,'" and thus he abandoned himself to an immoral life.[25] Contrast this story with that of Manasseh, the worst sinner among the kings of Judah. It is to this effect. When the captains of the King of Assyria defeated Manasseh and put him among thorns, and inflicted upon him the most cruel tortures, he invoked all the strange gods he was in the habit of worshipping, but no relief came. Suddenly he said, "I remember my father once made me read the following verses

(Deut. 4: 30, 31), 'When thou art in tribulation, and all these things are come upon thee, . . . return thou to the Lord thy God. For the Lord thy God is a merciful God; he will not forsake thee nor destroy thee.' " He then began to address his prayers to God. The angels—in a most unangelic way, I am sorry to say—shut up the gates of heaven against his prayer, but the Holy One, blessed be he, said, " 'If I do not receive him, I shut the gate in the face of repentance.' And thus he was entreated of him and heard his supplication.' " [26] The moral of the two stories is, that the "other one" trusted to fresh messages, and went to perdition, while Manasseh fell back upon the family Bible and was saved. It is probable that it was such moral catastrophes as recorded in the case of the "other one" which brought the voice of heaven into disrepute. The verdict of the Rabbis in the second century was that no attention is to be paid to it when it presumes to decide against the moral conviction of the majority. The Torah is not in heaven.[27] Its interpretation is left to the conscience of Catholic Israel.

Now it is this conscience of Israel which is not satisfied with the lesson to be derived from the Scriptures at the first glance, or rather the first hearing, but insists upon its expansion. Thus when interpreting Lev. 19: 36, the Rabbis somehow managed to derive from it the law of "let your speech be yea, yea; nay, nay." [28] Again, when commenting upon the seventh commandment, they interpreted it in such a way as to include the prohibition of even an unchaste look or immoral thought.[29] The rules of interpretation by which such maxims were derived from the Scriptures would perhaps not satisfy the modern philologian. They, indeed, belong to the "second sense" of the Scriptures, the sense which is the heart and soul of all history and development. "God hath spoken once, twice I have heard this" (Ps. 62: 12), which verse is interpreted by the Rabbis to mean that Scrip-

ture is capable of many interpretations or hearings.[30] But it
is interesting to find that these interpretations of the Scriptures tending to improve upon the "first sense" are sometimes introduced by the formula: "I might hear so-and-so,
therefore there is a teaching to say that," etc. תלמוד לומר . . .
שומע אני.[31] Put into modern language the formula means
this: The words of the Scriptures might be at the first glance
(or first hearing) conceived to have this or that meaning, but
if we consider the context or the way in which the sentences
are worded, we must arrive at a different conclusion. This
parallel may perhaps throw some light on the expression
ἠκούσατε, "you have heard that it was said . . . but I say unto
you," a phrase frequent in the Sermon on the Mount. After
the declaration made by Jesus of his attachment to the
Torah, it is not likely that he would quote passages from it
showing its inferiority. The only way to get over the difficulty is to assume that Jesus used some such phrase as the one
just quoted, שומע אני, "I might hear," or "one might hear,"
that is to say, "one might be mistaken in pressing the literal
sense of the verses in question too closely." Against such a
narrow way of dealing with Scripture he warned his disciples
by some formula, as תלמוד לומר, "there is a teaching to say
that the words must not be taken in such a sense." But the
formula being a strictly Rabbinic idiom, it was not rendered
quite accurately by the Greek translator. Hence the apparent
contradiction between Matt. 3: 17, 20, and the matter following upon these verses. I only wish to add that in Rabbinic
literature it is sometimes God himself who undertakes such
rectifications. Thus we read in an ancient Midrash with
reference to Jer. 4: 2, "And thou shalt swear as the Lord
liveth, in truth and in judgment": "The Holy One, blessed
be he, said unto Israel, 'Think not that you may swear by my
name, even in truth. You may not do so unless you have
obtained that high degree of sanctity by which Abraham,

Joseph, and Job were distinguished, who were called God-fearing men (יראי אלהים).' " This limitation of swearing, even in truth, is indicated according to the Rabbis in Deut. 20: 10, which verse is interpreted to mean, "If thou fearest thy God, and art exclusively in his service, thou mayest swear by his name," not otherwise.[32]

Having mentioned the name of the patriarch, I may perhaps state the fact that, beside the epithets "the God-fearing" Abraham, or Abraham "the friend of God," Abraham also bears in Rabbinic literature the title of Rock. The wording of the Rabbinical passage and the terms used in it will not be uninteresting to the student of the New Testament. In Matt. 16: 18 we read: "And I also say unto thee, that thou art *Petros,* and upon this *petra* I will build my church." The Rabbinic passage forms an illustration of Num. 23: 9, "For from the top of the rocks I see him," and runs thus: There was a king who desired to build, and to lay foundations he dug constantly deeper, but found only a swamp. At last he dug and found a *petra* (this is the very word the Rabbi uses). He said, "On this spot I shall build and lay the foundations." So the Holy One, blessed be he, desired to create the world, but meditating upon the generations of Enoch and the deluge, he said, "How shall I create the world seeing that those wicked men will only provoke me?" But as soon as God perceived that there would rise an Abraham, he said, "Behold, I have found the *petra* upon which to build and to lay foundations." Therefore he called Abraham Rock, as it is said, "Look unto the rock whence ye are hewn. Look unto Abraham, your father" (Isa. 51: 1, 2).[33]

The parallels given so far have been more according to the letter. I will now give one or two parallels according to the spirit.

I have already referred to the attempts made by various

authors to describe the life and times of Jesus Christ. The best book of this class is undoubtedly Schürer's *History of the Jewish People in the Age of Jesus Christ*. It is a very learned work, particularly as far as the Greek and Roman documents are concerned. Its treament of such topics as the geography of Palestine, the topography of Jerusalem, the plan of the Temple, and kindred subjects, is almost perfect. A most excellent feature in it is the completeness of its bibliography, there being hardly any dissertation or article in any of the learned periodicals which is not duly registered by the author. But all these fine things are, to use a quaint Rabbinic phrase, only "after-courses of wisdom." Bibliography in particular is not even an after-course. It partakes more of the nature of the menu served sometimes by very ignorant waiters, possessing neither judgment nor discretion. The general vice attaching to this whole class of works is, that no attempt is made in them to gain acquaintance with the inner life of the Jewish nation at the period about which they write. Take, for instance, the subject of prayer. Considering that pre-Christian Judaism gave to the world the Psalms, and that post-Christian Judaism produced one of the richest liturgies; considering again that among the various prayers which have come down to us through the medium of the Talmud, there is also one that forms a close parallel to the "Lord's Prayer"; considering all this, one might expect that also in the times of Jesus the Jews were able to pray, and in fact did pray. The contents of their prayers might be of the greatest importance for the student, expressing as they probably did the religious sentiments of the age and the ideal aspirations of the nation. But what our theological waiters dish up is a minimum of prayer dressed up in a quantity of rubrics, in such a fashion as to stigmatise their authors as miserable pedants. And no attempt is made to enter into the spirit of even this minimum. No explanation is given, for

instance, of the meaning of the terms "the kingdom of
heaven," the yoke of which the Rabbi was supposed to receive upon himself, the "Hear, O Israel," etc. The terms
"sanctification of the name of God," "Father in heaven," and
"renewed world," are also frequent in Jewish literature and
in the Jewish prayer-book, but no sufficient attention is given
to them. To my knowledge Dalman is the only modern
Christian scholar who recognises the importance of these
terms, and similar ones, in their bearing upon a clearer
understanding of the New Testament, and has at least made
an attempt at their analysis in his book, *Die Worte Jesu*.

Another important point, which has never been properly
examined, is the unique position which the *Keneseth Israel*,
the congregation of Israel, or ideal Israel, occupies in Rabbinic theology. Yet it forms a striking parallel to that held by
Jesus in Christian theology. The Keneseth Israel was, like
the Spirit of the Messiah, created before the world was called
into existence. "She is the beloved of God, in whom he rejoices"; and there is no endearing epithet in the language,
such as son, daughter, brother, sister, bride, mother, lamb,
or eye, which is not, according to the Rabbis, applied by the
Scriptures to express the intimate relation between God and
the Keneseth Israel. Not even the title of "god," of which
God is otherwise so jealous, is denied to Israel, as it is written,
"I have said, Ye are gods." Nay, God even says to Moses,
"Exalt Israel as much as thou canst, for it is as if thou wert
exalting me"; whilst he who denies Israel or rises against
Israel denies God. In fact, it is only through the witness of
Israel that God is God, and he would cease to be so were
Israel to disappear, as it is written, "Ye are my witnesses,
. . . and I am God." [34] But there is no fear of such a calam-
ity. Israel is as eternal as the universe, and forms the rock on
which the world was built. As a rock towering up in the sea,
so the Keneseth Israel stands out in history, defying all

tempests and temptations; for "many waters cannot quench the love" between God and the Keneseth Israel.[35] She is, indeed, approached by Satan and the nations of the world with the seducing words, "What is thy beloved more than another? Beautiful and lovely thou art, if thou wilt mingle among us. Why dost thou permit thyself to go through fire for his sake, to be crucified for his name? Come unto us, where all the dignities in our power await thee." But Israel resists all temptations; they point to their connexion with God throughout their history, to His love unto them, shown by conferring upon them the gift of holiness, which even a Balaam envied, and to the promise held out to them of the Messianic times, when suffering will cease and Israel will revel in the glory of God.[36] These few quotations suffice to show what an interesting chapter might be added to our knowledge of comparative theology.

Again, our knowledge of the spiritual history of the Jews during the first centuries of our era might be enriched by a chapter on miracles. Starting from the principle that miracles can be explained only by more miracles, an attempt was made some years ago by a student to draw up a list of the wonder-workings of the Rabbis recorded in the Talmud and the Midrashim. He applied himself to the reading of these works, but his reading was only cursory. The list therefore is not complete. Still it yielded a harvest of not less than two hundred and fifty miracles. They cover all classes of supernatural workings recorded in the Bible, but occur with much greater frequency.

A repetition of these miracles would be tiresome. I will content myself with reproducing a story from Tractate *Chagigah*, which will illustrate to you how much even the individual Jew shared in the glories conferred upon the Keneseth Israel. I am speaking, of course, of that individual who is described by the Rabbis as one "who labours in the

Torah for its own sake, who is called a lover of God and a lover of humanity. Unto him kingdom and authority are given. Unto him the secrets of the Torah are revealed." The term "authority," by the way, is given with the word ממשלה, suggested probably by Ben Sira 45: 17, וימשילהי בחוק ומשפט, "and he made him have authority over statute and judgment"; whilst Matt. 7: 29, "and he taught them as one having authority," was probably suggested by Ben Sira 3: 10, ומושל בה ילמדנה, "and he who has authority over it shall teach it." As a man of such authority we may consider R. Johanan ben Zakkai, the hero of the story I am about to relate. He was the younger member of the "Eighty Club" of the school of Hillel, and thus a contemporary of the Apostles, though he survived them. He was an eye-witness of the terrible catastrophe of the destruction of the Temple by the Romans, an event which he prophesied forty years before it took place. He is best known by the school he established in Jabneh, whither the Sanhedrin, and with them the Divine Presence presiding over this assembly, emigrated after the fall of Jerusalem. There (in Jabneh) he died about 108 C.E.

It is related that Rabbi Johanan ben Zakkai was riding upon his ass on the road, while his pupil, R. Eleazar ben Arach, was walking behind him. Said R. Eleazar to him, "Master, teach me a chapter about the matter relating to the chariot," that is, the vision in the first chapter of Ezekiel. The master declined, preferring to hear the pupil. R. Eleazar said again, "Wilt thou permit me to repeat in thy presence one thing which thou has taught me?" to which he gave his assent. R. Johanan then dismounted from his ass, and wrapped himself in his gown, and seated himself upon a stone under an olive-tree. He said it was disrespectful that he should be riding on his beast, whilst his pupil was lecturing on such awful mysteries, and the *Shechinah* (the Divine Presence) and the *Malache ha-Shareth* (the angels-in-waiting) were accompanying them. Immediately R. Eleazar began his exposition. And there came down fire from heaven and encircled them and the whole field. And the angels assembled and came to hearken, as the sons of men assemble and come to look on at the festivities of bride and bridegroom. And the terebinth-trees in the field opened their mouths and uttered a song, "Praise the Lord from the earth, ye dragons and all deeps. . . . Fruitful trees and all cedars, . . . praise ye the Lord." And an angel answered from the fire and said, "This is the matter of the chariot." When he had finished, R. Johanan ben Zakkai stood up and kissed him on his head, saying, "Praised be the God of Abraham, Isaac, and Jacob, who has given our father Abraham a wise son, who knows how to discourse on the glory of our Father in heaven." So much for the story. I need hardly recall to your mind the parallels in the Book of Enoch and in the New Testament.[37]

My lecture is at an end, not so the subject it treats. To accomplish the latter in a properly critical and scientific manner the aid of fellow-workers is necessary. I have often heard the wish expressed that a history of the rise of Christianity might be written by a Jew who could bring Rabbinic learning to bear upon the subject. I do not think that the time is as yet ripe for such an experiment. The best thing to be done at present is, that Christians devote themselves to the study of Rabbinic literature. The history which would be written after such study would certainly be more scientific and more critical, though perhaps less edifying.

3

THE DOGMAS OF JUDAISM

THE object of this essay is to say about the dogmas of Judaism a word which I think ought not to be left unsaid.

In speaking of dogmas it must be understood that Judaism does not ascribe to them any saving power. The belief in a dogma or a doctrine without abiding by its real or supposed consequences (*e.g.* the belief in *creatio ex nihilo* without keeping the Sabbath) is of no value. And the question about certain doctrines is not whether they possess or do not possess the desired charm against certain diseases of the soul, but whether they ought to be considered as characteristics of Judaism or not.

It must again be premised that the subject, which occupied the thoughts of the greatest and noblest Jewish minds for so many centuries, has been neglected for a comparatively long time. And this for various reasons. First, there is Mendelssohn's assertion, or supposed assertion, in his *Jerusalem*, that Judaism has no dogmas—an assertion which has been accepted by the majority of modern Jewish theologians as the only dogma Judaism possesses. You can hear it pronounced in scores of Jewish pulpits; you can read it written in scores of Jewish books. To admit the possibility that Mendelssohn was in error was hardly permissible, especially for those with whom he enjoys a certain infallibility. Nay, even the fact that he himself was not consistent in his theory, and on another occasion declared that Judaism *has* dogmas, only that they are purer and more in harmony with reason than those of other religions; or even the more important fact that he published a school-book for children, in which the so-called Thirteen Articles were embodied, only that instead of the formula "I believe," he substituted "I am convinced," —even such patent facts did not produce much effect upon many of our modern theologians.[1] They were either over-looked or explained away so as to make them harmonise with the great dogma of dogmalessness. For it is one of the attributes of infallibility that the words of its happy possessor must always be reconcilable even when they appear to the eye of the unbeliever as gross contradictions.

Another cause of the neglect into which the subject has fallen is that our century is an *historical* one. It is not only books that have their fate, but also whole sciences and literatures. In past times it was religious speculation that formed the favourite study of scholars, in our time it is history with its critical foundation on a sound philology. Now as these two most important branches of Jewish science were so long neglected—were perhaps never cultivated in the true meaning of the word, and as Jewish literature is so vast and Jewish history so far-reaching and eventful, we cannot wonder that these studies have absorbed the time and the labour of the greatest and best Jewish writers in this century.

There is, besides, a certain tendency in historical studies that is hostile to mere theological speculation. The historian deals with realities, the theologian with abstractions. The latter likes to shape the universe after his system, and tells us how things *ought to be,* the former teaches us how they *are* or *have been,* and the explanation he gives for their being so and not otherwise includes in most cases also a kind of justification for their existence. There is also the *odium theologicum,* which has been the cause of so much misfortune that it is hated by the historian, whilst the superficial, rationalistic way in which the theologian manages to explain everything which does not suit his system is most repulsive to the critical spirit.

But it cannot be denied that this neglect has caused much confusion. Especially is this noticeable in England, which is essentially a theological country, and where people are but little prone to give up speculation about things which concern their most sacred interest and greatest happiness. Thus whilst we are exceedingly poor in all other branches of Jewish learning, we are comparatively rich in productions of a theological character. We have a superfluity of essays on such delicate subjects as eternal punishment, immortality of the soul, the day of judgment, etc., and many treatises on the definition of Judaism. But knowing little or nothing of the progress recently made in Jewish theology, of the many protests against all kinds of infallibility, whether canonised in this century or in olden times, we in England still maintain that Judaism has no dogmas as if nothing to the contrary had ever been said. We seek the foundation of Judaism in political economy, in hygiene, in everything except religion. Following the fashion of the day to esteem religion in proportion to its ability to adapt itself to every possible and impossible metaphysical and social system, we are anxious to squeeze out of Judaism the last drop of faith and hope, and strive to make it so flexible that we can turn it in every direction which it is our pleasure to follow. But alas! the flexibility has progressed so far as to classify Judaism among the invertebrate species, the lowest order of living things. It strongly resembles a certain Christian school which addresses itself to the world in general and claims to satisfy everybody alike. It claims to be socialism for the adherents of Karl Marx and Lassalle, worship of man for the followers of Comte and St. Simon; it carefully avoids the word "God" for the comfort of agnostics and sceptics, whilst on the other hand it pretends to hold sway over paradise, hell, and immortality for the edification of believers. In such illusions many of our theologians delight. For illusions they are; you cannot be everything if you want to be anything. Moreover, illusions in themselves are bad enough, but we are menaced with what is still worse. Judaism, divested of every higher religious motive, is in danger of falling into gross materialism. For what else is the meaning of such declarations as "Believe what you like, but conform to this or that mode of life"; what else does it mean but "We cannot expect you to believe that the things you are bidden to do are commanded by a higher authority; there is not such a thing as belief, but you ought to do them for conventionalism or for your own convenience."

But both these motives—the good opinion of our neighbours, as well as our bodily health—have nothing to do with our nobler and higher sentiments, and degrade Judaism to a matter of expediency or diplomacy. Indeed, things have advanced so far that well-meaning but ill-advised writers even think to render a service to Judaism by declaring it to be a kind of enlightened Hedonism, or rather a moderate Epicureanism.

I have no intention of here answering the question, What is Judaism? This question is not less perplexing than the problem, What is God's world? Judaism is also a great Infinite, composed of as many endless Units, the Jews. And these Unit-Jews have been, and are still, scattered through all the world, and have passed under an immensity of influences, good and bad. If so, how can we give an exact definition of the Infinite, called Judaism?

But if there is anything sure, it is that the highest motives which worked through the history of Judaism are the strong belief in God and the unshaken confidence that at last this God, the God of Israel, will be the God of the whole world; or, in other words, Faith and Hope are the two most prominent characteristics of Judaism.

In the following pages I shall try to give a short account of the manner in which these two principles of Judaism found expression, from the earliest times down to the age of Mendelssohn; that is, to present an outline of the history of Jewish Dogmas. First, a few observations on the position of the Bible and the Talmud in relation to our theme. Insufficient and poor as they may be in proportion to the importance of these two fundamental documents of Judaism, these remarks may nevertheless suggest a connecting link between the teachings of Jewish antiquity and those of Maimonides and his successors.

I begin with the Scriptures.

The Bible itself hardly contains a command bidding us *to believe*. We are hardly ordered, *e.g.,* to believe in the existence of God. I say hardly, but I do not altogether deny the existence of such a command. It is true that we do not find in the Scripture such words as: "You are commanded to believe in the existence of God." Nor is any punishment assigned as awaiting him who denies it. Notwithstanding these facts, many Jewish authorities—among them such important men as Maimonides, R. Judah Hallevi, Nachmanides —perceive, in the first words of the Ten Commandments, "I am the Lord thy God," the command to believe in His existence.[2]

Be this as it may, there cannot be the shadow of a doubt that the Bible, in which every command is dictated by God, and in which all its heroes are the servants, the friends, or the ambassadors of God, presumes such a belief in every one to

whom those laws are dictated, and these heroes address themselves. Nay, I think that the word "belief" is not even adequate. In a world with so many visible facts and invisible
causes, as life and death, growth and decay, light and darkness; in a world where the sun rises and sets; where the stars
appear regularly; where heavy rains pour down from the sky,
often accompanied by such grand phenomena as thunder and
lightning; in a world full of such marvels, but into which no
notion has entered of all our modern true or false explanations—who but God is behind all these things? "Have the
gates," asks God, "have the gates of death been open to thee?
or hast thou seen the doors of the shadow of death? . . .
Where is the way where light dwelleth? and as for darkness,
where is the place thereof? . . . Hath the rain a father? or
who hath begotten the drops of dew? . . . Canst thou bind
the sweet influences of Pleiades, or loose the bands of Orion?
. . . Canst thou send lightnings, that they may go, and say
unto thee, Here we are?" (Job xxxviii). Of all these wonders,
God was not merely the *prima causa;* they were the result of
His direct action, without any intermediary causes. And it is
as absurd to say that the ancient world believed in God, as
for a future historian to assert of the nineteenth century that
it believed in the effects of electricity. We *see* them, and so
antiquity *saw* God. If there was any danger, it lay not in
the denial of the existence of a God, but in having a wrong
belief. Belief in as many gods as there are manifestations in
nature, the investing of them with false attributes, the misunderstanding of God's relation to men, lead to immortality.
Thus the greater part of the laws and teachings of the Bible
are either directed against polytheism, with all its low ideas
of God, or rather of gods; or they are directed towards regulating God's relation to men. Man is a servant of God, or His
prophet, or even His friend. But this relationship man
obtains only by his conduct. Nay, all man's actions are care-

fully regulated by God, and connected with his holiness. The 19th chapter of Leviticus, which is considered by the Rabbis as the portion of the Law in which the most important articles of the Torah are embodied, is headed, "Ye shall be holy, for I the Lord your own God am holy." And each law therein occurring, even those which concern our relations to each other, is *not* founded on utilitarian reasons, but is ordained because the opposite of it is an offense to the holiness of God, and profanes His creatures, whom He desired to be as holy as He is.[3]

Thus the whole structure of the Bible is built upon the visible fact of the existence of a God, and upon the belief in the relation of God to men, especially to Israel. In spite of all that has been said to the contrary, the Bible *does* lay stress upon belief, where belief is required. The unbelievers are rebuked again and again. "For all this they sinned still, and believed not for His wondrous work," complains Asaph (Ps. lxxviii. 32). And belief is praised in such exalted words as, "Thus saith the Lord, I remember thee, the kindness of thy youth, the love of thine espousals, when thou wentest after me in the wilderness, in a land that was not sown" (Jer. ii. 2). The Bible, especially the books of the prophets, consists, in great part, of promises for the future, which the Rabbis justly termed the "Consolations." [4] For our purpose, it is of no great consequence to examine what future the prophets had in view, whether an immediate future or one more remote, at the end of days. At any rate, they inculcated hope and confidence that God would bring to pass a better time. I think that even the most advanced Bible critic—provided he is not guided by some modern Aryan reasons—must perceive in such passages as, "The Lord shall reign for ever and ever," "The Lord shall rejoice in his works," and many others, a hope for more than the establishment of the "national Deity among his votaries in Palestine."

We have now to pass over an interval of many centuries, the length of which depends upon the views held as to the date of the close of the canon, and examine what the Rabbis, the representatives of the prophets, thought on this subject. Not that the views of the author of the *Wisdom of Solomon*, of Philo and Aristobulus, and many others of the Judæo-Alexandrian school would be uninteresting for us. But somehow their influence on Judaism was only a passing one, and their doctrines never became authoritative in the Synagogue. We must here confine ourselves to those who, even by the testimony of their bitterest enemies, occupied the seat of Moses.

The successors of the prophets had to deal with new circumstances, and accordingly their teachings were adapted to the wants of their times. As the result of manifold foreign influences, the visible fact of the existence of God as manifested in the Bible had been somewhat obscured. Prophecy ceased, and the Holy Spirit which inspired a few chosen ones took its place. Afterwards this influence was reduced to the hearing of a Voice from Heaven, which was audible to still fewer. On the other hand the Rabbis had this advantage, that they were not called upon to fight against idolatry as their predecessors the prophets had been. The evil inclination to worship idols was, as the Talmud expresses it allegorically, killed by the Men of the Great Synagogue, or, as we should put it, it was suppressed by the sufferings of the captivity in Babylon. This change of circumstances is marked by the following fact:—Whilst the prophets mostly considered idolatry as the cause of all sin, the Rabbis show a strong tendency to ascribe sin to a defect in, or a want of, belief on the part of the sinner. They teach that Adam would not have sinned unless he had first denied the "Root of all" (or the main principle), namely, the belief in the Omnipresence of God. Of Cain they say that before murdering his brother he declared: "There is no judgment, there is no judge, there is no world to come, and there is no reward for the just, and no punishment for the wicked." [5]

In another place we read that the commission of a sin in secret is an impertinent attempt by the doer to oust God from the world. But if unbelief is considered as the root of all evil, we may expect that the reverse of it, a perfect faith, would be praised in the most exalted terms. So we read: Faith is so great that the man who possesses it may hope to become a worthy vessel of the Holy Spirit, or, as we should express it, that he may hope to obtain by this power the highest degree of communion with his Maker. The Patriarch Abraham, notwithstanding all his other virtues, only became "the possessor of both worlds" by the merit of his strong faith. Nay, even the fulfilment of a single law when accompanied by true faith is, according to the Rabbis, sufficient to bring man nigh to God. And the future redemption is also conditional on the degree of faith shown by Israel. [6]

It has often been asked what the Rabbis would have thought of a man who fulfils every commandment of the Torah, but does not believe that this Torah was given by God, or that there exists a God at all. It is indeed very difficult to answer this question with any degree of certainty. In the time of the Rabbis people were still too simple for such a diplomatic religion, and conformity in the modern sense was quite an unknown thing. But from the foregoing remarks it would seem that the Rabbis could not conceive such a monstrosity as atheistic orthodoxy. For, as we have seen, the Rabbis thought that unbelief must needs end in sin, for faith is the origin of all good. Accordingly, in the case just supposed they would have either suspected the man's orthodoxy, or would have denied that his views were really what he professed them to be.

Still more important than the above cited Agadic passages

is one which we are about to quote from the tractate Sanhe-drin. This tractate deals with the constitution of the supreme law-court, the examination of the witnesses, the functions of the judges, and the different punishment to be inflicted on the transgressors of the law. After having enumerated various kinds of capital punishment, the Mishnah adds the following words: "These are (the men) who are excluded from the life to come: He who says there is no resurrection from death; he who says there is no Torah given from heaven, and the Epikurus." [7] This passage was considered by the Rabbis of the Middle Ages, as well as by modern scholars, the *locus classicus* for the dogma question. There are many passages in the Rabbinic literature which exclude man from the world to come for this or that sin. But these are more or less of an Agadic (legendary) character, and thus lend them-selves to exaggeration and hyperbolic language. They cannot, therefore, be considered as serious legal dicta, or as the general opinion of the Rabbis.

The Mishnah in Sanhedrin, however, has, if only by its position in a legal tractate, a certain *Halachic* (obligatory) character. And the fact that so early an authority as R. Akiba made additions to it guarantees its high antiquity. The first two sentences of this Mishnah are clear enough. In modern language, and positively speaking, they would represent articles of belief in Resurrection and Revelation. Great dif-ficulty is found in defining what was meant by the word *Epikurus*. The authorities of the Middle Ages, to whom I shall again have to refer, explain the Epikurus to be a man who denies the belief in reward and punishment; others identify him with one who denies the belief in Providence; while others again consider the Epikurus to be one who denies Tradition. But the parallel passages in which it occurs incline one rather to think that this word cannot be defined by one kind of heresy. It implies rather a frivolous treatment of the words of Scripture or of Tradition. In the case of the latter (Tradition) it is certainly not honest difference of opinion that is condemned; for the Rabbis themselves differed very often from each other, and even Mediæval authorities did not feel any compunction about explaining Scripture in variance with the Rabbinic interpretation, and sometimes they even went so far as to declare that the view of this or that great authority was only to be considered as an isolated opinion not deserving particular attention. What they did blame was, as already said, scoffing and impiety. We may thus safely assert that reverence for the teachers of Israel formed the third essential principle of Judaism.[8]

I have still to remark that there occur in the Talmud such passages as "the Jew, even if he has sinned, is still a Jew," or "He who denies idolatry is called a Jew." These and similar passages have been used to prove that Judaism was not a positive religion, but only involved the negation of idolatry. But it has been overlooked that the statements quoted have more a legal than a theological character. The Jew belonged to his nationality even after having committed the greatest sin, just as the Englishman does not cease to be an Englishman—in regard to treason and the like—by having committed a heinous crime. But he has certainly acted in a very un-English way, and having outraged the feelings of the whole nation will have to suffer for his misconduct. The Rabbis in a similar manner did not maintain that he who gave up the belief in Revelation and Resurrection, and treated irreverently the teachers of Israel, severed his connection with the Jewish nation, but that, for his crime, he was going to suffer the heaviest punishment. He was to be excluded from the world to come.

Still, important as is the passage quoted from Sanhedrin, it would be erroneous to think that it exhausted the creed of the Rabbis. The liturgy and innumerable passages in the

Midrashim show that they ardently clung to the belief in the advent of the Messiah. All their hope was turned to the future redemption and the final establishment of the Kingdom of Heaven on earth. Judaism, stripped of this belief, would have been for them devoid of meaning. The belief in reward and punishment is also repeated again and again in the old Rabbinic literature. A more emphatic declaration of the belief in Providence than is conveyed by the following passages is hardly conceivable. "Everything is foreseen, and free will is given. And the world is judged by grace." Or, "the born are to die, and the dead to revive, and the living to be judged. For to know and to notify, and that it may be known that He (God) is the Framer and He the Creator, and He the Discerner, and He the Judge, and He the Witness," etc.[9]

But it must not be forgotten that it was not the habit of the Rabbis to lay down, either for conduct or for doctrine, rules which were commonly known. When they urged the three points stated above there must have been some historical reason for it. Probably these principles were controverted by some heretics. Indeed, the whole tone of the passage cited from Sanhedrin is a protest against certain unbelievers who are threatened with punishment. Other beliefs, not less essential, but less disputed, remain unmentioned, because there was no necessity to assert them.

It was not till a much later time, when the Jews came into closer contact with new philosophical schools, and also new creeds which were more liable than heathenism was to be confused with Judaism, that this necessity was felt. And thus we are led at once to the period when the Jews became acquainted with the teachings of the Mohammedan schools. The Caraites came very early into contact with non-Jewish systems. And so we find that they were also the first to formulate Jewish dogmas in a fixed number, and in a systematic order. It is also possible that their separation from the

Tradition, and their early division into little sects among themselves, compelled them to take this step, in order to avoid further sectarianism.

The number of their dogmas amounts to ten. According to Judah Hadasi (1150), who would appear to have derived them from his predecessors, their dogmas include the following articles: 1. *Creatio ex nihilo;* 2. The existence of a Creator, God; 3. This God is an absolute unity as well as incorporeal; 4. Moses and the other prophets were sent by God; 5. God has given to us the Torah, which is true and complete in every respect, not wanting the addition of the so-called Oral Law; 6. The Torah must be studied by every Jew in the original (Hebrew) language; 7. The Holy Temple was a place elected by God for His manifestation; 8. Resurrection of the dead; 9. Punishment and reward after death; 10. The Coming of the Messiah, the son of David.

How far the predecessors of Hadasi were influenced by a certain Joseph Albashir (about 950), of whom there exists a manuscript work, "Rudiments of Faith," I am unable to say. The little we know of him reveals more of his intimacy with Arabic thoughts than of his importance for his sect in particular and for Judaism in general. After Hadasi I shall mention here Elijah Bashazi, a Caraite writer of the end of the fifteenth century. This author, who was much influenced by Maimonides, omits the second and the seventh articles. In order to make up the ten he numbers the belief in the eternity of God as an article, and divides the fourth article into two. In the fifth article Bashazi does not emphasise so strongly the completeness of the Torah as Hadasi, and omits the portion which is directed against Tradition. It is interesting to see the distinction which Bashazi draws between the Pentateuch and the Prophets. While he thinks that the five books of Moses can never be altered, he regards the words of the Prophets as only relating to their contempo-

raries, and thus subject to changes. As I do not want to antic-
ipate Maimonides' system, I must refrain from giving here
the articles laid down by Solomon Troki in the beginning of
the eighteenth century. For the articles of Maimonides are
copied by this writer with a few slight alterations so as to
dress them in a Caraite garb.

I must dismiss the Caraites with these few remarks, my
object being chiefly to discuss the dogmas of the Synagogue
from which they had separated themselves. Besides, as in
everything Caraitic, there is no further development of the
question. As Bashazi laid them down, they are still taught by
the Caraites of to-day. I return to the Rabbanites.[10]

As is well known, Maimonides (1130-1205), was the first
Rabbanite who formulated the dogmas of the Synagogue.
But there are indications of earlier attempts. R. Saadiah
Gaon's (892-942) work, *Creeds and Opinions,* shows such
traces. He says in his preface, "My heart sickens to see that
the belief of my co-religionists is impure and that their
theological views are confused." The subjects he treats in
this book, such as creation, unity of God, resurrection of the
dead, the future redemption of Israel, reward and punishment, and other kindred theological subjects might thus,
perhaps, be considered as the essentials of the creed that the
Gaon desired to present in a pure and rational form. R.
Hannaneel, of Kairowan,[11] in the first half of the eleventh
century, says in one of his commentaries that to deserve
eternal life one must believe in *four* things: in God, in the
prophets, in a future world where the just will be rewarded,
and in the advent of the Redeemer. From R. Judah Hallevi's
Cusari, written in the beginning of the twelfth century, we
might argue that the belief in the election of Israel by God
was the cardinal dogma of the author.[12] Abraham Ibn Daud,
a contemporary of Maimonides, in his book *The High
Belief,*[13] speaks of *rudiments,* among which, besides such

metaphysical principles as unity, rational conception of God's attributes, etc., the belief in the immutability of the Law, etc., is included. Still, all these works are intended to furnish evidence from philosophy or history for the truth of religion rather than to give a definition of this truth. The latter task was undertaken by Maimonides.

I refer to the thirteen articles embodied in his first work, *The Commentary to the Mishnah.* They are appended to the Mishnah in Sanhedrin, with which I dealt above. But though they do not form an independent treatise, Maimonides' remarks must not be considered as merely incidental.

That Maimonides was quite conscious of the importance of this exposition can be gathered from the concluding words addressed to the reader: "Know these (words) and repeat them many times, and think them over in the proper way. God knows that thou wouldst be deceiving thyself if thou thinkest thou hast understood them by having read them once or even ten times. Be not, therefore, hasty in perusing them. I have not composed them without deep study and earnest reflection."

The result of this deep study was that the following Thirteen Articles constitute the creed of Judaism. They are: 1. The belief in the existence of a Creator; 2. The belief in His Unity; 3. The belief in His Incorporeality; 4. The belief in His Eternity; 5. The belief that all worship and adoration are due to Him alone; 6. The belief in Prophecy; 7. The belief that Moses was the greatest of all Prophets, both before and after him; 8. The belief that the Torah was revealed to Moses on Mount Sinai; 9. The belief in the Immutability of this revealed Torah; 10. The belief that God knows the actions of men; 11. The belief in Reward and Punishment; 12. The belief in the coming of the Messiah; 13. The belief in the Resurrection of the dead.

The impulse given by the great philosopher and still

greater Jew was eagerly followed by succeeding generations, and Judaism thus came into possession of a dogmatic literature such as it never knew before Maimonides. Maimonides is the centre of this literature, and I shall accordingly speak in the remainder of this essay of Maimonists and Anti-Maimonists. These terms really apply to the great controversy that raged round Maimonides' *Guide of the Perplexed,* but I shall, chiefly for brevity's sake, employ them in these pages in a restricted sense to refer to the dispute concerning the Thirteen Articles.

Among the Maimonists we may probably include the great majority of Jews, who accepted the Thirteen Articles without further question. Maimonides must indeed have filled up a great gap in Jewish theology, a gap, moreover, the existence of which was very generally perceived. A century had hardly elapsed before the Thirteen Articles had become a theme for the poets of the Synagogue. And almost every country where Jews lived can show a poem or a prayer founded on these Articles. R. Jacob Molin (1420) of Germany speaks of metrical and rhymed songs in the German language, the burden of which was the Thirteen Articles, and which were read by the common people with great devotion. The numerous commentaries and homilies written on the same topic would form a small library in themselves.[14] But on the other hand it must not be denied that the Anti-Maimonists, that is to say those Jewish writers who did not agree with the creed formulated by Maimonides, or agreed only in part with him, form also a very strong and respectable minority. They deserve our attention the more as it is their works which brought life into the subject and deepened it. It is not by a perpetual Amen to every utterance of a great authority that truth or literature gains anything.

The Anti-Maimonists can be divided into two classes. The one class categorically denies that Judaism has dogmas. I shall have occasion to touch on this view when I come to speak of Abarbanel. Here I pass at once to the second class of Anti-Maimonists. This consists of those who agree with Maimonides as to the existence of dogmas in Judaism, but who differ from him as to what these dogmas are, or who give a different enumeration of them.

As the first of these Anti-Maimonists we may regard Nachmanides, who, in his famous *Sermon in the Presence of the King,* speaks of three fundamental principles: Creation (that is, non-eternity of matter), Omniscience of God, and Providence. Next comes R. Abba Mari ben Moses, of Montpellier. He wrote at the beginning of the fourteenth century, and is famous in Jewish history for his zeal against the study of philosophy. We possess a small pamphlet by him dealing with our subject, and it forms a kind of prologue to his collection of controversial letters against the rationalists of his time.[15] He lays down three articles as the fundamental teachings of Religion: 1. Metaphysical: The existence of God, including His Unity and Incorporeality; 2. Mosaic: *Creatio ex nihilo* by God—a consequence of this principle is the belief that God is capable of altering the laws of nature at His pleasure; 3. Ethical: Special Providence—*i.e.* God knows all our actions in all their details. Abba Mari does not mention Maimonides' Thirteen Articles. But it would be false to conclude that he rejected the belief in the coming of the Messiah, or any other article of Maimonides. The whole tone and tendency of this pamphlet is polemical, and it is therefore probable that he only urged those points which were either doubted or explained in an unorthodox way by the sceptics of his time.

Another scholar, of Provence, who wrote but twenty years later than Abba Mari—R. David ben Samuel d'Estella (1320)—speaks of the seven pillars of religion. They are: Revelation, Providence, Reward and Punishment, the Coming of the Messiah, Resurrection of the Dead, *Creatio ex nihilo,* and Free Will.[16]

Of authors living in other countries, I have to mention here R. Shemariah, of Crete, who flourished at about the same time as R. David d'Estella, and is known from his efforts to reconcile the Caraites with the Rabbanites. This author wrote a book for the purpose of furnishing Jewish students with evidence for what he considered the five fundamental teachings of Judaism, viz.: 1. The Existence of God; 2. The Incorporeality of God; 3. His Absolute Unity; 4. That God created heaven and earth; 5. That God created the world after His will 5106 years ago—5106 (1346 A.C.) being the year in which Shemariah wrote these words.[17]

In Portugal, at about the same time, we find R. David ben Yom-Tob Bilia adding to the articles of Maimonides thirteen of his own, which he calls the "Fundamentals of the Thinking Man." Five of these articles relate to the functions of the human soul, that, according to him, emanated from God, and to the way in which this divine soul receives its punishment and reward. The other eight articles are as follows: 1. The belief in the existence of spiritual beings—angels; 2. *Creatio ex nihilo;* 3. The belief in the existence of another world, and that this other world is only a spiritual one; 4. The Torah is above philosophy; 5. The Torah has an outward (literal) meaning and an inward (allegorical) meaning; 6. The text of the Torah is not subject to any emendation; 7. The reward of a good action is the good work itself, and the doer must not expect any other reward; 8. It is only by the "commands relating to the heart," for instance, the belief in one eternal God, the loving and fearing Him, and not through good actions, that man attains the highest degree of perfection.[18] Perhaps it would be suitable to mention here another contemporaneous writer, who also enumerates twenty-six articles. The name of this writer is unknown, and his articles are only gathered from quotations by later authors. It would seem from these quotations that the articles of his unknown author consisted mostly of statements emphasising the belief in the attributes of God: as, His Eternity, His Wisdom and Omnipotence, and the like.[19]

More important for our subject are the productions of the fifteenth century, especially those of Spanish authors. The fifteen articles of R. Lipman Muhlhausen, in the preface to his well-known *Book of Victory*[20] (1410), differ but slightly from those of Maimonides. In accordance with the anti-Christian tendency of his polemical book, he lays more stress on the two articles of Unity and Incorporeality, and makes of them four. We can therefore dismiss him with this short remark, and pass at once to the Spanish Rabbis.

The first of these is R. Chasdai Ibn Crescas, who composed his famous treatise, *The Light of God,* about 1405. Chasdai's book is well known for its attacks on Aristotle, and also for its influence on Spinoza. But Chasdai deals also with Maimonides' Thirteen Articles, to which he was very strongly opposed. Already in his preface he attacks Maimonides for speaking, in his *Book of the Commandments,* of the belief in the existence of God as an "affirmative precept." Chasdai thinks it absurd; for every commandment must be dictated by some authority, but on whose authority can we dictate the acceptance of this authority? His general objection to the Thirteen Articles is that Maimonides confounded dogmas or *fundamental beliefs* of Judaism, without which Judaism is inconceivable, with beliefs or *doctrines* which Judaism inculcates, but the denial of which, though involving a strong heresy, does not make Judaism impossible. He maintains that if Maimonides meant only to count fundamental teachings, there are not more than seven; but that if he intended also to include doctrines, he ought to have enumerated sixteen. As beliefs of the first class—namely, fundamental beliefs—he considers the following articles: 1. God's knowledge of our actions; 2. Providence; 3. God's omnipotence—even to act against the laws of nature; 4. Prophecy; 5. Free will; 6. The aim of the Torah is to make man long after the closest communion with God. The belief in the existence of God, Chasdai thinks, is an axiom with which every religion must begin, and he is therefore uncertain whether to include it as a dogma or not. As to the doctrines which every Jew is bound to believe, but without which Judaism is not impossible, Chasdai divides them into two sections: (a) 1. *Creatio ex nihilo;* 2. Immortality of the soul; 3. Reward and Punishment; 4. Resurrection of the dead; 5. Immutability of the Torah; 6. Superiority of the prophecy of Moses; 7. That the High Priest received from God the instructions sought for, when he put his questions through the medium of the Urim and Thummim; 8. The coming of the Messiah. (b) Doctrines which are expressed by certain religious ceremonies, and on belief in which these ceremonies are conditioned: 1. The belief in the efficacy of prayer—as well as in the power of the benediction of the priests to convey to us the blessing of God; 2. God is merciful to the penitent; 3. Certain days in the year—for instance, the Day of Atonement—are especially qualified to bring us near to God, if we keep them in the way we are commanded. That Chasdai is a little arbitrary in the choice of his "doctrines," I need hardly say. Indeed, Chasdai's importance for the dogma-question consists more in his critical suggestions than in his positive results. He was, as we have seen, the first to make the distinction between fundamental teachings which form the basis of Judaism, and those other simple Jewish doctrines without which Judaism is not impossible. Very daring is his remark, when proving that Reward and Punishment, Immortality

of the soul, and Resurrection of the dead must not be considered as the basis of Judaism, since the highest ideal of
religion is to serve God without any hope of reward. Even
more daring are his words concerning the Immutability
of the Law. He says: "Some have argued that, since God is
perfection, so must also His law be perfect, and thus un-
susceptible of improvement." But he does not think this
argument conclusive, though the fact in itself (the Immutability of the Law) is true. For one might answer that this
perfection of the Torah could only be in accordance with
the intelligence of those for whom it was meant; but as soon
as the recipients of the Torah have advanced to a higher state
of perfection, the Torah must also be altered to suit their
advanced intelligence. A pupil of Chasdai illustrates the
words of his master by a medical parallel. The physician has
to adapt his medicaments to the various stages through which
his patient has to pass. That he changes his prescription does
not, however, imply that his medical knowledge is imperfect,
or that his earlier remedies were ignorantly chosen; the vary-
ing condition of the invalid was the cause of the variation in
the doctor's treatment. Similarly, were not the Immutability
of the Torah a "doctrine," one might maintain that the perfection of the Torah would not be inconsistent with the assumption that it was susceptible of modification, in accordance with our changing and progressive circumstances. But
all these arguments are purely of a theoretic character; for,
practically, every Jew, according to Chasdai, has to accept
all these beliefs, whether he terms them fundamental teachings or only Jewish doctrines.[21]

Some years later, though he finished his work in the same
year as Chasdai, R. Simeon Duran (1366-1444), a younger
contemporary of the former, made his researches on dogmas.
His studies on this subject form a kind of introduction to his
commentary on Job, which he finished in the year 1405.

Duran is not so strongly opposed to the Thirteen Articles as Chasdai, or as another "thinker of our people," who thought them an arbitrary imitation of the thirteen attributes of God. Duran tries to justify Maimonides; but nevertheless he agrees with "earlier authorities," who formulated the Jewish creed in Three Articles—The Existence of God, Revelation, and Reward and Punishment—under which Duran thinks the Thirteen Articles of Maimonides may be easily classed. Most interesting are his remarks concerning the validity of dogmas. He tells us that only those are to be considered as heretics who abide by their own opinions, though they know that they are contradictory to the views of the Torah. Those who accept the fundamental teachings of Judaism, but are led by their deep studies and earnest reflection to differ in details from the opinions current among their co-religionists, and explain certain passages in the Scripture in their own way, must by no means be considered as heretics. We must, therefore, Duran proceeds to say, not blame such men as Maimonides, who gave an allegorical interpretation to certain passages in the Bible about miracles, or R. Levi ben Gershom, who followed certain un-Jewish views in relation to the belief in *Creatio ex nihilo*. Only the views are condemnable, not those who cherish them. God forbid, says Duran, that such a thing should happen in Israel as to condemn honest inquirers on account of their differing opinions. It would be interesting to know of how many divines as tolerant as this persecuted Jew the fifteenth century can boast.[22]

We can now pass to a more popular but less original writer on our theme. I refer to R. Joseph Albo, the author of the *Roots*,[23] who was the pupil of Chasdai, a younger contemporary of Duran, and wrote at a much later period than these authors. Graetz has justly denied him much originality. The chief merit of Albo consists in popularising other people's thoughts, though he does not always take care to mention their names. And the student who is a little familiar with the contents of the *Roots* will easily find that Albo has taken his best ideas either from Chasdai or from Duran. As it is of little consequence to us whether an article of faith is called "stem," or "root," or "branch," there is scarcely anything fresh left to quote in the name of Albo. The late Dr. Löw, of Szegedin, was indeed right, when he answered an adversary who challenged him—"Who would dare to declare me a heretic as long as I confess the Three Articles laid down by Albo?" with the words "Albo himself." For, after all the subtle distinctions Albo makes between different classes of dogmas, he declares that every one who denies even the immutability of the Law or the coming of the Messiah, which are, according to him, articles of minor importance, is a heretic who will be excluded from the world to come. But there is one point in his book which is worth noticing. It was suggested to him by Maimonides, indeed; still Albo has the merit of having emphasised it as it deserves. Among the articles which he calls "branches" Albo counts the belief that the perfection of man, which leads to eternal life, can be obtained by the fulfilling of *one* commandment. But this command must, as Maimonides points out, be done without any worldly regard, and only for the love of God. When one considers how many platitudes are repeated year by year by certain theologians on the subject of Jewish legalism, we cannot lay enough stress on this article of Albo, and we ought to make it better known than it has hitherto been.[24]

Though I cannot enter here into the enumeration of the Maimonists, I must not leave unmentioned the name of R. Nissim ben Moses of Marseilles, the first great Maimonist, who flourished about the end of the thirteenth century, and was considered as one of the most enlightened thinkers of his age.[25] Another great Maimonist deserving special attention is R. Abraham ben Shem-Tob Bibago, who may perhaps be regarded as the most prominent among those who undertook to defend Maimonides against the attacks of Chasdai and others. Bibago wrote *The Path of Belief*[26] in the second half of the fifteenth century, and was, as Dr. Steinschneider aptly describes him, a *Denkgläubiger*. But, above all, he was a believing Jew. When he was once asked, at the table of King John II, of Aragon, by a Christian scholar, "Are you the Jewish philosopher?" he answered, "I am a Jew who believes in the Law given to us by our teacher Moses, though I have studied philosophy." Bibago was such a devoted admirer of Maimonides that he could not tolerate any opposition to him. He speaks in one passage of the prudent people of his time who, in desiring to be looked upon as orthodox by the great mob, calumniated the Teacher (Maimonides), and depreciated his merits. Bibago's book is very interesting, especially in its controversial parts; but in respect to dogmas he is, as already said, a Maimonist, and does not contribute any new point on our subject.

To return to the Anti-Maimonists of the second half of the fifteenth century. As such may be considered R. Isaac Aramah, who speaks of three foundations of religion: *Creatio ex nihilo,* Revelation (?), and the belief in a world to come.[27] Next to be mentioned is R. Joseph Jabez, who also accepts only three articles: *Creatio ex nihilo,* Individual Providence, and the Unity of God.[28] Under these three heads he tries to classify the Thirteen Articles of Maimonides.

The last Spanish writer on our subject is R. Isaac Abarbanel. His treatise on the subject is known under the title *Top of Amanah,*[29] and was finished in the year 1495. The greatest part of this treatise forms a defence of Maimonides, many points in which are taken from Bibago. But, in spite of this fact, Abarbanel must not be considered a Maimonist. It is only a feeling of piety towards Maimonides, or perhaps rather a fondness for argument, that made him defend Maimonides against Chasdai and others. His own view is that it is a mistake to formulate dogmas of Judaism, since every word in the Torah has to be considered as a dogma for itself. It was only, says Abarbanel, by following the example of non-Jewish scholars that Maimonides and others were induced to lay down dogmas. The non-Jewish philosophers are in the habit of accepting in every science certain indisputable axioms from which they deduce the propositions which are less evident. The Jewish philosophers in a similar way sought for first principles in religion from which the whole of the Torah ought to be considered as a deduction. But, thinks Abarbanel, the Torah as a revealed code is under no necessity of deducing things from each other, for all the commands came from the same divine authority, and, therefore, all are alike evident, and have the same certainty. On this and similar grounds Abarbanel refused to accept dogmatic articles for Judaism, and he thus became the head of the school that forms a class by itself among the Anti-Maimonists to which many of the greatest Cabbalists also belong. But it is idle talk to cite this school in aid of the modern theory that Judaism has no dogmas. As we have seen, it was rather an *embarras de richesse* that prevented Abarbanel from accepting the Thirteen Articles of Maimonides. To him and to the Cabbalists the Torah consists of at least six hundred and thirteen Articles.

Abarbanel wrote his book with which we have just dealt, at Naples. And it is Italy to which, after the expulsion of the Jews from Spain, we have to look chiefly for religious speculation. But the philosophers of Italy are still less independent of Maimonides than their predecessors in Spain. Thus we find that R. David Messer Leon, R. David Vital, and others were Maimonists. Even the otherwise refined and original thinker, R. Elijah Delmedigo (who died about the end of the fifteenth century), becomes almost impolite when he speaks of the adversaries of Maimonides in respect to dogmas. "It was only," he says, "the would-be philosopher that dared to question the articles of Maimonides. Our people have always the bad habit of thinking themselves competent to attack the greatest authorities as soon as they have got some knowledge of the subject. Genuine thinkers, however, attach very little importance to their objections." [30]

Indeed, it seems as if the energetic protests of Delmedigo scared away the Anti-Maimonists for more than a century. Even in the following seventeenth century we have to notice only two Anti-Maimonists. The one is R. Tobijah, the Priest (1652), who was of Polish descent, studied in Italy, and lived as a medical man in France. He seems to refuse to accept the belief in the Immutability of the Torah, and in the coming of the Messiah, as fundamental teachings of Judaism.[31] The other, at the end of the seventeenth century (1695), is R. Abraham Chayim Viterbo, of Italy. He accepts only six articles: 1. Existence of God; 2. Unity; 3. Incorporeality; 4. That God was revealed to Moses on Mount Sinai, and that the prophecy of Moses is true; 5. Revelation (including the historical parts of the Torah); 6. Reward and Punishment. As to the other articles of Maimonides, Viterbo, in opposition to other half-hearted Anti-Maimonists, declares that the man who denies them is *not* to be considered as a heretic; though he ought to believe them.[32]

I have now arrived at the limit I set to myself at the beginning of this essay. For, between the times of Viterbo and those of Mendelssohn, there is hardly to be found any serious opposition to Maimonides worth noticing here. Still I must mention the name of R. Saul Berlin (died 1794); there is much in his opinions on dogmas which will help us the better to understand the Thirteen Articles of Maimonides. As the reader has seen, I have refrained so far from reproducing here the apologies which were made by many Maimonists in behalf of the Thirteen Articles. For, after all their elaborate pleas, none of them was able to clear Maimonides of the charge of having confounded dogmas or fundamental teachings with doctrines. It is also true that the Fifth Article—that prayer and worship must only be offered to God—cannot be considered even as a doctrine, but as a simple precept. And there are other difficulties which all the distinctions of the Maimonists will never be able to solve. The only possible justification is, I think, that suggested by a remark of R. Saul. This author, who was himself—like his friend and older contemporary Mendelssohn—a strong Anti-Maimonist, among other remarks, maintains that dogmas must never be laid down but with regard to the necessities of the time.[33]

Now R. Saul certainly did not doubt that Judaism is based on eternal truths which can in no way be shaken by new modes of thinking or changed circumstances. What he meant was that there are in every age certain beliefs which ought to be asserted more emphatically than others, without regard to their theological or rather logical importance. It is by this maxim that we shall be able to explain the articles of Maimonides. He asserted them, because they were necessary for his time. We know, for instance, from a letter of his son and from other contemporaries, that it was just at his time that the belief in the incorporeality of God was, in the opinion of Maimonides, a little relaxed. Maimonides, who thought such low notions of the Deity dangerous to Judaism, therefore laid down an article against them. He tells us in his

Guide that it was far from him to condemn anyone who was
not able to demonstrate the Incorporeality of God, but he
stigmatised as a heretic one who refused to believe it. This
position might be paralleled by that of a modern astronomer
who, while considering it unreasonable to expect a mathe-
matical demonstration of the movements of the earth from an
ordinary unscientific man, would yet regard the person who
refused to believe in such movements as an ignorant faddist.

Again, Maimonides undoubtedly knew that there may be
found in the Talmud—that bottomless sea with its innumerable undercurrents—passages that are not quite in harmony
with his articles; for instance, the well-known dictum of R.
Hillel, who said, there is no Messiah for Israel—a passage
which has already been quoted *ad nauseam* by every opponent of Maimonides from the earliest times down to the
year of grace 1896. Maimonides was well aware of the existence of this and similar passages. But, being deeply convinced of the necessity of the belief in a future redemption
of *Israel*—in opposition to other creeds which claim this
redemption exclusively for their own adherents—Maimonides simply ignored the saying of R. Hillel, as an isolated
opinion which contradicts all the consciousness and traditions
of the Jew as expressed in thousands of other passages, and
especially in the liturgy. Most interesting is Maimonides'
view about such isolated opinions in a letter to the wise men
of Marseilles. He deals there with the question of free will
and other theological subjects. After having stated his own
view he goes on to say: "I know that it is possible to find in
the Talmud or in the Midrash this or that saying in contradiction to the views you have heard from me. But you
must not be troubled by them. One must not refuse to accept
a doctrine, the truth of which has been proved, on account
of its being in opposition to some isolated opinion held by

this or that great authority. Is it not possible that he overlooked some important considerations when he uttered this
strange opinion? It is also possible that his words must not be
taken literally, and have to be explained in an allegorical
way. We can also think that his words were only to be applied
with regard to certain circumstances of his time, but never
intended as permanent truths. . . . No man must surrender
his private judgment. The eyes are not directed backwards
but forwards." In another place Maimonides calls the sup-
pression of one's own opinions—for the reason of their being
irreconcilable with the isolated views of some great authority
—a moral suicide.

By such motives Maimonides was guided when he left
certain views hazarded in the Rabbinic literature unheeded,
and followed what we may perhaps call the religious instinct,
trusting to his own conscience. We may again be certain that
Maimonides was clear-headed enough to see that the words
of the Torah: "And there arose no prophet since in Israel
like unto Moses" (Deut. xxxiv. 10), were as little intended to
imply a doctrine as the passage relating to the king Josiah,
"And like unto him was there no king before him that turned
to the Lord with all his heart . . . neither after him arose
there any like him" (2 Kings xxiii. 25). And none would
think of declaring the man a heretic who should believe
another king to be as pious as Josiah. But living among
followers of the "imitating creeds" (as he calls Christianity
and Mohammedism), who claimed that their religion had
superseded the law of Moses, Maimonides, consciously or un-
consciously, felt himself compelled to assert the superiority
of the prophecy of Moses. And so we may guess that every
article of Maimonides which seems to offer difficulties to us
contains an assertion of some relaxed belief, or a protest
against the pretensions of other creeds, though we are not

always able to discover the exact necessity for them. On the other hand, Maimonides did not assert the belief in free will, for which he argued so earnestly in his *Guide*. The common "man," with his simple unspeculative mind, for whom these Thirteen Articles were intended, "never dreamed that the will was not free," and there was no necessity of impressing on his mind things which he had never doubted.[34]

So much about Maimonides. As to the Anti-Maimonists, it could hardly escape the reader that in some of the quoted systems the difference from the view of Maimonides is only a logical one, not a theological. Of some authors again, especially those of the thirteenth and fourteenth centuries, it is not at all certain whether they intended to oppose Maimonides. Others again, as for instance R. Abba Mari, R. Lipman, and R. Joseph Jabez, acted on the same principle as Maimonides, urging only those teachings of Judaism which they thought endangered. One could now, indeed, animated by the praiseworthy example given to us by Maimonides, also propose some articles of faith which are suggested to us by the necessities of our own time. One might, for instance, insert the article, "I believe that Judaism is, in the first instance, a divine religion, *not* a mere complex of racial peculiarities and tribal customs." One might again propose an article to the effect that Judaism is a proselytising religion, having the mission to bring about God's kingdom on earth, and to include in that kingdom all mankind. One might also submit for consideration whether it would not be advisable to urge a little more the principle that religion means chiefly a *Weltanschauung* and worship of God by means of holiness both in thought and in action. One would even not object to accept the article laid down by R. Saul, that we have to look upon ourselves as sinners. Morbid as such a belief may be, it would, if properly impressed on our mind, have perhaps the wholesome effect of cooling down a little our self-importance and our mutual admiration that makes all progress among us almost impossible.

But it was not my purpose to ventilate here the question whether Maimonides' articles are sufficient for us, or whether we ought not to add new ones to them. Nor do I attempt to decide what system we ought to prefer for recitation in the Synagogue—that of Maimonides or that of Chasdai, or of any other writer. I do not think that such a recital is of much use. My object in this sketch has been rather to make the reader *think* about Judaism, by proving that it regulates not only our actions, but also our thoughts. We usually urge that in Judaism religion means life; but we forget that a life without guiding principles and thoughts is a life not worth living. At least it was so considered by the greatest Jewish thinkers, and hence their efforts to formulate the creed of Judaism, so that men should not only be able to do the right thing, but also to think the right thing. Whether they succeeded in their attempts towards formulating the creed of Judaism or not will always remain a question. This concerns the logician more than the theologian. But surely Maimonides and his successors *did* succeed in having a religion depending directly on God, with the most ideal and lofty aspirations for the future; whilst the Judaism of a great part of our modern theologians reminds one very much of the words with which the author of *Marius the Epicurean* characterises the Roman religion in the days of her decline: a religion which had been always something to be done rather than something to be thought, or believed, or loved.

Political economy, hygiene, statistics, are very fine things. But no sane man would for them make those sacrifices which Judaism requires from us. It is only for God's sake, to fulfil His commands and to accomplish His purpose, that religion becomes worth living and dying for. And this can only be possible with a religion which possesses dogmas.

It is true that every great religion is "a concentration of many ideas and ideals," which make this religion able to adapt itself to various modes of thinking and living. But there must always be a point round which all these ideas concentrate themselves. This centre is Dogma.

4

THE DOCTRINE OF DIVINE RETRIBUTION IN RABBINICAL LITERATURE

"BLESSED be he who knows." These are the words with which Nachmanides, in his classical treatise, *Gate of Reward*, dismisses a certain theory of the Gaonim with regard to this question; after which he proceeds to expound another theory, which seems to him more satisfactory. This mode of treatment implies that, unsatisfactory as the one or other theory may appear to us, it would be presumptuous to reject either entirely, there being only One who knows the exact truth about the great mystery. But we may indicate our doubt about one doctrine by putting by its side another, which we may affirm to be not more absolutely true, but more probable. This seems to have been the attitude, too, of the compilers of the ancient Rabbinical literature, in which the most conflicting views about this grave subject were embodied. Nor did the Synagogue in general feel called upon to decide between these views. There is indeed no want of theodicies, for almost every important expounder of Job, as well as every Jewish philosopher of note, has one with its own system of retribution. Thus Judaism has no fixed doctrine on the subject. It refused a hearing to no theory, for fear that it should contain some germ of truth, but on the same ground it accepted none to the exclusion of the others.

These theories may, perhaps, be conveniently reduced to the two following main doctrines that are in direct opposition to each other, whilst all other views about the subject will be treated as the more or less logical results of the one or other doctrine.

1. There is no death without (preceding) sin, nor affliction without (preceding) transgression.[1] This view is cited in the name of R. Ammi, who quoted in corroboration the verses Ez. xviii. 20, and Ps. lxxxix. 33. Though this Rabbi flourished towards the end of the third century, there is hardly any doubt that his view was held by the authorities of a much earlier date. For it can only be under the sway of such a notion of Retribution that the Tannaim were so anxious to assign some great crime as the antecedent to every serious calamity by which mankind was visited. The following illustrations will suffice:—"Pestilence comes into the world for capital crimes mentioned in the Torah, which are not brought before the earthly tribunal. . . . Noisome beasts come into the world for vain swearing and for profanation of the name (of God). Captivity comes upon the world for strange worship and incest, and for shedding of blood and for (not) giving release to the land." As an example of the misfortune befalling the individual I will merely allude to a passage in another tractate of the Talmud, according to which leprosy is to be regarded as the penalty for immorality, slander, perjury, and similar sins.[2]

If we were now to complement R. Ammi's view by adding that there is no happiness without some preceding merit— and there is no serious objection to making this addition —then it would resolve itself into the theory of Measure for Measure, which forms a very common standard of reward and punishment in Jewish literature. Here are a few instances:—

"Because the Egyptians wanted to destroy Israel by water (Exod. i. 22), they were themselves destroyed by the waters of the Red Sea, as it is said, Therefore I will *measure* their former work into their bosom (Is. lxv. 7)"; whilst, on the other hand, we read, "Because Abraham showed himself hospitable towards strangers, providing them with water (Gen. xviii. 4), God gave to his children a country blessed with plenty of water (Deut. viii. 1)." Sometimes this form of retribution goes so far as to define a special punishment to that part of the body which mostly contributed to the committing of the sin. Thus we read, "Samson rebelled against God with his eyes, as it is said, Get her (the Philistine woman) for me, for she pleases *my eyes* (Judg. xvi. 21); therefore his *eyes* were put out by the Philistines (Judg. xviii. 9)"; whilst Absalom, whose sinful pride began by his *hair* (2 Sam. xiv. 25), met his fate by his *hair* (2 Sam. xviii. 9).[3] Nahum of Gemzo himself explained his blindness and the maimed condition of his arms and legs as a consequence of a specific offence in having neglected the duty of succouring a poor man. Addressing the dead body of the suppliant who perished while Nahum was delaying his help, he said, "Let my eyes (which had no pity for your pitiful gaze) become blind; may my hands and legs (that did not hasten to help thine) become maimed, and finally my whole body be covered with boils." [4] "This was the hand that wrote it," said Cranmer at the stake; "therefore it shall first suffer punishment."

It is worth noticing that this retribution does not always consist in a material reward, but, as Ben Azzai expressed it: "The reward of a command is a command, and the reward of a transgression is a transgression." [5] So again: "Because Abraham showed himself so magnanimous in his treatment of the king of Sodom, and said, I will not take from thee a thread; therefore, his children enjoyed the privilege of having the command of Zizith, consisting in putting a thread or fringe in the border of their garments." In another passage we read, "He who is anxious to do acts of charity will be rewarded by having the means enabling him to do so." [6] In more general terms the same thought is expressed when the Rabbis explained the words, Ye shall sanctify yourselves, and ye shall be holy (Lev. xi. 44), to the effect that if man takes the initiative in holiness, even though in a small way, Heaven will help him to reach it to a much higher degree.[7]

Notwithstanding these passages, to which many more might be added, it cannot be denied that there are in the Rabbinical literature many passages holding out promises of *material* reward to the righteous as well as threatening the wicked with *material* punishment. Nor is there any need of denying it. Simple-minded men—and such the majority of the Rabbis were—will never be persuaded into looking with indifference on pain and pleasure; they will be far from thinking that poverty, loss of children, and sickness are no evil, and that a rich harvest, hope of posterity, and good health, are not desirable things. It *does* lie in our nature to consider the former as curses and the latter as blessings; "and if this be wrong there is no one to be made responsible for it but the Creator of nature." Accordingly the question must arise, How can a just and omnipotent God allow it to happen that men should suffer innocently? The most natural suggestion towards solving the difficulty would be that we are *not* innocent. Hence R. Ammi's assertion that affliction and death are both the outcome of sin and transgression; or, as R. Chanina ben Dossa expressed it, "It is not the wild beast but sin which kills." [8]

We may thus perceive in this theory an attempt "to justify the ways of God to man." Unfortunately it does not correspond with the real facts. The cry wrung from the prophets against the peace enjoyed by the wicked, and the pains inflicted on the righteous, which finds its echo in so many

Psalms, and reaches its climax in the Book of Job, was by no means silenced in the times of the Rabbis. If long experience could be of any use, it only served to deepen perplexity. For all this suffering of the people of God, and the prosperity of their wicked persecutors, which perplexed the prophets and their immediate followers, were repeated during the death-struggle for independence against Rome, and were not lessened by the establishment of Christianity as the dominant religion. The only comfort which time brought them was, perhaps, that the long continuance of misfortune made them less sensible to suffering than their ancestors were. Indeed, a Rabbi of the first century said that his generation had by continuous experience of misery become as insensible to pain as the dead body is to a prick of a needle.[9] The anæsthetic effect of long suffering may, indeed, help one to endure pain with more patience, but it cannot serve as an apology for the deed of the inflictors of the pain. The question, then, how to reconcile hard reality with the justice of God, remained as difficult as ever.

The most important passage in Rabbinical literature relating to the solution of this problem is the following:— With reference to Exod. xxxiii. 13, R. Johanan said, in the name of R. José, that, among other things, Moses also asked God to explain to him the method of his Providence, a request that was granted to him. He asked God, Why are there righteous people who are prosperous, and righteous who suffer; wicked who are prosperous and wicked who suffer? The answer given to him was, according to the one view, that the prosperity of the wicked and the suffering of the righteous are a result of the conduct of their ancestors, the former being the descendants of righteous parents and enjoying their merits, whilst the latter, coming from a bad stock, suffer for the sins of those to whom they owe their existence. This view was suggested by the Scriptural words, "Keeping mercy for thousands (of generations) . . . visiting the iniquity of the fathers upon the children" (Exod. xxxiv. 7), which were regarded as the answer to Moses' question in the preceding chapter of Exodus.[10] Prevalent, however, as this view may have been in ancient times, the Rabbis never allowed it to pass without some qualification. It is true that they had no objection to the former part of this doctrine, and they speak very frequently of the "Merits of the Fathers" for which the remotest posterity is rewarded; for this could be explained on the ground of the boundless goodness of God, which cannot be limited to the short space of a lifetime. But there was no possibility of overcoming the moral objection against punishment of people for sins they have not committed.

It will suffice to mention here that, with reference to Joshua vii. 24, 25, the Rabbis asked the question, If he (Achan) sinned, what justification could there be for putting his sons and daughters to death? And by the force of this argument they interpreted the words of the Scriptures to mean that the children of the criminal were only compelled to be present at the execution of their father.

Such passages, therefore, as would imply that children have to suffer for the sins of their parents are explained by the Rabbis as referring to cases in which the children perpetuate the crimes of their fathers.[11] The view of R. José, which I have already quoted, had, therefore, to be dropped, and another version in the name of the same Rabbi is accepted. According to this theory the sufferer is a person either "entirely wicked" or "not perfectly righteous," whilst the prosperous man is a person either "perfectly righteous," or "not entirely wicked."

It is hardly necessary to say that there is still something wanting to supplement this view, for the given classification would place the not entirely wicked on the same level with the perfectly righteous, and on a much higher level than the imperfectly righteous, who are undoubtedly far superior. The following passage may be regarded as supplying this missing something:—"The wicked who have done some good work are as amply rewarded for it in *this* world as if they were men who have fulfilled the whole of the Torah, so that they may be punished for their sins in the next world" (without interruption); whilst the righteous who have committed some sin have to suffer for it (in this world) as if "they were men who burned the Law," so that they may enjoy their reward in the world to come (without interruption).[12] Thus the real retribution takes place in the next world, the fleeting existence on earth not being the fit time either to compensate righteousness or to punish sin. But as, on the one hand, God never allows "that the merit of any creature should be cut short," whilst, on the other hand, He deals very severely with the righteous, punishing them for the slightest transgression; since, too, this reward and punishment are only of short duration, they must take place in this short terrestrial existence. There is thus established a sort of divine economy, lest the harmony of the next world should be disturbed.

Yet another objection to the doctrine under discussion remains to be noticed. It is that it justifies God by accusing man, declaring every sufferer as more or less of a sinner. But such a notion, if carried to its last consequences, must result in tempting us to withhold our sympathies from him. And, indeed, it would seem that there were some non-Jewish philosophers who argued in this way. Thus a certain Roman official is reported to have said to R. Akiba, "How can you be so eager in helping the poor? Suppose only a king, who, in his wrath against his slave, were to set him in the gaol, and give orders to withhold from him food and drink; if, then, one dared to act to the contrary, would not the king be angry with him?" [13] There is some appearance of logic in this notion put into the mouth of a heathen. The Rabbis, however, were inconsistent people, and responded to the appeal which suffering makes to every human heart without asking too many questions. Without entering here into the topic of charity in the Rabbinic literature, which would form a very interesting chapter, I shall only allude now to the following incident, which would show that the Rabbis did not abandon even those afflicted with leprosy, which, according to their own notion, given above, followed only as a punishment for the worst crimes. One Friday, we are told, when the day was about to darken, the Chassid Abba Tachnah was returning home, bearing on his shoulders the baggage that contained all his fortune; he saw a leprous man lying on the road, who addressed him: "Rabbi, do me a deed of charity and take me into the town." The Rabbi now thought, "If I leave my baggage, where shall I find the means of obtaining subsistence for myself and my family? But if I forsake this leprous man I shall commit a mortal sin." In the end, he allowed the good inclination to prevail over the evil one, and first carried the sufferer to the town.[14] The only practical conclusion that the Rabbis drew from such theories as identify suffering with sin were for the sufferer himself, who otherwise might be inclined to blame Providence, or even to blaspheme, but would now look upon his affliction as a reminder from heaven that there is something wrong in his moral state. Thus we read in tractate *Berachoth:*[15] "If a man sees that affliction comes upon him, he ought to inquire into his actions, as it is said, Let us search and try our ways, and turn again to the Lord" (Lam. iii. 40). This means to say that the sufferer will find that he has been guilty of some offence. As an illustration of this statement we may perhaps consider the story about R. Huna, occurring in the same tractate.[16] Of this Rabbi it is said that he once experienced heavy pecuniary losses, whereupon his friends came to his house and said to him, "Let the master but examine his conduct a little closer." On this R. Huna answered, "Do you suspect me of having committed some misdeed?" His friends rejoined, "And do you think that God would pass judgment without justice?" R. Huna then followed their hint, and found that he did not treat his tenant farmer so generously as he ought. He offered redress, and all turned out well in the end. Something similar is to be found in the story of the martyrdom of R. Simeon ben Gamaliel and R. Ishmael ben Elisha. Of these Rabbis we are told that on their way to be executed the one said to the other, "My heart leaves me, for I am not aware of a sin deserving such a death"; on which the other answered, "It might have happened that in your function as judge you sometimes—for your own convenience —were slow in administering justice." [17]

But even if the personal actions of the righteous were blameless, there might still be sufficient ground for his being afflicted and miserable. This may be found in his relations to his kind and surroundings, or, to use the term now more popular, by reason of human solidarity. Now, after the above remarks on the objections entertained by the Rabbis against a man's being punished for the sins of others, it is hardly necessary to say that their idea of solidarity has little in common with the crude notions of it current in very ancient times. Still, it can hardly be doubted that the relation of the individual to the community was more keenly felt by the Rabbis than by the leaders in any other society, modern or ancient. According to the view given by an ancient Rabbi whose name is unknown, it would, indeed, seem that to them the individual was not simply a member of the Jewish commonwealth, or a co-religionist, but a limb of the great and single body "Israel," and that as such he communicated both for good and evil the sensations of the one part to the whole. In the *Midrash,* where a parallel is to be found to this idea, the responsibility of the individual towards the community is further illustrated by R. Simeon ben Yochai, in the following way: "It is," we read there, "to be compared to people sitting on board a ship, one of the passengers of which took an awl and began to bore holes in the bottom of the vessel. Asked to desist from his dangerous occupation, he answered, 'Why, I am only making holes on my own seat,' forgetting that when the water came in it would sink the whole ship." Thus the sin of a single man might endanger the whole of humanity. It was in conformity with the view of his father that R. Eliezer, the son of R. Simeon (ben Yochai) said, "The world is judged after the merits or demerits of the majority, so that a single individual by his good or bad actions can decide the fate of his fellow-creatures, as it may happen that he is just the one who constitutes this majority." [18] Nor does this responsibility cease with the man's own actions. According to the Rabbis man is responsible even for the conduct of others—and as such liable to punishment —if he is indifferent to the wrong that is being perpetrated about him, whilst an energetic protest from his side could have prevented it. And the greater the man the greater is his responsibility. He may suffer for the sins of his family which is first reached by his influence; he may suffer for the sins of the whole community if he could hope to find a willing ear among them, and he may even suffer for the sins of the whole world if his influence extend so far, and he forbear from exerting it for good.[19] Thus the possibility is given that the righteous man may suffer with justice, though he himself has never committed any transgression.

As a much higher aspect of this solidarity—and as may have already suggested itself to the reader from the passage cited above from the anonymous Rabbi—we may regard the suffering of the righteous as an atonement for the sins of their contemporaries. "When there will be neither Tabernacle nor the Holy Temple," Moses is said to have asked God, "what will become of Israel?" Whereupon God answers, "I will take from among them the righteous man whom I shall consider as pledged for them, and will forgive all their sins"; the death of the perfect man, or even his suffering being looked upon as an expiation for the shortcoming of his generation.[20]

It is hardly necessary to remind the reader of the affinity of this idea with that of sacrifices in general, as in both cases it is the innocent being which has to suffer for the sins of another creature. But there is one vital point which makes all the difference. It is that in our case the suffering is not enforced, but is a voluntary act on the part of the sacrifice, and is even desired by him. Without entering here on the often-discussed theme of the suffering of the Messiah, I need only mention the words of R. Ishmael who, on a very slight provocation, exclaimed, "I am the atonement for the Jews," which means that he took upon him all their sins to suffer for them.[21] This desire seems to have its origin in nothing else than a deep sympathy and compassion with Israel. To suffer *for,* or at least *with* Israel was, according to the Rabbis, already the ideal of Moses. He is said, indeed, to have broken the Two Tables with the purpose of committing some sin, so that he would have either to be condemned together with Israel (for the sin of the golden calf), or to be pardoned together with them.[22] And this conduct was expected not only from the leaders of Israel, but almost from every Jew. "When Israel is in a state of affliction (as, for instance, famine) one must not say, I will rather live by myself, and eat and drink, and peace be unto thee, my soul. To those who do so the words of the Scriptures are to be applied: And in that day did the Lord God of Hosts call to weeping and to mourning, . . . and behold joy and gladness. . . . Surely this iniquity shall not be purged out from you till ye die" (Is. xxii. 12-14). Another passage is to the effect that, when a man shows himself indifferent to the suffering of the community, there comes the two angels (who accompany every Jew), put their hands on his head, and say, "This man who has separated himself shall be excluded from their consolations." [23]

We might now characterise this sort of suffering as the chastisement of love (of the righteous) to mankind, or rather to Israel. But we must not confuse it with the Chastisement of Love often mentioned in the Talmud, though this idea also seems calculated to account for the suffering of the righteous. Here the love is not on the side of the sufferer, but proceeds from him who inflicts this suffering. "Him," says R. Huna, "in whom God delights he crushes with suffering." As a proof of this theory the words of Is. liii. 10 are given, which are interpreted to mean: him whom the Lord delights in He puts to grief. Another passage, by the same authority, is to the effect that where there is no sufficient cause for punishment (the man being entirely free from sin), we have to regard his suffering as a chastisement of love, for it is said: "Whom the Lord loveth He correcteth" (Proverbs iii. 11).[24] To what purpose He corrects him may, perhaps, be seen from the following passage: "R. Eleazar ben Jacob says: If a man is visited by affliction he has to be thankful to God for it: for suffering draws man to, and reconciles him with God, as it is said: For whom God loveth he correcteth." [25]

It is in conformity with such a high conception that affliction, far from being dreaded, becomes almost a desirable end, and we hear many Rabbis exclaim, "Beloved is suffering," for by it fatherly love is shown to man by God; by it man obtains purification and atonement, by it Israel came in possession of the best gifts, such as the Torah, the Holy Land, and eternal life.[26] And so also the sufferer, far from being considered as a man with a suspected past, becomes an object of veneration, on whom the glory of God rests, and he brings salvation to the world if he bears his affliction with joyful

submission to the will of God.[27] Continuous prosperity is by
no means to be longed after, for, as R. Ishmael taught, "He
who has passed forty days without meeting adversity has already received his (share of the) world (to come) in this
life." [28] Nay, the standing rule is that the really righteous
suffer, whilst the wicked are supposed to be in a prosperous
state. Thus, R. Jannai said, "We (average people) enjoy
neither the prosperity of the wicked nor the afflictions of the
righteous," [29] whilst his contemporary, Rab, declared that he
who experiences no affliction and persecution does not belong to them (the Jews).[30]

2. The second main view on Retribution is that recorded
by the Rabbis as in direct opposition to that of R. Ammi. It
is that there is suffering as well as death without sin and
transgression. We may now just as well infer that there is
prosperity and happiness without preceding merits. And this
is, indeed, the view held by R. Meir. For in contradiction
to the view cited above, R. Meir declares that the request of
Moses to have explained to him the mysterious ways of Providence was *not* granted, and the answer he received was, "And
I will shew mercy on whom I will shew mercy" (Exod. xxxiii.
19), which means to say, even though he to whom the mercy
is shown be unworthy of it. The old question arises how such
a procedure is to be reconciled with the justice and omnipotence of God. The commentaries try to evade the difficulty by
suggesting some of the views given above, as that the real reward and punishment are only in the world to come, or that
the affliction of the righteous is only chastisement of love,
and so on. From the passages I am about to quote, however,
one gains the impression that some Rabbis rather thought
that this great problem will indeed not bear discussion or
solution at all. Thus we have the legend: "The angels said
to God, why have you punished Adam with death? He answered, On account of his having transgressed my command-

ment (with regard to the eating of the tree of knowledge). But why had Moses and Aaron to die? The reply given to them is the words, Eccl. ix. 2: 'All things come alike to all; there is one event to the righteous and to the wicked, to the good and to the clean and to the unclean.' " [31] Another legend records, "When Moses ascended to heaven, God showed him also the great men of futurity. R. Akiba was sitting and interpreting the law in a most wonderful way. Moses said to God: Thou hast shown me his worth, show me also his reward; on which he is bidden to look back. There he perceives him dying the most cruel of deaths, and his flesh being sold by weight. Moses now asks: Is this the reward of such a life? whereupon God answers him: Be silent; this I have determined." [32]

It is impossible not to think of the fine lines of the German poet:

> Warum schleppt sich blutend, elend,
> Unter Kreuzlast der Gerechte,
> Während glücklich als ein Sieger
> Trabt auf hohem Ross der Schlechte?
> Also fragen wir beständig,
> Bis man uns mit einer Handvoll
> Erde endlich stopft die Mäuler—
> Aber ist das eine Antwort?

Still, one might perhaps suggest that these passages when examined a little closer, not only contain a rebuke to man's importunity in wanting to intrude into the secrets of God, but also hint at the possibility that even God's omnipotence is submitted to a certain law—though designed by His own holy will—which He could not alter without detriment to the whole creation. Indeed, in one of the mystical accounts of the martyrdom of R. Akiba and other great Rabbis, God is represented as asking the sufferers to accept His hard decree without protest, unless they wish Him to destroy the whole world. In another place again, we read of a certain renowned Rabbi, who lived in great poverty, that once in a dream he asked the divine Shechinah how long he would have still to endure this bitter privation? The answer given to him was: "My son, will it please you that I destroy the world for your sake?" [33] It is only in this light that we shall be able to understand such passages in the Rabbinic litera- ture as that God almost suffers Himself when He has to in- flict punishment either on the individual or on whole com- munities. Thus God is represented as mourning for seven days (as in the case when one loses a child) before He brought the deluge on the world; He bemoans the fall of Israel and the destruction of the Temple, and the Shechinah laments even when the criminal suffers his just punishment. And it is not by rebelling against these laws that He tries to redeem His suffering. He himself has recourse to prayer, and says: "May it be my will that my mercy conquer my wrath, that my love over-rule my strict justice, so that I may treat my children with love." [34] If now man is equal to God, he has nevertheless, or rather on that account, to submit to the law of God without any outlook for reward or punishment; or, as Antigonos expressed it, "Be not as slaves that minister to the Lord with a view to receive recompense." [35] Certainly it would be hazardous to maintain that Antigonos's saying was a consequence of this doctrine; but, at any rate, we see a clear tendency to keep the thought of reward (in spite of the prom- inent part it holds in the Bible) out of view. Still more clearly is it seen when, with reference to Ps. cxii, "Blessed is the man . . . that delighteth greatly in his commandments," Rabbi Eleazar remarks that the meaning is that the man de- sires only to do His commandments, but he does not want the rewards connected with them.[36] This is the more remarkable, as the whole contents of this psalm are nothing else than a long series of promises of various rewards, so that the explanation of Rabbi Eleazar is in almost direct contradiction to the simple meaning of the words. On the other hand, also, every complaint about suffering must cease. Not only is affliction no direct chastisement by God in the way of revenge; but even when it would seem to us that we suffer innocently, we have no right to murmur, as God himself is also suffering, and, as the Talmud expresses it, "It is enough for the slave to be in the position of his master." [37]

This thought of the compassion—in its strictest sense of fellow-suffering—of God with His creatures becomes a new motive for avoiding sin. "Woe to the wicked," exclaims a Rabbi, "who by their bad actions turn the mercy of God into strict justice." [38] And the later mystics explain distinctly that the great crime of sin consists in causing pain, so to speak, to the Shechinah. One of them compared it with the slave who abuses the goodness of his master so far as to buy with his money arms to wound him. But, on the other hand, it becomes, rather inconsistently, also a new source of comfort; for, in the end, God will have to redeem Himself from this suffering, which cannot be accomplished so long as Israel is still under punishment.[39] Most interesting is the noble prayer by a Rabbi of a very late mystical school: "O God, speedily bring about the redemption. I am not in the least thinking of what I may gain by it. I am willing to be condemned to all tortures in hell, if only the Shechinah will cease to suffer." [40]

If we were now to ask for the attitude of the Synagogue towards these two main views, we should have to answer that—as already hinted at the opening of this paper—it never decided for the one or the other. R. David Rocca Martino dared even to write a whole book in Defence of Adam proving that he committed no sin in eating the fruit

of the tree of knowledge against the literal sense of the
Scriptures, which were also taken by the Rabbis literally.[41]
By this he destroyed the prospects of many a theodicy, but
it is not known to me that he was severely rebuked for it.
It has been said by a great writer that the best theology is that
which is not consistent, and this advantage the theology of
the Synagogue possesses to its utmost extent. It accepted with
R. Ammi the stern principle of divine retribution, in as far
as it makes man feel the responsibility of his actions, and
makes suffering a discipline. But it never allowed this principle to be carried so far as to deny the sufferer our sympathy,
and by a series of conscious and unconscious modifications,
he passed from the state of a sinner into the zenith of the
saint and the perfectly righteous man. But, on the other hand,
the Synagogue also gave entrance to the very opposite view
which, abandoning every attempt to account for suffering,
bids man do his duty without any hope of reward, even as
God also does His. Hence the remarkable phenomenon in
the works of later Jewish moralists, that, whilst they never
weary of the most detailed accounts of the punishments awaiting the sinner and the rewards in store for the righteous, they
warn us most emphatically that our actions must not be
guided by these unworthy considerations, and that our only
motive should be the love of God and submission to His
holy will.

Nor must it be thought that the views of the Rabbis are
so widely divergent from those enunciated in the Bible. The
germ of almost all the later ideas is already to be found in the
Scriptures. It only needed the process of time to bring into
prominence those features which proved at a later period
most acceptable. Indeed, it would seem that there is also
a sort of domestication of religious ideas. On their first association with man there is a certain rude violence about them

which, when left to the management of untutored minds, would certainly do great harm. But, let only this association last for centuries, during which these ideas have to be subdued by practical use, and they will, in due time, lose their former roughness, will become theologically workable, and turn out the greatest blessing to inconsistent humanity.

5

SAINTS AND SAINTLINESS [1]

SOME two years ago, in a conversation with a lady of the Jewish persuasion, of high culture and wide reading, she made the remark to me that, as far as she knows, Judaism is the only one among the great religions which has never produced a saint, and that there is, indeed, no room in it for that element of saintliness which, in other creeds, forms the goal the true believer endeavors to reach. The conclusion which she drew from this alleged fact was, that good enough as Judaism may prove for the daily wear and tear of life, men and women of finer texture of soul than the common run of humanity must look to other religions for higher aspirations than to that which had come down to her from her ancestors.

Strange as such an assertion must appear to the student of Hebrew literature, I was not altogether surprised at her statements, considering the religious environment in which she had been brought up. Carlyle said of Voltaire that "he dearly loved truth, but of the triumphant kind." My lady-friend loved Judaism fairly in her own patronising way, but her Judaism was of the sane and plausible kind. It made no demand on faith. It was devoid of dogma, and shunned everything in the nature of a doctrine. Its great virtue consisted in its elasticity, in being adaptable to the latest result of the latest reconstruction of the Bible, and in being compatible with any system of philosophy ever advanced—provided, of course, that the system in question was still a subject of languid conversation in fashionable drawing-rooms. Above all, Judaism was with her a sober religion, hostile to all excesses of mysticism and enthusiasm, all prudence and common sense, but little of wisdom and less of soul and emotion. But enthusiasm and mysticism are the very soil upon which saintliness thrives best. It is, therefore, not to be wondered at if Saints and Saintliness were excluded from Judaism as conceived by her and her teachers.

It is not my intention to enter into a controversy as to such a conception of Judaism. Starting afresh in the world as we did, to a certain extent, at the end of the eighteenth century, it was only natural that with the zeal of new converts we should be eager to assimilate all sorts of ideas; and whilst we have learned a good deal of Latin, a good deal of Greek, a good deal of history, and also acquired some methodical habits in our scientific work—for all of which benefits we ought to feel truly grateful—we have been at the same time too much accessible to all kinds of rationalistic platitudes, and to a sort of free-thinking and materialistic dogmatism long ago obsolete among the great majority of thinkers. It is ample time that we become free men, and begin to use our powers of discretion. We ought to remember that we live now in the twentieth century, not at the end of the eighteenth. True, the twentieth century is still in its infancy, and has hardly had time to develop a line of thought of its own. But as it is the heir of the past, we know that among the ideals bequeathed to it by the last decades of the nineteenth century which it cherishes most, are the following: That in religion catholicity is good, sectarianism is bad; that great religions can live only on ideas and ideals, not on mere

organisation; that plausibility is more often a sign of mediocrity than a test of truth; that soberness is good, but that
inspiration and enthusiasm are better, and that every religion
wanting in the necessary sprinkling of Saints and Saintliness
is doomed in the end to degenerate into commonplace virtues in action, and Philistinism in thought, certain to disappear at the first contact with higher life and higher thought.

It will readily be perceived that under these altered conditions of thought there must be much in the scheme of salvation drawn up some seventy or eighty years ago that is badly
in need of revision. And this revision does take place, in spite
of all the frenzied attacks upon romanticism, mysticism, and
Orientalism. The only section of humanity never afflicted
with this last vice were, as far as I know, the Red Indians.
They were good Western gentlemen *sans reproche*, without a
taint of Orientalism and all its terrible consequences. However, I do not wish to argue this point just now. Here we
shall confine ourselves to the subject of Saints and Saintliness
in Judaism, an aspect of Judaism almost entirely neglected
by our "theologians."

The best Hebrew equivalent for the term saint is the adjective חסיד, commonly used in the sense of pious, devout,
reverend, godly; but the noun חסד is found together with חן
and רחמים, thus implying the qualities of grace, graciousness,
gracefulness, and kindness. Thus we read of Esther, "And
the King loved Esther above all the women, and she obtained
חן and חסד in his sight" (Esther 2: 17); that is to say, she
found grace and kindness in his sight. Of the virtuous woman
it is said, "She opens her mouth with wisdom, and in her
tongue is תורת חסד, the law of kindness (or graciousness)"
(Prov. 31: 26). When God reminds Israel of the honeymoon
at the outset of her spiritual career, when she was wedded
to the Torah, he says, "I remember thee the grace (חסד) of
thy youth," etc. (Jer. 2: 2). When an ancient Rabbi wanted

to be polite to a newly-married couple, he would compliment the bride with the words, וחמודה נאה (beautiful and graceful).[2] Applied to matters spiritual, the best equivalent for חסידים or חסידות would be "beautiful souls."

Closely connected with the terms Chasiduth and Chasid are the terms Kedushah (holiness) and Kadosh (holy). The two ideas are so naturally allied with each other that they are interchangeably used in Rabbinic texts. But it must be remarked that the term Kedushah does not entirely cover the English word holiness, the mystical and higher aspect of it being better represented by the term Chasiduth (saintliness). Whilst I shall thus consider myself at liberty to utilise freely such Biblical and Rabbinic matter as gives evidence of the existence and nature of Kedushah in Judaism, I shall, on the other hand, try to sift the material in such a way as to give prominence to the element of Chasiduth, and all that this term implies.

The notion of Chasiduth, or saintliness, is variously described by different Jewish writers. The only point about which they fairly agree is the feature of individualism that distinguishes the Chasid, or saint, from other religionists.[3] The golden mean, so much praised by philosophers and teachers of ethics, has no existence for him, and he is rather inclined to excesses. Nor can he be measured by the standard of the Law, for it is one of the characteristics of the saint that he never waits for a distinctive commandment. The various precepts of the Bible are for him so many memoranda, or head-lines, each leading to new trains of thought and suggestive of any number of inferences. But inferences are subject to different interpretations.[4] Hence the fact that each writer emphasises the special feature in the saint with which he was most in sympathy by reason of his own bent of mind or particular religious passion. The saint thus belonging to the subjective species, our theme would be best treated by a series of monographs, or lives of the various saints. But those could hardly be brought within the compass of an essay. It will therefore be best for our purpose to combine the various features characteristic of the saint into a general sketch, though such a mode of treatment will necessarily bring more into prominence the thing saintliness, than the person practising it.

In speaking of saints it should be premised that I am not referring to organisations or societies bearing this name. The references in Jewish literature to such organisations are few and of a doubtful nature, and will certainly not stand the test of any scientific criticism. Besides, one does not become a saint by reason of a corporate act, or by subscribing to a certain set of rules, though a man may be a saint despite his being a member of a society or community composed of professional saints. Saintliness is essentially a subjective quality. An ancient Rabbi put the matter well when he said, "As often as Israel perceived the Holy One, blessed be he, they became saints." [5] Put in a modern equivalent, we should say that saintliness is the effect of a personal religious experience when man enters into close communion with the Divine. Some New England mystic describes such communion as the mingling of the individual soul with the universal soul. This is just as obscure as any other term the new or the old world may choose to describe old ideas. When the Rabbis spoke of perceiving God, they probably thought of Psalm 17: 15, "I will behold thy face in righteousness; I will be satisfied when I awake with thine image." [6] Some versions paraphrase the second half of the just quoted verse: "I will be satisfied by gazing on thy likeness," an expression denoting the highest fellowship with God, almost, as it were, a fellowship of the senses.

As to the way in which these blissful moments of close communion with the Divine might be made lasting and effective, the Rabbis give us a hint when they say that Israel, when they became saints, sang a song.[7] The same thought may also perhaps be divined in the words of another Rabbi, who maintained that saintliness consists in man's zealous compliance with the prescriptions in Berachoth, the Talmudic tractate dealing mostly with matter appertaining to benediction and prayer.[8] Under song and prayer we have to understand all those manifestations of the soul in which the individual attempts to reciprocate his revelation of the Divine. As was pointed out in another place[9] with regard to the Bible, its unique character consists in furnishing us with both the revelation of God to man, as given in the Pentateuch and in the Prophets, and the revelation of man to God, as contained in the Psalms and in other portions of the Scriptures of a liturgical nature.[10] Hence the value the saint attached to prayer. He longs for the moments when he can pour out his soul before his God in adoration and supplication. The hours of the day appointed for the three prayers, evening, morning, and noon, are for him, a Jewish saint expresses it, the very heart of the day.[11] Apparently, however, the saint is not satisfied with these appointed times. He is so full of expectation of the time of prayer that he devotes a whole hour of preparation to put himself in the proper frame of mind for it, and he is so reluctant to sever himself from such blissful moments that he lingers for a whole hour after the prayer, in "after-meditation." It was in this way that the ancient saints spent nine hours of the day in meditation and supplication.[12] The ancient Rabbis had a special formula of thanksgiving for the privilege of prayer, and the saints availed themselves of this privilege to its full extent.[13] Besides the obligatory prayers, the Jewish saint had his own individual prayers, some of which have come down to us. The burden of these is mostly an appeal to God's mercy for help, that He may find him worthy to do his will. "May it be thy will," runs one of

these prayers, "that we be single-hearted in the fear of thy
name; that thou remove us from all thou hatest; that thou
bring us near to all thou lovest, and that thou deal with us
graciously for thy name's sake." [14] Another Rabbi prayed, "It
is revealed before thee, God, that we have not the power to
resist the evil inclination. May it be thy will to remove it
from us, so that we may accomplish thy will with a perfect
heart." [15] In such prayer God and man meet, for, as an old
Agadist expressed it, in a rather hyperbolic way, "From the
beginning of the world, the Holy One, blessed be he, established a tent for himself in Jerusalem, in which, if one may
say so, he prayed, 'May it be my will that my children accomplish my will.' " [16]

Midnight, with its awe-inspiring silence and the feeling of
utter isolation which comes upon man, was considered by the
saints as another favourable moment for prayer. In allusion
to Psalm 119: 62, the Rabbis report that above the couch of
David there hung a harp.[17] "The midnight breeze, as it rip-
pled over the strings, made such music that the poet-king was
constrained to rise from his bed, and, till the dawn flushed
the Eastern skies, he wedded words to the strains." The music
was not silenced with the disappearance of the harp of David.
It kept awake many a Jewish saint even during the Middle
Ages. Of one of these saints the record is that he used to rise
up in the depths of the night and pray: "My God, thou hast
brought upon me starvation and penury. Into the depths of
darkness thou hast driven me, and thy might and strength
hast thou taught me. But even if they burn me in fire, only
the more will I love thee and rejoice in thee, for so said the
Prophet, 'And thou shalt love thy God with all thy heart.' " [18]
In the later Middle Ages, a whole liturgy was developed,
known under the name of תיקון חצות, or "The Order of
Prayers for Midnight." It is composed of a collection of
Psalms and Biblical verses, mostly of a mournful nature, ex-

pressing Israel's grief over the destruction of the Holy Temple and the suffering of God's children in the dispersion. It is accompanied by a number of soul-stirring hymns, composed by the poets of the Synagogue. They are mostly of a deep, spiritual nature, of matchless beauty, infinitely superior to any we have acquired lately in our modern hymn books.[19] It is one of the great tragedies of modern Judaism that it knows itself so little. A people that has produced the Psalmists, a R. Judah Hallevi, a R. Israel Nagara, and other hymnologists and liturgists counted by hundreds, has no need to pass round the hat to all possible denominations begging for a prayer or a hymn. It contains further a confession of sins which are the cause of deferring the manifestation of the glory of God and the establishing of the kingdom of heaven on earth. Perhaps I may remark that confession of sin is an especial feature of the Jewish liturgy, which the Jew is eager to repeat as often as the opportunity offers itself. The Occidental man, in his self-complacency, thinks this a mark of Oriental cringing, unworthy of a citizen who believes himself good, and is prosperous. Perhaps the reader will be more reconciled to this feature in our liturgy if I quote the following from a letter of Lincoln to Thurlow Weed. It probably refers to a passage in his second inaugural, in which, if I am not mistaken, he makes the whole nation a participant in the sin of slavery. He writes: "I believe it is not immediately popular. Men are not flattered by being shown that there has been a difference of purpose between them and the Almighty. To deny it, however, in this case, is to deny that there is a God governing the world. It is a truth which I thought needed to be told, and, as whatever of humiliation there is in it falls most directly on myself, I thought others might afford for me to tell it." [20] When the Jewish saint said, "We have sinned, we have betrayed," and so on, he meant chiefly himself, and others might at least afford for him to tell it.

The Sabbath, with its opportunities for rest and devotion, is described as the harvest of the week,[21] the advent of which is impatiently awaited by the saint. It is a gift of the Lord, and the saint shows his gratitude by the preparations he makes to accept it. Indeed, he would avoid anything which in some circuitous way might lead to the breaking of the Sabbath, even in such cases where breaking it would be permitted by the Law. Queen Sabbath is met by him on her way with song and praise, and greeted royally; and when she has arrived, he experiences that sense of the plus-soul, or over-soul,[22] which imparts to his devotion and his rest a foretaste of the bliss to come. Other nations, it is pointed out, have also days of rest, but they stand in the same relation to the Jewish Sabbath as a copy to the original—wanting in life and soul.[23] The Sabbath is mystically described as the mate of Israel.[24] Hence, with the saint, every profane or secular thought would be considered as a breach of connubial duty. And when, against his will, his thoughts were directed to money transactions, or improvement in his estate, the saint would decline to profit by them.[25] But, as a rule, his very thoughts rest on that day. Even in the prayers nothing concerning mundane affairs is allowed to come in.[26] It is all joy and no contrition. It is entirely the day of the Lord.

The same may be applied to the festivals, which the saint observes with similar strictness; for they are so many occasions of enjoying fellowship with the Divine. The Penitential Days, extending from the first to the tenth of the month of Tishri, with the opportunity they afford for reconciliation with God, are the subject of his special solicitude. A well-known saint expressed himself, that all the year he does nothing but listen impatiently to catch the sound of the hammer, knocking at the doors in the early hours of the morning, calling the faithful to the synagogue, when the Penitential Days are about to arrive.[27]

The saint is further described as a regent,[28] having absolute control over all his organs. Of these the mouth is one of the most important. The maxim of Judaism, as conceived by the great moralists, is that the things which enter the mouth as well as those which proceed from the mouth may be unclean. Accordingly the Jewish saint would constantly watch both the imports and the exports of his mouth. With regard to the former it is hardly necessary to say that the saint would refrain from all those various forbidden foods which the Bible describes as "unclean, an abomination," and fetid. These have, according to the general Jewish opinion, the effect of polluting the soul, and there is no difference upon this point between the teachings of the Pentateuch and those of the Prophets, unless we choose to interpret these latter in the spirit of Paul and Marcion, and their modern successors. The saint, with his abhorrence of anything impure, would avoid the least contact with them. True, the saint is an individualist, but an extensive menu and the indulgence of other appetites forbidden by the Scriptures, are no mark of a strong personality. We Occidentals are greatly proud and jealous of our right of private judgment. But the first condition for private judgment is that the judge should not be bribed by considerations of comfort and convenience. The great majority of Jewish saints had no difficulty in reconciling themselves to any observance or ceremony. Speech about the Divine has to be in metaphors, and action corresponding to such speech can be only in signs and symbols. Those mystically inclined perceived in them the reflex of things unseen, assuming proportions in the regions above never dreamt of by the vulgar. Certainly, there were a few, especially among the mystics, who had antinominian tendencies, but they never stopped at the ritual part. They equally resented the moral restraint imposed upon them by the Torah. They all became notorious profligates, and terminated in apostasy.

The individualism of the saint found expression in the following principle: "Sanctify thyself even in that which is permitted to thee." [29] As Nachmanides points out, the Torah has forbidden us certain kinds of food, but allowed the eating of meat and the drinking of wine, but even within these limits can the man of impure appetite become a drunkard and a glutton. From doing this, man is warded off by the general commandment of holiness, which keeps him aloof from all animal desires.[30] R. Joseph Caro had his menu regulated by his angel, or the spirit of the Mishnah, created by his devotion to that part of the oral law, who, again and again, impresses upon him the fact that every morsel of food and drop of drink not absolutely necessary to support life is a sacrifice to the strange god. Even the luxury of drinking too much water is considered by him a concession to the Evil One.[31]

On the whole, the saint would be rather inclined to asceticism. His inference from such commandments as, for instance, that regarding the Nazarite who had to abstain from wine, or that concerning the refraining from food altogether on the Day of Atonement, would be, that restraint and discipline in every respect are pleasing to his Father in Heaven. The statement is often made that Judaism is not an ascetic religion, and, indeed, there are passages in Jewish literature which might be cited in corroboration of this view. But the saint, by reason of his aspirations to superior holiness, will never insist on privileges and concessions. His models will be the heroic Elijah, with his rough mantle of camel's hair, his dwelling in the cherit, and sleeping under a desert-broom, and preparing himself for a revelation on Mount Horeb by a fast of forty days; or the Psalmist, who says, "My knees are weak from fasting, and my flesh faileth of fatness"; or the laymen of the Second Temple, called "Men of the Station," representing the Third Estate in the Holy Temple, where they fasted four days a week, and spent their time in meditation and prayer.[32] And thus we find any number of saints in Jewish history, as notorious for their asceticism with all its extravagances as those of any other religion. Long lists might be drawn up of Jewish saints who fasted, as the phrase is, from the beginning of the week to the end, except the Sabbath; or, at least, Monday and Thursday of every week. Others again confined themselves to vegetable food and plain water; whilst others inflicted upon themselves all sorts of torture, taking snow baths in winter and exposing themselves to the heat in summer.[33] The remarkable thing about these saints is, that many among them warned their disciples against asceticism. Of the Gaon of Wilna, the story is, that when he remonstrated with his disciple R. Zalman against wasting himself by frequent fasts and keeping vigils through the night, he answered him, "But I understand the master himself lived such an ascetic life in his younger days." "Yes," answered the Rabbi, "I did; but I regret it deeply now." The rejoinder of Rabbi Zalman was, "I also wish to have something to regret." [34] The reader will probably have noticed that even the modern man, notwithstanding all his admiration for flesh and muscle, speaks of a fine ascetic face, which he usually identifies with spirituality and inner worth. Even the community at large, which could not afford to spend itself in fasts and vigils, never doubted that self-denial is better than self-indulgence. They were all strongly impressed with the truth that the man insisting upon his three square meals a day, and everything else in correspondence, is less accessible to discipline and self-sacrifice than the man who follows the rule of the sages: "A morsel of bread with salt thou must eat, and water by measure thou must drink, thou must sleep upon the ground, and live a life of trouble the while thou toilest in the Torah." [35] The toiler in the Torah is hardly conscious of the trouble. The story is of a famous Jewish saint who indulged in the luxury of fasting the first six days in the week; when asked how he accomplished this feat, he answered that he never meant to fast: he simply forgot to eat.

Even more stringent was the watch which the saint would keep over the things which proceed from the mouth. "Be careful not to utter an untruth," says an old Jewish saint, even in the way of a joke, or in the way of over-emphasis, "for," an old Jewish moralist tells us, "against the most weighty sins we are warned in the Bible with only one prohibitive command, whilst the law forbidding the speaking of untruth is ever so many times repeated in the Scriptures." [36] Indeed, truth is one of the specialties of the Jewish saint. "The soul," the moralist remarks, "is extracted from the place of the holy spirit, hewn out from a place all purity. She is created of the superior splendour, the throne of glory. In the Holy of Holies, there is no falsehood; all is truth; as it is said: 'God—truth.' . . . He who will meditate over these things, that his soul is extracted from the very source of truth, will do truth; never allow a lie an inlet into the place of the holiness of truth." [37] "Truth," again the ancient Rabbis said, "is the seal of the Holy One, blessed be he," and everything proceeding from the saint, either in thought, or in word, or in deed, would bear this impress. He speaks the truth in his very heart. Untruth has no existence for him, and he would, under no consideration, agree to any concession or compromise in this direction. Thus, one of the saints prescribes, "Guard thyself against anger, flattery, and falsehood. If untruth has become a matter of habit with thee, make it a rule to tell people, 'I lied,' and thus thou wilt accustom thyself that no falsehood escape thy mouth." [38] "The Messiah will come," a Jewish saint said, "only when the world will have realised that to speak an untruth is as heinous a crime as adultery." [39] The same saint was wont to say to his disciples, "Rather allow your soul to expire than that an untruth should proceed from your mouth," and considered this prohibitive commandment among the precepts of the Torah for which man is bound to undergo martyrdom.[40] It is of this saint, or a pupil of his, that the story is recorded that the Russian Government, suspecting the Jews of his town of smuggling, consented to withdraw the charge if he declared his brethren innocent. Having no alternative but either to bring misfortune on his brethren or to tell an untruth, he prayed to God to save him from this dilemma by sending death upon him. And, lo, a miracle happened! When the officials came to fetch him before the law court, they found him dead.

The last paragraph brings us to that part in the programme of the saint which the Talmud calls "laws regulating the relations between man and man," and which we would classify under the general heading of conduct. "He who is desirous of being a saint," one Rabbi remarked, "let him fulfil the precepts of that part of the law which deals with 'damages.'" [41] In observing these, he avoids everything that might result in an injury to his fellow-man. We need not enlarge here upon matters of commonplace integrity, "which it is no honour to have, but simply a disgrace to want." Lying, backbiting, slandering, and the acquisition of wealth by dishonest means come under the prohibitive laws, the transgression of which has, according to the Rabbis, a defiling effect, and they are put into the same category as murder and idolatry.[42] It is thus no special mark of saintliness to avoid these deadly sins. But the saint would go further: he would speak the truth in his very heart. He would, for instance, consider himself bound to a money transaction even when the promise made never assumed the shape of a committal by word of mouth, having been only a determination of the heart.[43] As to avoiding injury, he would do this at the very risk of his life, though not bound to do so by the letter of the law. Thus, when the Roman Government once besieged the town of Lydda, and insisted upon the extradition of a certain Ula bar Koseheb, threatening the defenders with the destruction of the place and the massacre of its inhabitants in the case of further resistance, R. Joshua ben Levi exerted his influence with Ula, that he would voluntarily deliver himself to the Romans, so that the place might be saved. Thereupon, the Prophet Elijah, who often had communion with R. Joshua ben Levi, stopped his visits. After a great deal of penance, which the Rabbi imposed upon himself, Elijah came back and said, "Am I expected to reveal myself to informers?" Whereupon the Rabbi asked, "Have I not acted in accordance with the strict letter of the law?" "But," retorted Elijah, "this is not the law of the saints." [44]

By injury is also understood anything which might cause one's fellow-man the feeling of nausea or disgust. As it would seem, these were cases which the court could not well reach. They fell under the class of secret things, but the rabbis applied to them the verse in Ecclesiastes (12: 14), "God shall bring every work into judgment with every secret thing." But we have on record that there were saints who made it a specialty to go about cleaning such public places as by the carelessness of passers-by might have proved offensive to the public.[45]

Altogether, there is no room in the soul of the saint for those ugly qualities which, in one way or another, are bound to impair the proper relations between man and his fellow-man. These are, according to one authority, "pride, anger, petulance, despair, hatred, jealousy, dissipation, covetousness, desire for power, and self-assertion." They all belong to the ugly qualities of man, making man's communion with God impossible, and hence are incompatible with saintliness.[46] "Pride," or vanity, it is pointed out, "is at the root of all evils," man setting up himself as an idol, worshipping his own self, and thus bound to come into collision with both God and fellow-man.[47] Hence, the prayer at the conclusion of the Eighteen Benedictions: "O my God! Guard my tongue from evil and my lips from speaking guile; and to such as curse me let my soul be dumb, yea, let my soul be unto all as the dust." [48] Man's love of self is, however, too deeply rooted to be overcome by these reminders, few and too far between. We therefore read of a saint who was overheard constantly whispering the prayer: "May the Merciful save me from pride." "The man who has a taint of pride or insolence, though he be righteous and upright in all other respects, is worth nothing. Indeed, a man may fulfil ever so many laws and fast six days in the week, and be nevertheless a disciple of the wicked Balaam," who though a prophet was of a haughty spirit and a swelled soul, and thus destined to perdition.[49] The same saint was in the habit of saying, "The devil will make man all possible concessions, if he can only succeed in impressing upon him the fact of his prominence and his greatness. He will show him what a great scholar he is, what a pious man he is, what a great orator he is, what a clear fine hand he writes, what a fine figure he makes when dancing, and so on." [50] "Should a man happen to be devoid of all accomplishments, and a fool in the bargain, he will compliment him on his sagacity and wisdom. Should he be lacking in all sympathy with religion, especially of the practical and living kind, he will congratulate him on his deep spirituality. Infatuated with his own importance, man before long will be in opposition to man and God, who keep his due from him. The best remedy against this ugly quality is love. Hence the warning of the saint: 'He who hates an Israelite, hates Abraham, Isaac, and Jacob, and grandsires of Israel.'"

Again, he who hates man, hates the Holy One, blessed be he, who created man. We are all children unto the Lord our God, all souls rooting in him.[51] The injunction of the saint is, therefore, "Let man love all creatures, including Gentiles, and let him envy none." [52] This, by the way, is the distinct precept of the Jewish saint of the sixteenth century. It is not known to me that any Christian saint of the same period made the love of the Jew a condition of saintliness. This is a love which leaves no room for self. Man will not succeed in attaining to this love until he has acquired the virtues of humility and meekness. There is hardly any Jewish moralist who does not enlarge upon the significance of humility, and the references to it would easily fill a volume. One of the most emphatic is, "Be exceedingly lowly of spirit, since the hope of man is but the worm." [53]

Man must be so thoroughly convinced of his own unworthiness, that he is even bidden to love those who rebuke him and hate those who praise him.[54] Nay, he should feel under torture when he hears his own praise, as it is sure to be undeserved.[55] In addition to this, there is with the saint the conception of the superiority of his fellow-man, which proves another stimulus toward the cultivation of meekness and humbleness. When man quits the world, he is asked, according to an ancient Midrash, "Hast thou been busy in the study of the Torah, and in works of lovingkindness? Hast thou declared thy Maker as King morning and evening? Hast thou acknowledged thy fellow-man as king over thee in meekness of spirit?" [56] Man should accordingly perceive in his fellow-man not only an equal whose rights he is bound to respect, but a superior whom he is obliged to revere and love. In every person, it is pointed out by these saints, precious and noble elements are latent, not to be found with anybody else. In fact, every human being is a servant of God *in posse*. One of these saints declined to be considered as one of the righteous of his generation, saying he had no right to this distinction so long as he felt that he loved his children better than the rest of mankind.[57] Whenever the saint heard of a birth in the community, he used to break out in wild joy, welcoming the new-born child as a future volunteer in the service of God, taking his or her place in the rank and file of militant Judaism. Hence, the prayer of certain of these saints: "May it be thy will that we shall not sin either against thee or against thy creatures";[58] whilst another saint used to add to his morning prayer, the short prayer, "O God, establish in my heart faith, humility, and meekness," and his favourite saying was, "As a man is anxious for his very life, so should he be anxious to be permeated by the thought that he is less important than anybody else." [59] He used especially to be very severe with his family when they dared be unkind to his domestics. Another of the saints expresses it, "Let each man be considered in thy eyes as better than thou, even the servant in thy house." [60] Of one of these godly men legend reports that he was in the habit of addressing all the people with whom he came in contact as "saints," or "righteous ones," and, indeed, believing them to be so. One day, the story is, when walking in the street, he saw two cabmen fighting over the right of way, giving force to their arguments with the whips which they applied to each other. The godly man was embarrassed, and he prayed, "Lord of the universe, it is my duty to separate them, but who dares interfere between two saints?"

Another consequence of this love is that men should never break out in anger against any one. This is a precept to be found in all the moralist literature of the different ages, but R. Joseph Caro, even the author of the *Shulchan Aruch*, in the special manual for his own guidance adds, that anger should be avoided even in the cause of religion, where zeal for the glory of God might give some justification for it.[61]

Indeed, we should love all, including those who have gone astray, this being the only means of bringing them back into the fold. When a certain pious man came to the saint, asking his advice as to what he should do with his son who had left the faith of his ancestors, the answer was, "Love him. The influence of thy love will be his salvation." And so it came to pass. Of another saint, the story is that he used to make special journeys to places settled by converts to the dominant religion. To these converts he made a gift of his share of the bliss awaiting the pious in the world to come, at the same time eliciting the promise that they would read every day the verse, שמע ישראל, "Hear, O Israel, the Lord our God, the Lord is One." This proved a link between them and the faith they had left, to which, in time, many of them returned.[62] Indeed, prayer must be universal. He who prays shall not direct his attention to himself. Any prayer in which the whole of Israel is not included, is no prayer. Nay, one must pray even for the wicked among the Gentiles.[63] Of course, there were other saints who were distinguished more by their zeal than by their powers of persuasion. They were good haters, and Elijah was their model, but it may be said in their favour, that so far as Judaism is concerned their motives were pure; their zeal was never dictated by consideration of self or by ambition. Sometimes I am inclined to think that the haters and the lovers were both right.

In matters of philanthropy, the saint would be inclined to extravagance. "It is a strange though true thing," some philosopher has remarked, "that virtue itself has need of limits." At a certain epoch in history, when mendicancy was made a special sign of holiness, the Rabbis drew the limit when they said, "He who wishes to be lavish in his philanthropic work, let him not spend more than twenty per cent of his income." [64] The saint transgresses this limit, taking as his norm, "What is mine is thine, and what is thine is thine." [65] He would also remove any barrier or obstacle preventing the poor from reaching him personally, whilst he would, at the same time, save no effort to make others do their duty to the poor.[66] And this duty practically means to make the poor equal partners in one's property. Thus, in the sacred letter of R. Shneor (Senior) Zalman, a well-known saint of Russia, he writes to his adherents to the following effect:

My beloved ones, my brethren and my friends:—I have no doubt about the distress of the time. The means of getting a livelihood have become very small, and certain acquaintances of mine, whom I knew to have been in prosperous circumstances, are now compelled to borrow in order to maintain their families. May the Lord have mercy upon them. Nevertheless, they do not act properly when they shut their hands and refuse to supply the poor with their needs. If we have no mercy with them, who will? It is true that the law teaches that man's own life comes first, but this is to be applied only to things on which life depends, as, for instance, when men are in a desert, and there is sufficient water to quench the thirst of only one person, and save him from death. In this case we say that the owner has first right upon it. But if it is a question of bread and clothes and wood on one side, and dinners with fish and meat and fruit on the other side, the latter have to be given up as things superfluous. First the poor must be provided with the necessaries of life. This is the real meaning of the law, but it is indeed not worthy of a man to insist upon the law in such cases. He ought not to think of his life. We are all in need of the mercy of heaven, and those who have no mercy on earth, be their reason what it may, can never hope for God's mercy.[67]

He then proceeds, in a long, mystical discourse, to show how this grace of heaven can be encouraged to flow into the proper channels, as the term is, only by manifestations of grace on earth, heaven and earth acting in harmony to reveal the great attribute of love.

The literature and stories bearing on charity and the saint's share in it are too extensive to be entered upon here, even in a casual way. The greatest sacrifice is told of a certain Rabbi who used to save the whole of the year enough money to enable him to buy an *Ethrog* for the Feast of Tabernacles (Lev. 23: 40). When he was in possession of six rubles he made a special journey from his village to Brody, to buy the *Ethrog*. But on the way he met a poor man who made a livelihood by means of his horse-cart, on which he carried water for the neighbourhood. Unfortunately, the horse died on the way. Thereupon the Rabbi gave him his six rubles to buy another beast, saying, "What is the difference? To buy an *Ethrog* is a command of God, and to help this poor man is also a command of God." Naturally, a miracle happened afterwards. The Rabbi was presented by some rich man with a fine *Ethrog* for the feast.[68] I will only remark that charity belongs, according to the mystics, to the commandments that work a certain re-birth in man, or rather give a new soul to those who make strenuous efforts to fulfil them.[69]

It will, perhaps, be interesting to hear, that these saints were by no means so unpractical as their mystical discourses would lead us to imagine. The successor of this R. Shneor Zalman, Rabbi Beer, in an epistle written in a time of great distress and persecution, writes to his followers not to engage so much in commerce.

"The best for you," he says, "is to learn proper trades, in factories, under the superintendence of practical men." He also gives them counsel to take up agricultural pursuits, buy land either from the great landlords, or from the Government, and employ for the first two or three years non-Jews who will teach them this new vocation. "Did we not," he says, "in Palestine derive all our livelihood from our labour in field and in vineyard? It is only in this way," he says, "that we can hope to find favour with the Government. Who knows what will be our end? They may, God forbid, expel us to some far-away country." [70]

Sympathy and tenderness are by the saint not confined to the human species. They extend also to dumb creation. Thus we read in the "Little Book of Saints," "Refrain thy kindness and thy mercy from nothing which the Holy One, blessed be he, created in this world. Never beat nor inflict pain on any animal, beast, bird, or insect; nor throw stones at a dog or a cat; nor kill flies or wasps." [71] Indeed, man will be punished who will make his animal carry larger burdens than it is able to bear. In connexion with this, we read the story of a man who was cruel to his dog. The dog, however, sought refuge under the robes of a sage. When the man approached the dog with the purpose of beating him, the sage protested with the words, "Since this dog sought my protection, you shall not touch it," and applied to him the verse in Genesis (19: 8), "Only unto these do nothing, for they came under the shadow of my roof." [72] Another story illustrating the same trait in the saint is the following: R. Isaac Loria was once the guest of a good and upright man. Before he left, the saint said to his host, "How can I compensate you for your kind hospitality?" The master of the house then answered that his only grief was that God had not given him the blessing of children. Whereupon Loria, who knew everything going on in heaven and earth, said to him, "The cause of your misfortune is, that you were not kind to animals." After making inquiries it turned out that the man had poultry in his yard, with a cistern in it. In this cistern there was a ladder by means of which the water at the bottom could be reached by the young chickens as yet unable to use their wings. Once his wife inadvertently had the ladder removed, which fact was the cause of great suffering to the animals. The man replaced the ladder, and the children came in due time.[73]

The relations between the sexes are regulated by the law. Judaism, as we know, not only did not encourage, but distinctly objected to celibacy. Only one or two instances are recorded of Jewish saints who remained single all their lives.

But, on the other hand, if marriage was not made a sacrament in the Roman Catholic sense, it was a thing holy. Maimonides, with that fine tact so characteristic of him, grouped the marriage laws under the general heading of "Kedushah" (Holiness); whilst Nachmanides wrote a whole treatise called the "Sacred Letter," dealing exclusively with the most intimate moments in the lives of the sexes, and showing how even such functions as were declared by other religions as distinctly animalic, can with the saint be elevated into moments of worship and religious exaltation. It is, in fact, a vindication of the flesh from a religious point of view. All the more strongly did the Jewish saint insist upon making these relations pure and chaste, stigmatising even an impure thought as being as bad as an impure action, if not worse. It was only by reason of the purification of these relations and their thorough sanctification, that the whole vocabulary of love could afterwards, in moments of rapture and ecstasy, be used by the saints in their prayers and hymns, to symbolise the relation between the human and the Divine, and the longing of man for the moment of total absorption in the Deity. The Song of Songs became the great allegory, picturing the connexion between God and Israel. The act of revelation is described as the wedding between heaven and earth. The death of the righteous, when the soul returns unto God, is described as a kiss; whilst each individual mystic considered his particular action of losing himself in the Divine as a new matrimonial act.

I have referred once or twice to saints who were visited by angels, who had peculiar visions, and who even wrought miracles. Writing for a modern public, I consider it due to these true saints that the reader should not suspect them of untruth, because of failure to reconcile these happenings with his own experiences. Things absolutely impossible to us may have been, and, indeed, were, an actual reality with them. Ruskin, in his lecture, "Pleasures of Faith," given in a not less sceptical age than ours, thus said to his hearers:

> You have all been taught by Lord Macaulay and his school that because you have carpets instead of rushes for your feet; and feather-beds instead of fern for your backs; and kickshaws instead of beef for your eating; and drains instead of holy wells for your drinking;—that, therefore, you are the cream of creation, and every one of you a seven-headed Solomon. Stay in those pleasant circumstances and convictions, if you please; but don't accuse your roughly-bred and fed fathers of telling lies about the aspect the earth and sky bore to *them,*—till you have trodden the earth as they, barefoot, and seen the heavens as they, face to face.

I grudge no one his Persian rugs or his mineral-waters. I have even personally a sneaking desire for such things, and do prefer the electric light to the tallow-candle with which I was brought up. But one has a right to resent the superior smile which one meets when speaking of those times and those men. I find that the terms saints, mystics, and Cabbalists, are used as terms of reproach nowadays. This attitude is quite inconceivable to me. Has the German nation ever disowned its Master Ekkehart, or its Boehme? Has the French nation ever looked with contempt on the School of the Jansenists, or is it not even more proud of Pascal's *Pensées* than of his scientific discoveries? If one will attempt to live like these saints, he will have the same experiences. Let him try only to spend nine hours a day in prayer, and the rest in the study of the Law, and in the relief of suffering; to fast six days out of seven, and break the fast on bread and water; to give to sleep three hours out of twenty-four, and these on a stone instead of a feather-bed. Let him make martyrdom the dwelling-point of his thoughts for a time, and the death of a martyr the goal of his ambitions and achievements. Let him make this experiment for half a year only, and see whether the experiences which he will have to relate will not be the same as those of a Loria, a Caro, and other saints.

The saint must not be judged by the common standard of humanity. Consciousness of sin and the assurance of grace are the two great motive powers in the working of religion. Without them, religion sinks to the level of a mere cult, or a kind of ethico-æsthetico-spiritual sport in which there is no room for devotion and submission; but what is with the common religionist a mere dogma, is with the saint an awful reality, dominating all his actions and pervading all his being. Under these two realities—the reality of sin and the reality of grace—the saint is constantly labouring. "My sin is ever before me," is the cry of the Psalmist, and it is echoed by every Jewish saint. Hence the tendency toward self-accusation so manifest in many a composition by the Jewish saints. Sometimes it is the sin of his fellow-man for which he holds himself fully responsible. We possess formulas of confessions written and read by Jewish saints, in which they arraign themselves for the most heinous offences, and which it would take a dozen lifetimes to commit. This is rightly explained on the ground that the sense of solidarity and responsibility was so keen with the Jewish saint that he saw nothing incongruous in pleading guilty to the sum total of iniquities committed by his contemporaries.[74] But, with the Psalmist, he is equally certain of the assurance expressed in the passage, "I have set God before me continually: for with him at my right hand I cannot be moved. Therefore my heart is glad and my glory exults, my flesh also dwells in safety." [75] One of our higher critics thinks that these verses may, without effort, be called Christian. I am proud to call them Jewish. The notion of the permanency of the Divine Presence is the great safeguard against sin. The exhortation to feel shame before the Holy One, blessed be he, who is present everywhere and witnesses man's deeds, is a favourite appeal with all the Jewish moralists. The saint, however, is so strongly overawed by the shame before God, that he said: "A sinful thought should bring a blush to man's face, and make him experience the same sensation of confusion and shame, as he would at the sudden appearance of an intimate friend at the moment when he is about to engage in some disgraceful action." Thus the saint "cannot be moved," but when a slip happens, there is the Divine grace surviving sin, which latter is only an outcome of human frailty. The very realisation on the part of man of his loss through his departure from God has brought him back to God; or, as a Jewish liturgical poet expressed it, "And where shall I flee, if not from thee to thee?" Hence the despondency bordering on despair which you will find in the composition of many a saint, but which suddenly passes into exaltation and joy. For, indeed, for him the world is God-full, though disfigured by sin and misery; but, even in the depths of this misery and sin, the saint divines those "inshinings of the pure rays of holy celestial light," which, in God's own time, will lift and purify fallen creation. The Devil himself is an angel of God, though a fallen angel, and he has to be prayed for, whilst the hope is expressed that Hell itself will, with the disappearance of sin, be converted into a Paradise.[76]

The period of struggle in the life of the saint, and the stage of serenity and peace following upon it, are described by one of the saints in the following words:

And when the soul has realised God's omnipotence and his greatness, she prostrates herself in dread before his greatness and glory, and remains in this state till she receives his assurance, when her fear and anxiety cease. Then she drinks of the cup of love to God. She has no other occupation than his service, no other thought than of him, no other intent than the accomplishment of his will, and no other utterance than his praise.[77]

But even during his struggle the fear of the saint is not of punishment, for suffering is looked upon by him as another token of God's love, indeed, as a gift of heaven; nor is his hope connected with reward, which he would consider unworthy and mercenary. Death has no terrors for him. "When I am afar from thee," prayed an ancient Jewish saint, "my death is in my life; when I cleave to thee, my life is in my death." [78] What he dreads is separation from God, what he longs for is fellowship with God.

Some mystics defined the saint, or the Chasid, as one who acts Chasid-like with his Maker, which may be interpreted to mean that not only does he not insist upon the letter of the Law, but all his worship is an act of grace without any hope of reward or fear of punishment.[79]

One of the saints expressed this thought in the following rather bold words:

"I have no wish for thy Paradise, nor any desire for the bliss in the world to come. I want thee and thee alone." [80]

6

THE CHASSIDIM [1]

THROUGHOUT the whole of that interesting field of Theological Literature which deals with the genesis and course of
religious movements, there is probably none whose history,
even whose name, is so little known to English students, as
that of the Chassidim. And yet it would be difficult to point,
in comparatively recent times, to a dissenting movement
more strikingly complete in its development, more suggestive
of analogy, more full of interest in its original purpose, more
pregnant of warning in its decay.

The Hebrew word "Chassidim" [2] merely means "the
Pious," and appears to have been complacently adopted by
the early apostles of the sect. But the thing—Chassidism—
was, in its inception at all events, a revolt among the Jews of
Eastern Europe against the excessive casuistry of the contemporary Rabbis. It was in fact one more manifestation of the
yearning of the human heart towards the Divine idea, and
of its ceaseless craving for direct communion with God. It
was the protest of an emotional but uneducated people
against a one-sided expression of Judaism, presented to them
in cold and over-subtle disquisitions which not only did they
not understand, but which shut out the play of the feelings

and the affections, so that religion was made almost impossible to them.

Some account of the sect is the more necessary because, although the Chassidim have not been wholly ignored by historians or novelists, the references to them have generally, for perfectly intelligible reasons, been either biassed or inaccurate. The historians who have treated of them have been almost exclusively men saturated with Western culture and rationalism. To them the rude and uncouth manifestations of an undisciplined religious spirit could not be other than repellent; to them Chassidism was a movement to be dismissed as unæsthetic and irrational.

To the purposes of fiction the romantic side of Chassidism lends itself readily, but the novelists who have used this material have confined themselves to its externals. Indeed, to have done more would have involved a tedious and unremunerative study of difficult Hebrew texts, an undertaking not to be expected from the most conscientious writers of this class. Thus Franzos in his references to the Jews of Barnow describes faithfully the outer signs of the man, his long coat and tangled curls, but the inner life, the world in which the Chassid moved and had his being, was unknown to him and is therefore unrecorded.

As to my treatment of the subject, I confess that there was a time when I loved the Chassidim as there was a time when I hated them. And even now I am not able to suppress these feelings. I have rather tried to guide my feelings in such a way as to love in Chassidism what is ideal and noble, and to hate in it what turned out bad and pernicious for Judaism. How far I have been successful is another question. At least I have endeavoured to write this paper in such a spirit. But of one thing I must warn the reader—the desire to give some clear notion of the leading ideas of Chassidism has compelled me to quote some passages in which the Chas-

sidim have spoken in very offensive terms of their opponents. In justice to these I must remark that unfortunately
religious struggles are usually conducted on the most irre-
ligious principles. Thus the Chassidim imputed to their
antagonists, the contemporary Rabbis, many vices from
which they were free. Certainly, there was, as one can read in
every history of Jewish religion, something wrong in the
state of Judaism. But I know people who maintain that there
is something very wrong in the present state of Judaism, and
who despair of a regeneration. But surely this is a silly exaggeration. The Chassidim also exaggerated. It would be better
to take but little notice of their accusations and dwell more
on that which was spoken in a kind and loving spirit.

As to the literature of the subject, I can only say here that
I have made use of every book I could consult, both in
English and in foreign libraries. But I cannot pledge myself
to be what early Jewish writers called "a donkey which carries books." I exercise my own choice and my own judgment
on many points.

As an active force for good, Chassidism was short-lived.
For, as I propose to show, there lurked among its central
tenets the germs of the degeneracy which so speedily came
upon it. But its early purposes were high, its doctrines fairly
pure, its aspirations ideal and sublime.

The founder of the sect was one Israel Baalshem,[3] and the
story of his parentage, birth, and childhood, and the current
anecdotes of his subsequent career play a considerable part
in Chassidic literature. But the authentic materials for his
biography are everywhere interwoven with much that is pure
legend and with much more that is miraculous. This was,
perhaps, inevitable, and is certainly not an unfamiliar feature in the personal histories of religious reformers as presented by their followers and devotees.

The sayings and doings of Baalshem are an essential—

perhaps the most essential—portion of any account of the sect. For Baalshem is the centre of the Chassidic world, and Chassidism is so intimately bound up with the personality of its founder that any separation between them is well nigh impossible. To the Chassidim Baalshem is not a man who established a theory or set forth a system; he himself was the incarnation of a theory and his whole life the revelation of a system.

Even those portions of his history which are plainly legendary have their uses in indicating the ideals and in illustrating the aspirations of the early Chassidim; while their circulation and the ready credence they received are valuable evidence of the real power and influence of Baalshem's personality.

In the tale as told by the sect little is omitted of those biographical accessories which are proper to an Avatar. There is all the conventional heralding of a pre-ordained advent; all the usual signs and portents of a new dispensation may be recognised in the almost preternatural virtues of Baalshem's parents, in the miraculous annunciation and exceptional circumstances of his nativity, and in the early indication of a strong and fearless individuality. Everywhere it seems to be suggested that Baalshem from his infancy was conscious of a lofty mission. It is already in tender years that he is made to give evidence of an indifference to conventional restraints and accepted ideals.

Rabbi Eliezer and his wife, the parents of Baalshem, dwelt, as the story goes, in Moldavia. They are described as a pious and God-fearing couple, who, when they had already reached old age, were still childless. They are accredited with a spotless rectitude, which was unimpaired by a long series of strange vicissitudes and misfortunes.

Ultimately, an angel of God appeared to Eliezer and announced that, as he had successfully withstood all the tempta-

tions and sufferings by which he had been tried, God was
about to reward him with a son, who was destined to en-
lighten the eyes of all Israel. Therefore his name should be
Israel, for in him the words of Scripture were to be fulfilled,
"Thou art my servant, Israel, in whom I will be glorified."
In due course the promise was fulfilled, and to the aged
couple a son was born, who was named Israel according to
the angel's word. The date of Baalshem's birth is about 1700;
his birthplace, in Bukowina, in a hitherto unidentified
village which the authorities call Ukop, then still belonging
to Roumania. The child's mother died soon after he was
weaned, and his father did not long survive her. But before
Eliezer died he took his child in his arms, and blessing him,
bade him fear naught, for God would always be with him.

As Eliezer had been greatly honoured in the community
in which he lived, his orphan son was carefully tended and
educated. He was early supplied with an instructor in the
Holy Law. But though he learned with rare facility, he rejected the customary methods of instruction. One day, while
still quite young, his teacher missed him, and on seeking
found him sitting alone in the forest that skirted his native
village, in happy and fearless solitude. He repeated this
escapade so often that it was thought best to leave him to
follow his own bent. A little later we find him engaged as
assistant to a schoolmaster. His duty was not to teach, but to
take the children from their homes to the synagogue and
thence on to the school. It was his wont while accompanying
the children to the synagogue to teach them solemn hymns
which he sang with them. In the synagogue he encouraged
them to sing the responses, so that the voices of the children
penetrated through the heavens and moved the Divine father
to compassion. Satan, fearing lest his power on earth should
thereby be diminished, assumed the shape of a werewolf,
and, appearing before the procession of children on their

way to the synagogue, put them to flight. In consequence of this alarming incident the children's services were suspended. But Israel, recollecting his father's counsel to fear naught, besought the parents to be allowed to lead the children once more in the old way. His request was granted, and when the werewolf appeared a second time Israel attacked him with a club and routed him.

In his fourteenth year Israel became a beadle at the Beth Hammidrash.[4] Here he assiduously but secretly pursued the study of the Law. Yet, being anxious that none should know his design, he read and worked only at night, when the schoolroom was empty and the usual scholars had retired. During the daytime he slept, so that he was popularly believed to be both ignorant and lazy. Despite these precautions, however, his true character was revealed to one person. A certain holy man, the father of a young student at the college, had discovered some old manuscripts which contained the deepest secrets. Before his death he bade his son repair to Ukop, Israel's birthplace, telling him that he would find one Israel, son of Eliezer, to whom the precious documents were to be entrusted. They possessed, so the old man declared, a certain mystic and heavenly affinity with Israel's soul. The student carried out his father's instructions, and at last discovered the object of his search in the beadle of the Beth Hammidrash. Israel admitted him to his friendship and confidence on the condition of secrecy as to his real character. The student, however, paid dearly for this acquaintance with Israel. Contrary to Baalshem's advice, he entered upon a dangerous incantation in the course of which he made a mistake so serious that it cost him his life.

Upon the death of his friend, Baalshem left his native village and settled as a teacher in a small town near Brody. Here, although his true mission and character were still unknown, he became much respected for his rigid probity, and was frequently chosen as umpire in disputes among Jews. On one of these occasions he arbitrated with so much learning and impartiality that not only did he satisfy both parties, but one of them, a learned man of Brody, named Abraham, offered him his own daughter in marriage. Israel, to whom it had been revealed that Abraham's daughter was his pre-destined wife, immediately accepted the offer and the act of betrothal was drawn up. But wishing his true character to remain unknown he stipulated that Abraham, although a "Talmid Chacham" (student)[5] himself and therefore pre-sumably desirous that his daughter should marry a scholar, should omit from the betrothal-deed all the titles of honour usually appended to the name of a learned bridegroom. While returning to Brody, Abraham died, and Gershon his son, a scholar still greater and more celebrated than his father, was surprised and shocked to find a deed of betrothal among his father's papers, from which it appeared that his sister was to wed a man with apparently no claim to scholar-ship or learning. He protested to his sister, but she declined to entertain any objections to a marriage which her father had arranged. When the time for the wedding was at hand, Israel gave up his post as teacher, and repaired to Brody. Disguised as a peasant he presented himself before his future brother-in-law, who was then fulfilling some high judicial function. Gershon taking him for a beggar offered him alms, but Israel, refusing the money, asked for a private interview, stating that he had an important secret to reveal. He then, to Gershon's surprise and disgust, explained who he was and that he had come to claim his bride. As the girl was deter-mined to obey her father's will the affair was settled and the day fixed. On the morning of the wedding Israel revealed to his bride his real character and mission, at the same time enjoining secrecy. Evil fortunes would befall them, he said, but a better time would eventually follow.

After the wedding, Gershon, having in vain attempted to instruct his seemingly ignorant brother-in-law, decided to rid himself of his presence. He gave his sister the choice of being separated from her husband, or of leaving the town in his company. She chose the latter, and thereupon the two left Brody and began a life of hardship and suffering. Israel chose for his new home a spot on one of the spurs of the Carpathian Mountains. No Jews lived there, and Israel and his wife were thus separated from the society of their fellows in a life of complete and unchanging solitude. Israel dug lime in the ravines among the mountains, and his wife conveyed it for sale to the nearest town. Their life at this period seems to have been one of great privation, but the harder Israel's outward lot, the more he increased in spiritual greatness. In his solitude he gave himself up entirely to devotion and religious contemplation. His habit was to climb to the summit of the mountains and wander about rapt in spiritual ecstasies. He fasted, prayed, made continual ablutions, and observed all the customary outward and inward exercises of piety and devotion.

After seven years, Gershon, who was well aware of the bitter poverty which his sister endured, relented and brought her and her husband back to Brody. At first he employed Baalshem as his coachman, but as he proved wholly unfit for this work Gershon rented a small inn in a remote village, and there established his sister and her husband. The business of the inn was managed by the wife, while Baalshem passed most of his time in a hut in a neighbouring forest. Here he once more gave himself up to meditation and preparation for his future work, and here, a little later, when nearly forty-two years of age, to a few chosen spirits, afterwards his most fervent disciples, he first revealed his true character and mission.

From this point unfortunately the materials for a continuous biography are wanting; we next hear of Baalshem discharging the functions of an ordinary Rabbi at Miedziboz in Podolia, but for the remainder of his personal history we have to be content with detached anecdotes and fragmentary passages in his life, the sum total of which goes to show that he resided in Podolia and Wallachia, teaching his doctrines to his disciples and "working Wonders." He does not seem to have figured as a public preacher, nor has he left behind him any written work. He appears rather to have used the method, familiar to students of Greek philosophy, of teaching by conversations with his friends and disciples. These conversations, and the parables with which they were largely interspersed, were remembered and stored up by his hearers. By his neighbours the country folk, Baalshem was regarded simply as "a man of God." He was allowed to pursue his course undisturbed by persecution of the serious character which his more aggressive successors provoked. Such of the Rabbis as were aware of his existence despised him and his ways, but the Rabbinical world was at that time too much occupied in the controversy between Eybeschütz and Emden to concern itself with the vagaries of an obscure and apparently "unlearned" eccentric. Baalshem also took part in the disputes which were held in Lemberg, the capital of Galicia (1757?), between the Rabbis and the Frankists,[6] who denounced the Talmud to the Polish Government and wanted to have all the Rabbinical books destroyed. Baalshem suffered from this excitement in a most terrible way. The abrogation of the Oral Law meant for him the ruin of Judaism.

Baalshem, in forming the little band of devoted followers who were destined to spread a knowledge of his creed, travelled considerably about Wallachia. He at one time decided to make a pilgrimage to Palestine, but when he reached Constantinople he felt himself inspired to return and continue his work at home. He died at Miedziboz on the eve of Pentecost, 1761.

After his death his disciples, of whom one Beer of Mizriez was the most prominent, undertook the proselytising mission for which Baalshem had prepared them, but from which he himself appears to have abstained. They preached and taught in all the provinces of Russia where Jews may reside, and in Roumania, and Galicia. The number of the sect at the present day is probably about half a million.

Returning now to Baalshem the founder, it may be noted that his appearance as a teacher and reformer was accompanied and justified by a customary and adequate number of miracles. To one disciple he revealed secrets which could have become known to him only by divine revelation; to another he appeared with a nimbus round his head. On the evidence of the Chassidim we learn that Baalshem performed all the recognised signs and marvels which have ever been the customary minor characteristics of men of similar type in similar environment. When Baalshem desired to cross a stream, he spread forth his mantle upon the waters, and standing thereupon passed safely to the other side. Ghosts evacuated haunted houses at the mere mention of his name. Was he alone in the forest on a wintry night, he had but to touch a tree with his finger tips and flames burst forth. When his spirit wandered through the angelic spheres, as was frequently the case, he obtained access to Paradise for millions of pining souls who had vainly waited without through long thousands of mournful years. These and other miracles need not be examined. Here, as in the case of other such blissful seasons of grace, they were the ephemeral though important accessories in establishing the inspired character of his utterances and the authority of his injunctions. It is not as a worker of miracles, but as a religious teacher and reformer, that Baalshem is interesting.

Properly to understand the nature and special direction of his teaching, it is necessary in some measure to realise the character of the field in which he worked; to consider, in other words, the moral and religious condition of the Jews in those districts where Chassidism first took root.

In a Hebrew Hymn, written about 1000 A.C., and still recited in the synagogue on the Day of Atonement, the poet expresses the strange and bitter fortunes of his race in touching words of mingled sorrow and exultation.

> Destroyed lies Zion and profaned,
> Of splendour and renown bereft,
> Her ancient glories wholly waned,
> One deathless treasure only left;
> Still ours, O Lord,
> Thy Holy Word.

And this Divine Word it was, which a persecuted religion has sought to preserve intact through so many centuries of persecution, and for the sake of which no labour seemed too severe, no sacrifice too large. "Bethink Thee, O God," exclaimed one of our Jewish sages who flourished about the same period, "bethink Thee of Thy faithful children who, amid their poverty and want, are busy in the study of Thy Law. Bethink Thee of the poor in Israel who are willing to suffer hunger and destitution if only they can secure for their children the knowledge of Thy Law." And so indeed it was. Old and young, weak and strong, rich and poor, all pursued that single study, the Torah. The product of this prolonged study is that gigantic literature which, as a long unbroken chain of spiritual activity, connects together the various periods of the Jews' chequered and eventful history. All ages and all lands have contributed to the development of this supreme study. For under the word Torah was comprised not only the Law, but also the contributions of later times expressing either the thoughts or the emotions of holy and

sincere men; and even their honest scepticism was not entirely excluded. As in the canon of the Bible, Ecclesiastes
and the Song of Solomon found place in the same volume
that contains the Law and the Prophets, so at a later time
people did not object to put the philosophical works of Maimonides and the songs of Judah Hallevi on the same level
with the Code of the Law compiled by R. Isaac Alfasi, and
the commentaries on the Bible by R. Solomon b. Isaac.[7]
None of them was declared infallible, but also to none of
them, as soon as people were convinced of the author's sincerity, was denied the homage due to seekers after truth.
Almost every author was called Rabbi ("my master") or
Rabbenu ("our master"),[8] and nearly every book was regarded more or less as a contribution to the great bulk of the
Torah. It was called Writ,[9] and was treated with a certain
kind of piety. But, by a series of accidents too long to be
related here, sincerity ceased and sport took its place. I refer
to the casuistic schools commonly known by the name of
Pilpulists[10] (the "seasoned" or the "sharp" ones), who flourished in the last two centuries preceding ours. To the authors
of this unhappy period, a few glorious exceptions always
allowed, the preceding Jewish literature did not mean a
"fountain of living waters," supplying men with truth and
religious inspiration, but rather a kind of armoury providing
them with juristic cases over which to fight, and to out-do
each other in sophistry and subtlety. As a consequence they
cared little or nothing for that part of the Jewish literature
that appeals less to the intellect than to the feelings of men.
In short, religion consisted only of complicated cases and
innumerable ordinances, in which the wit of these men found
delight. But the emotional part of it, whose root is the Faith
and Love of men, was almost entirely neglected.

But it was precisely these higher religious emotions that
were Baalshem's peculiar province, and it was to them that

he assigned in his religious system a place befitting their importance and their dignity. And the locality where his ministration lay was curiously adapted for such propaganda. To that universal study of the Law of which I have just spoken there was one exception. That exception was amongst the Jews in the territories which bordered on the Carpathian Mountains, and comprise the principalities of Moldavia, and Wallachia, Bukowina, and the Ukraine.

It is historically certain that the first arrival of the Jews in Roumania was at a very early date, but there is no trace of any intellectual productivity among the immigrants until recent times, and it is admitted that the study of the Law was almost entirely neglected. It was in these districts of mental, and perhaps we might add of even spiritual, darkness that Chassidism took its rise and achieved its first success. "The sect of the Chassidim," says one of the bitterest but most trustworthy of their opponents, "first gained ground in the most uncivilised provinces; in the wild ravines of Wallachia and the dreary steppes of the Ukraine."

Apart from the genius of its founder, Chassidism owed its rapid growth to the intellectual barrenness of these districts as compared with the intellectual fertility of the other regions where Jews most thickly congregated. The Roumanian Jews were to some extent under the jurisdiction of the Rabbis of Poland. Now the Poles were celebrated even in Germany for the elaboration of their casuistry. These over-subtle Rabbis, delighting in the quibbles of their sophistry, and reducing religion to an unending number of juristic calculations and all sorts of possibilities and impossibilities, were but too apt to forget the claims of feeling in their eager desire to question and to settle everything. They may have been satisfactory guides in matters spiritual to the men of their own stamp, but they were of no avail to their Roumanian brethren who failed to recognise religion in the garb of casuistry.

It was, therefore, not surprising that a revolt against the excess of intellectualism should have sprung up and flourished in those districts where the inhabitants were constitutionally incapable of appreciating the delights of argument. The field was ready, and in the fulness of time came the sower in the person of Baalshem.

In the above estimate of the Polish Rabbis there undoubtedly lurks a touch of exaggeration. But it represents the view which the Chassidim took of their opponents. The whole life of Baalshem is a protest against the typical Rabbi thus conceived. The essential difference in the ideals of the two parties is perhaps best illustrated in those portions of their biographical literature where legend treads most closely upon the heels of fact.

The hero of Polish Rabbinic biography at five years of age can recite by heart the most difficult tractates of the Talmud; at eight he is the disciple of the most celebrated teacher of the time, and perplexes him by the penetrative subtlety of his questions; while at thirteen he appears before the world as a full-fledged Doctor of the Law.

The hero of the Chassidim has a totally different education, and his distinctive glory is of another kind. The legendary stories about Baalshem's youth tell us little of his proficiency in Talmudic studies; instead of sitting in the Beth Hammidrash with the folios of some casuistic treatise spread out before him, Baalshem passes his time singing hymns out of doors, or under the green trees of the forest with the children. Satan, however, says the Chassid, is more afraid of these innocent exercises than of all the controversies in the Maharam Shiff.[11] It was through external nature, the woods of his childhood, the hills and wild ravines of the Carpathians where he passed many of his maturer years, that Baalshem, according to his disciples, reached his spiritual confirmation. The Chassidic hero had no celebrated Rabbi for his master. He was his own teacher. If not self-taught, it was from angelic lips, or even the Divine voice itself, that he learned the higher knowledge. From the source whence the Torah flowed Baalshem received heavenly lore. His method of self-education, his ways of life, his choice of associates were all instances of revolt; not only did he teach a wholly different theory and practice, but he and his disciples seem to have missed no opportunity of denouncing the old teachers as misleading and ungodly. Among the many anecdotes illustrating this feature, it is told how once, on the evening before the great Day of Atonement, Baalshem was noticed by his disciples to be, contrary to his usual custom, depressed and ill at ease. The whole subsequent day he passed in violent weeping and lamentations. At its close he once more resumed his wonted cheerfulness of manner. When asked for the explanation of his behaviour, he replied that the Holy Spirit had revealed to him that heavy accusations were being made against the Jewish people, and a heavy punishment had been ordained upon them. The anger of heaven was caused by the Rabbis, whose sole occupation was to invent lying premisses and to draw from them false conclusions. All the truly wise Rabbis of the olden time (such as the Tannaim, the Amoraim[12] and their followers, whom Baalshem regarded as so many saints and prophets) had now stood forth as the accusers of their modern successors by whom their words were so grossly perverted from their original meaning. On this account Baalshem's tears had been shed, and his prayers as usual had been successful. The impending judgment was annulled. On another occasion, when he overheard the sounds of eager, loud discussion issuing from a Rabbinical college, Baalshem, closing his ears with his hands, declared that it was such disputants who delayed the redemption of Israel from captivity. Satan, he said, incites the Rabbis to study those portions of Jewish literature only on which they can whet the sharpness of their intellects, but from all writings of which the reading would promote piety and the fear of God he keeps them away. "Where there is much study," says a disciple of Baalshem, "there is little piety." "Jewish Devils" [13] is one of the numerous polite epithets applied to the Rabbis by the friends of Baalshem. "Even the worst sinners are better than they; so blind are they in the arrogance of their self-conceit that their very devotion to the Law becomes a vehicle for their sin." It will be found when we deal with the most positive side of Baalshem's teaching that this antagonism to the attitude and methods of the contemporary Rabbis is further emphasised, and it will readily be seen that his whole scheme of religion and of conduct in relation to God and man rendered this acknowledged hostility inevitable. In approaching this part of our subject it should be remembered that, as stated above, Baalshem himself wrote nothing. For a knowledge of his sayings we are therefore dependent on the reports of his friends and disciples. And it is not unfrequently necessary to supplement these by the teaching of his followers, whom we may suppose in large measure to have caught the spirit of their master. Unfortunately the original authorities are in a difficult Hebrew patois which often obscures the precise meaning of whole passages.

The originality of Baalshem's teaching has been frequently impugned, chiefly by the suggestion that he drew largely from the Zohar (Book of Brightness).[14] This mystical book, "the Bible of the Cabbalists," whether we regard its subject-matter or its history and influence, is unique in literature. Its pretended author is Simeon ben Yochai, a great Rabbi of the second century, but the real writer is probably one Moses de Leon, a Spanish Jew, who lived eleven centuries later. The book is one of the most interesting literary forgeries, and is a marvellous mixture of good and evil. A passage of delicate religious fancy is succeeded by another of gross obscenity in illustration and suggestion; true piety and wild blasphemy are strangely mingled together. Baalshem undoubtedly had studied the Zohar, and he even is reported to have said that the reading of the Zohar had enabled him to see into the whole universe of things. But, for all that, Baalshem was no copyist; and the Zohar, although it may have suggested a hint to him here and there, was not the source whence his inspiration was drawn.

Its attraction for Baalshem is sufficiently explained by the fantastic, imaginative, and emotional nature of its contents. It lent itself more easily than the older Rabbinical literature to new explanations unthought of by its author. But even the Talmud and its early commentaries became apocalyptic to the heroes of Chassidism. Nay, the driest and most legal disquisitions about *meum* and *tuum* could be translated into parables and allegories and symbols full of the most exalted meanings. Baalshem, like every other religious reformer, was partially the product of his age. The influences of the past, the history and literature of his own people, helped to make him what he was. But they do not rob him of his originality. He was a religious revivalist in the best sense; full of burning faith in his God and his cause; convinced utterly of the value of his work and the truth of his teaching.

Although there can be no real doubt of Baalshem's claim to originality, it should be borne in mind that his teaching is not only distinctively Jewish, but that for every part of it parallels and analogies could be found in the older Hebrew literature. Indeed it is not wonderful that in a literature, extending over 2000 years, of a people whose chief thoughts have been religion, and who have come in contact with so many external religious and philosophic influences, the germs can be discovered of almost every conceivable system, and the outline of almost every imaginable doctrine.

The keynote of all Baalshem's teachings is the Omnipresence, or more strictly the Immanence, of God. This is the source from which flows naturally every article of his creed; the universality of the Divinity is the foundation of the entire Chassidic fabric. The idea of the constant living presence of God in all existence permeates the whole of Baalshem's scheme; it is insisted on in every relation; from it is deduced every important proposition and every rule in conduct of his school.

All created things and every product of human intelligence owe their being to God. All generation and all existence spring from the thought and will of God. It is incumbent upon man to believe that all things are pervaded by the divine life, and when he speaks he should remember that it is this divine life which is speaking through him. There is nothing which is void of God. If we imagine for a moment such a thing to be, it would instantly fall into nothingness. In every human thought God is present. If the thought be gross or evil, we should seek to raise and ennoble it by carrying it back to its origin. So, if a man be suddenly overwhelmed by the aspect of a beautiful woman, he should remember that this splendour of beauty is owing to the all-pervading emanation from the divine. When he remembers that the source of corporeal beauty is God, he will not be content to let his thought abide with the body when he can rise to the inward contemplation of the infinite soul of beauty, which is God. A disciple of Baalshem has said: Even as in the jewels of his beloved the lover sees only the beauty of her he loves, so does the true lover of God see in all the appearances of this world, the vitalising and generative power of his divine master. If you do not see the world in the light of God you separate the creation from its Creator. He who does not fully believe in this universality of God's presence has never properly acknowledged God's

Sovereignty, for he excludes God from an existing portion of the actual world. The word of God (to Baalshem, a synonym for God himself), which "is settled in heaven" and "established on earth," is still and always speaking, acting, and generating throughout heaven and earth in endless gradations and varieties. If the vitalising word were to cease, chaos would come again. The belief in a single creation after which the Master withdrew from his completed work, is erroneous and heretical. The vivifying power is never withdrawn from the world which it animates. Creation is continuous; an unending manifestation of the goodness of God. All things are an affluence from the two divine attributes of Power and Love, which express themselves in various images and reflections.

This is the doctrine of universality in Chassidism. God, the father of Israel, God the Merciful, God the All-powerful, the God of Love, not only created everything but is embodied in everything. The necessity of believing this doctrine is the cardinal Dogma. But as creation is continuous so also is revelation. This revelation is only to be grasped by faith. Faith, therefore, is more efficacious than learning. Thus it is that in times of persecution, the wise and the foolish, the sinner and the saint, are wont alike to give up their life for their faith. They who could render no answer to the questions of the casuist are yet willing to die the most cruel of deaths rather than deny their faith in the One and Supreme God. Their strength to face danger and death is owing to that divine illumination of the soul which is more exalted than knowledge.

We should thus regard all things in the light of so many manifestations of the Divinity. God is present in all things; therefore there is good, actual or potential, in all things. It is our duty everywhere to seek out and to honour the good, and not to arrogate to ourselves the right to judge that which may seem to be evil. In thinking therefore of a fellow-man, we should above all things realise in him the presence of the spirit of good. Whence we have the Doctrine that each of us, while thinking humbly of himself, should always be ready to think well, and always slow to think evil, of another. This explains the Chassidic attitude towards erring humanity. Baalshem viewed human sin and infirmity in a very different light from that of the ordinary Rabbi. Ever conscious of the Divine side of Humanity, he vigorously combated the gratuitous assumption of sinfulness in man which was a fertile subject with contemporary preachers. They, among the Roumanian Jews as in other communities, delighted chiefly to dwell on the dark side of things, and found their favourite theme in elaborate descriptions of the infernal punishments that were awaiting the sinner after death. It is related how on one occasion Baalshem rebuked one of these. The preacher had been denouncing woe to an audience of whom he knew nothing whether for evil or for good. Baalshem, indignant at this indiscriminative abuse and conceited arrogation of the divine office of judgment, turned on him in the following words: "Woe upon thee who darest to speak evil of Israel! Dost not know that every Jew, when he utters ever so short a prayer at the close of day, is performing a great work before which the angels in heaven bow down?" Great, as it would seem, was the value set by Baalshem upon the smallest evidence of the higher nature in man, and few there were, as he believed, who, if their spirit was not darkened by pride, did not now and again give proof of the divine stamp in which God had created them. No sin so separates us from God that we need despair of return. From every rung of the moral ladder, no matter how low, let man seek God. If he but fully believe that nothing is void of God, and that God is concealed in the midst of apparent ruin and degradation, he will not fear lest God be far from him. God is regained in a moment of repentance, for repentance "transcends the limits of space and time." And he who leads the sinner to repentance causes a divine joy; it is as though a king's son had been in captivity and were now brought back to his father's gaze.

Baalshem refused to regard anyone as wholly irredeemable. His was an optimistic faith. God was to be praised in gladness by the dwellers in this glorious world. The true believer, recognising the reflection of God in every man, should hopefully strive, when that reflection was obscured by sin, to restore the likeness of God in man. The peculiar detestability of sin lies in this, that man rejects the earthly manifestations of the Divinity and pollutes them. One of Baalshem's disciples delighted in the saying that the most hardened sinners were not to be despaired of, but prayed for. None knows the heart of man, and none should judge his neighbour. Let him who burns with zeal for God's sake, exercise his zeal on himself, not others. Baalshem said, "Let no one think himself better than his neighbour, for all serve God; each according to the measure of understanding which God has given him."

From this position it is a natural step to Baalshem's view of prayer. He is reputed to have said that all the greatness he had achieved was the issue not of study but of prayer. But true prayer "must move," as Baalshem phrased it, "in the realms above," and not be concerned with affairs sublunary. Your prayer should not be taken up with your wishes and needs, but should be the means to bring you nigh to God. In prayer man must lay aside his own individuality, and not even be conscious of his existence; for if, when he prays, Self is not absolutely quiescent, the object of prayer is unattainable. Indeed it is only through God's grace that after true prayer man is yet alive; to such a point has the annihilation of self proceeded.

It may be necessary to caution the reader against ascribing to Baalshem any modern rationalistic notions on the subject of prayer. The power of prayer, in the old-fashioned sense, to produce an answer from God was never doubted by Baalshem for a moment. Baalshem's deity is not restricted towards any side by any philosophic considerations. All Baalshem meant was that any reference or regard to earthly requirements was unworthy and destructive of this communion of man with God. The wise man, says Baalshem, does not trouble the king with innumerable petitions about trifles. His desire is merely to gain admission into the king's presence and to speak with him without a go-between. To be with the king whom he loves so dearly is for him the highest good. But his love for the king has its reward; for the king loves him.

It has already been implied that, with regard to our duty towards our fellow-man, we must not only honour him for the good, and abstain from judging the evil that may be in him, but must pray for him. Furthermore we must work for his spiritual and moral reclamation. In giving practical effect in his own life to this doctrine, Baalshem's conduct was in striking contrast to that of his contemporaries. He habitually consorted with outcasts and sinners, with the poor and uneducated of both sexes, whom the other teachers ignored. He thus won for his doctrines a way to the heart of the people by adapting his life and language to their understanding and sympathies. In illustration of this, as well as of his hatred of vanity and display, it is told how, on the occasion of his being accorded a public reception by the Jews on his arrival at Brody, instead of addressing to them in the conventional fashion some subtle discourse upon a Talmudical difficulty, he contented himself with conversing upon trivial topics in the local dialect with some of the less important persons in the crowd.

This incident is perhaps the more noteworthy because it occurred in Brody, which was at that time a seat of learning and Rabbinic culture—a place where, for that very reason, Chassidism was never able to gain a foothold. It is probable enough that Baalshem in his visits to this town kept aloof from the learned and the wise, and sought to gather round him the neglected and humbler elements of Jewish society. It is well known that Baalshem consorted a good deal with the innkeepers of the district, who were held in very low repute among their brethren. The following remark by one of his followers is very suggestive in this respect. Just as only superficial minds attach a certain holiness to special places, whilst with the deeper ones all places are alike holy, so that to them it makes no difference whether prayers be said in the synagogue or in the forest; so the latter believe that not only prophecies and visions come from heaven, but that every utterance of man, if properly understood, contains a message of God. Those who are absorbed in God will easily find the divine element in everything which they hear, even though the speaker himself be quite ignorant of it.

This line of conduct gave a fair opening for attack to his opponents, an opportunity of which they were not slow to avail themselves. Baalshem was pointed at as the associate of the lowest classes. They avenged themselves for his neglect of and hostility to the learned by imputing the worst motives to his indifference to appearances. He was accused of idling about the streets with disreputable characters, and one polemical treatise draws the vilest inferences from his apparent familiarity with women. To this charge Baalshem's conduct, innocent in itself, gave some colour; for his views and habits in relation to women marked a strong divergence from current customs. The position of women in contemporary circles was neither debased nor inevitably unhappy, but it was distinctly subordinate. Their education was almost entirely neglected, and their very existence was practically ignored. According to the Chassidic doctrine of Universality, woman was necessarily to be honoured. "All Jews," says one Chassid, "even the uneducated and the women, believe in God." Baalshem frequently associated with women, assigning to them not only social equality, but a high degree of religious importance.

His own wife he reverenced as a saint; when she died he abandoned the hope of rising to heaven while yet alive, like Elijah of old, saying mournfully that undivided such translation might have happened, but for him alone it was impossible. Then again in a form of religion utilising so largely the emotions of Faith and Love there was a strong appeal to the female mind. The effect of this was soon evident, and Baalshem did not neglect to profit by it. Among the most devoted of his early adherents were women. One of them was the heroine of a favourite anecdote concerning Baalshem's work of Love and Rescue. It is related that in a certain village there dwelt a woman whose life was so disgraceful that her brothers at last determined to kill her. With this object they enticed her into a neighbouring wood, but guided by the Holy Spirit Baalshem intervened at the critical moment, and dissuading the men from their purpose rescued the sinner. The woman afterwards became a sort of Magdalen in the new community.

Above I have endeavoured to throw together in some order of sequence the doctrines and practical rules of conduct which Baalshem and his early disciples seem to have deduced from their central idea of the omnipresence of God. This was necessary in order to give a connected idea of their creed, but it is right to say that nowhere in Chassidic literature have these deductions been logically co-ordinated. Perhaps their solitary attempt to formulate and condense their distinctive views is confined to a statement of their idea of piety or service of God, and an examination of three cardinal virtues, Humility, Cheerfulness, and Enthusiasm. What the Chassidim held as to true service brings into relief Baalshem's characteristic manner of regarding the Law.

By the service of God was generally understood a life which fulfilled the precepts of the written and oral law. Baalshem understood by it a certain attitude towards life as a whole. For, as God is realised in life, each activity of life when rightly conceived and executed is at once a manifestation and a service of the Divine. All things have been created for the glory and service of God. The smallest worm serves Him with all its power. Thus, while eating, drinking, sleeping, and the other ordinary functions of the body are regarded by the old Jewish moralists as mere means to an end, to Baalshem they are already a service of God in themselves. All pleasures are manifestations of God's attribute of love; and, so regarded, they are at once spiritualised and ennobled. Man should seek to reach a higher level of purity and holiness before partaking of food and drink, than even before the study of the Law. For when the Torah had once been given by God the whole world became instinct with its grace. He who speaks of worldly matters and religious matters as if they were separate and distinct, is a heretic.

Upon the continual and uninterrupted study of the Law, Baalshem lays but little stress. He accepted the ordinary belief that the Law (under which term are included not only the Pentateuch, but the whole Old Testament and the major portion of the old Rabbinic literature) was a revelation of God. But, as the world itself is equally a divine revelation, the Torah becomes little more than a part of a larger whole. To understand it aright one needs to penetrate to the inward reality—to the infinite light which is revealed in it. We should study the Law not as we study a science for the sake of acquiring knowledge (he who studies it so has in truth

been concerning himself with its mere outward f
we should learn from it the true service of God.
study of the law is no end in itself. It is studied because, as
the word of God, God is more easily discerned and absorbed
in this revelation of Him than in any other. The Torah is
eternal, but its explanation is to be made by the spiritual
leaders of Judaism. It is to be interpreted by them in accordance with the Attribute of the age. For he regarded the
world as governed in every age by a different Attribute of
God—one age by the Attribute of Love, another by that of
Power, a third again, by Beauty, and so on—and the explanation of the Torah must be brought into agreement with it.
The object of the whole Torah is that man should become
a Torah himself. Every man being a Torah in himself, said
a disciple of Baalshem, has got not only his Abraham and
Moses, but also his Balaam and Haman: he should try to
expel the Balaam and develop the Abraham within him.
Every action of man should be a pure manifestation of God.

The reason why we should do what the Law commands is
not to gain grace thereby in the eyes of God, but to learn
how to love God and to be united to Him. The important
thing is not how many separate injunctions are obeyed, but
how and in what spirit we obey them. The object of fulfilling
these various ordinances is to put oneself, as it were, on the
same plane with God, and thus, in the ordinary phrase of
the religious mystic, to become one with Him, or to be
absorbed in Him. People should get to know, says Baalshem,
what the unity of God really means. To attain a part of this
indivisible unity is to attain the whole. The Torah and all
its ordinances are from God. If I therefore fulfil but one
commandment in and through the love of God, it is as
though I have fulfilled them all.

I have now briefly to refer to the three virtues to which
the Chassidim assigned the highest place of honour. Of these

the first is called in Hebrew "Shiphluth," [15] and is best rendered by our word "Humility," but in Chassidic usage it includes the ideas of modesty, considerateness, and sympathy. The prominence given to these qualities is in sharp contrast to the faults of conceit, vanity, and self-satisfaction, against which Baalshem was never weary of protesting. He regarded these as the most seductive of all forms of sin. But a few minutes before his death he was heard to murmur, "O vanity, vanity! even in this hour of death thou darest to approach me with thy temptations: 'Bethink thee, Israel, what a grand funeral procession will be thine because thou hast been so wise and good.' O vanity, vanity! beshrew thee." "It should be indifferent to man," says the master, "whether he be praised or blamed, loved or hated, reputed to be the wisest of mankind or the greatest of fools. The test of the real service of God is that it leaves behind it the feeling of humility. If a man after prayer be conscious of the least pride or self-satisfaction, if he think, for instance, that he has earned a reward by the ardour of his spiritual exercises, then let him know that he has prayed not to God but to himself. And what is this but disguised idolatry? Before you can find God you must lose yourself." The Chassidim treated Shiphluth from two sides: a negative side in thinking humbly of oneself, a positive in thinking highly of one's neighbour, in other words the love for our fellow-man.

He who loves the father will also love his children. The true lover of God is also a lover of man. It is ignorance of one's own errors that makes one ready to see the errors of others. "There is no sphere in heaven where the soul remains a shorter time than in the sphere of merit, there is none where it abides longer than in the sphere of Love."

The second Cardinal Virtue is "Cheerfulness," in Hebrew "Simchah." [16] Baalshem insisted on cheerfulness of heart as a necessary attitude for the due service of God. Once you believe that you are really the servant and the child of God, how can you fall again into a gloomy condition of mind? Nor should the inevitable sins which we all must commit disturb our glad serenity of soul. For is not repentance ready at hand by which we may climb back to God? Every penitent thought is a voice of God. Man should detect that voice in all the evidence of his senses, in every sight and sound of external nature. It is through his want of faith in the universality of God's presence that he is deaf to these subtle influences and can read only the lessons which are inscribed in books.

The reader will be prepared to learn that Baalshem, taking this cheerful view of things, was opposed to every kind of asceticism. Judaism, or rather Israelitism, it is true, was not originally much of an ascetic religion. But there can be little doubt that in the course of history there came in many ascetic doctrines and practices, quite enough at least to encourage such tender souls the bent of whose minds lay in this direction. To one of these, a former disciple, Baalshem wrote: "I hear that you think yourself compelled from religious motives to enter upon a course of fasts and penances. My soul is outraged at your determination. By the counsel of God I order you to abandon such dangerous practices, which are but the outcome of a disordered brain. Is it not written 'Thou shalt not hide thyself from thine own flesh'? Fast then no more than is prescribed. Follow my command and God shall be with you." On another occasion Baalshem was heard to observe that it is a machination of Satan to drive us into a condition of gloom and despondency in which the smallest error is regarded as a deadly sin. Satan's object is to keep us away from the true service of God, and God can only be truly served from a happy and confident disposition. Anxious scrupulosity in details is therefore to be avoided. It is the counsel of the Devil to persuade us that we never have done and shall never do our duty fully, and that moral progress is impossible. Such ideas beget melancholy and despair, which are of evil.

The third virtue is called in the Hebrew Chassidic literature "Hithlahabuth," [17] and is derived from a verb meaning "to kindle" or "set on fire." The substantive "Hithlahabuth," so far as I am aware, was first coined by Baalshem's followers. It is best rendered by our word "Enthusiasm." Every religious action, to be of any avail, must be done with enthusiasm. A mere mechanical and lifeless performance of an ordinance is valueless. A man is no step nearer the goal if he thinks, forsooth, that he has done his duty when he has gone through the whole round of laws in every section of the code. This essential enthusiasm is only begotten of Love. The service of fear, if not wholly useless, is yet necessarily accompanied by a certain repulsion and heaviness, which effectually prevent the rush and ardour of enthusiasm. The inspiration of true service is its own end. There is no thought of this world, and there is none of the world to come. In the Talmud there is frequent reference to one Rabbi Elisha ben Abuyah, an apostate from Judaism, who, when urged to repent, replied that repentance was useless, and that for this mournful belief he had direct divine authority. For he had been told by a voice from heaven that even though he repented he would be excluded from sharing the happiness of the world to come. Of him it was said by one of the Chassidim, "This man indeed missed a golden opportunity. How purely could he have served God, knowing that for his service there could never be a reward!"

From the conception of Enthusiasm springs the quality of mobility, suggesting spiritual progress, and commonly opposed by Baalshem and his followers to the dull religious stagnation of self-satisfied contemporaries. Man should not imagine himself to have attained the level of the righteous; let him rather regard himself as a penitent who should make progress every day. Always to remain on the same religious plane, merely repeating to-day the religious routine of yesterday, is not true service. There must be a daily advance in the knowledge and love of the Divine Master. Mere freedom from active sin is not sufficient; such negative virtue may be but another word for the chance absence of temptation. What boots it never to have committed a sin if sin lies concealed in the heart? It is only the uninterrupted communion with God which will raise and ennoble your thoughts and designs, and cause the roots of sin to die. The patriarch Abraham, without any command from God, fulfilled the whole Torah, because he perceived that the Law was the life of all created things. In the Messianic age the law will no longer seem to man as something ordained for him from without; but the law will be within the hearts of men; it will seem natural and self-evident to them, because they will realise that God and life are manifested through the law.

Baalshem, who dealt largely in parable, has left the following, which we may fitly add to our somewhat inadequate presentation of his doctrine.

There was once a king who built himself a glorious palace. By means of magical illusion it seemed as if the palace were full of devious corridors and mazes, preventing the approach to the royal presence. But as there was much gold and silver heaped up in the entrance halls, most people were content to go no further, but take their fill of treasure. The king himself they did not notice. At last the king's intimate had compassion upon them and exclaimed to them, "All these walls and mazes which you see before you do not in truth exist at all. They are mere illusions. Push forward bravely, and you shall find no obstacle."

We must not interpret the parable to mean that Baalshem denied the reality or even the importance of the actual phenomenal world. The very contrary is the truth. The world is for him full of God, penetrated through and through by the divine, and therefore as real as God himself. It was quite in Baalshem's manner when one of his disciples declared that only fools could speak of the world as vanity or emptiness. "It is in truth a glorious world. We must only learn how rightly to make use of it. Call nothing common or profane: by God's presence all things are holy."

Above we have reviewed the essential doctrines of Baalshem and his immediate followers; we have now to see how they fared at the hands of the sect which he founded. This is a sad part of our task, for the subsequent history of Chassidism is almost entirely a record of decay. As formulated by its founder the new creed amounted to a genuine Reformation, pure and lofty in ideal. After his death unhappily it was rapidly corrupted and perverted. This was due almost exclusively to the dangerous and exaggerated development of a single point in his teaching. That point, the honour due to the divine in man, was relatively a minor article in the original creed. But the later Chassidism has given it a distorted and almost exclusive importance wholly out of proportion to the grander and more essential features of Baalshem's teaching, until the distinctive feature of the Chassidism of to-day is an almost idolatrous service of their living leaders. What little there is to say of the history of the sect after Baalshem's death would be unintelligible without some explanation of the origin and growth of this unfortunate perversion.

It has been explained that Baalshem laid but little stress upon the study of the Law or the observance of its precepts in themselves, but regarded them only as means to an end. The end is union with God. Man has to discover the presence of God in the Divine word and will. Now this mystical service of God, although perhaps sufficing to sensitive and enthusiastic natures, is scarcely plain or definite enough for ordinary men. Few can realise abstractions: and yet fewer can delight in them and find in their contemplation sufficient nurture for their religious needs. What then had Chassidism to offer to the ordinary majority who could not recognise God in all the plenitude of His disguise? The want of something tangible whereon to fix the minds of the people, which has confronted the teachers of so many creeds, was also encountered by the Chassidim, and they unfortunately found their way out of the difficulty by relying on and developing their doctrine of man's position in the Universe. Man's ideal is to be a law himself; himself a clear and full manifestation of God. Now, not only is he God's servant and child, but in highest development he becomes himself a part of God, albeit in human shape, so that he may become wholly one with his divine Father. But if man may reach this highest level of holiness, he is virtually a kind of God-man, whom his fellow-men of lower levels perceive by reason of his manhood, but his essential office consists in raising them up to God by reason of his Divinity.

The few chosen spirits who through the successful persistency with which they have sought God in all things have become, though yet on earth, absorbed in Him, are known in Chassidic literature by the name of the "Zaddikim." The Hebrew word Zaddik[18] means "just" or "righteous," and the term was probably chosen in conscious opposition to the title of Rabbinic heroes, "disciples of the wise." For the Zaddik is not so much the product of learning as of intuition: his final consummation is reached by a sudden and direct illumination from God. The Zaddik not only resembles Moses, but, in virtue of his long communion with the Divine, he is also the true child of God. He is, moreover, a vivifying power in creation, for he is the connecting bond between God and his creatures. He is the source of blessing and the fount of grace. Man must therefore learn to love the Zaddik, so that through the Zaddik he may win God's grace. He who does not believe in the Zaddik is an apostate from God. Here then we have the fatal exaggeration to which I have alluded, and here its logical consequence. The step to man-worship is short.

This peculiar doctrine of the Intermediary soon became the distinguishing feature of Chassidism. By a Chassid was understood not a man who held such and such opinions in theology and religion, but a believer in the Zaddik, and one who sought to attain salvation through the worship of the Zaddik. Every other doctrine of Chassidism was rapidly pushed into the background and overlooked. Even the grand and fundamental doctrine of Omnipresence in the Creation was veiled by the special presence in the Zaddik. Chassidism became mere Zaddikism, and its subsequent history is identical with the downward development of that cult.

Whether Baalshem named his successor is doubtful. But the lead after his death was assumed by his disciple Beer of Mizriez. This man's conversion to Chassidism was an important event for the new community; his piety and learning were beyond dispute, and, whereas during Baalshem's life Chassidism had found its chief adherents among the lower classes of society, Beer managed to gather round him many of the most learned among his contemporaries. It was to these new and ardent disciples of Beer that the expansion of Chassidism was chiefly due. They came together from many quarters, and after Beer's death separated and preached the new doctrine far and wide. Many even went forth during the lifetime of their master, and at his command, to found fresh branches of the new sect. Like Beer himself, they directed their efforts mainly to winning over the educated sections of the Jews. The elder men paid little heed to their word, but the youths, just fresh from their casuistic studies, which had sharpened their wits and starved their souls, lent a ready ear and an eager heart to the new doctrine. The uneducated were by no means excluded; to them Chassidism held out a deeper consolation and a grander hope than the current Rabbinism of the age; they therefore joined the young community in large numbers without any special effort being necessary to gain them over.

In their methods of Prayer the Chassidim most conspicuously differed from the older communities. Laying as they did supreme stress on the importance and efficacy of prayer, they soon found it necessary to secede from the existing synagogues and erect separate buildings for themselves. The usual salaried Reader "with the beautiful voice and empty head," who naturally regarded his function as a matter of business, was done away with and his place taken either by the Zaddik himself or by some other distinguished person in the community. The Chassidim also effected many changes in the liturgy. Instead of the German they adopted the Spanish ritual. They excised many prayers which, lacking the authority of antiquity, were cumbrous in form or objectionable in matter. They inserted new prayers and hymns of their own. They paid little regard to the prescribed hours at which public worship should be held. Prayer began when they had got themselves into the proper devotional frame of mind. Frequent ablutions, perusal of mystical writings, introspective meditation were the means by which they sought to gain the befitting mood. The prayers themselves were accompanied by the usual phenomena of religious excitement. Some in the zeal of their devotion began to dance; others were rapt in a motionless ecstasy; some prayed aloud; others in solemn silence. They justified their abrogation of fixed hours for prayer by saying that you cannot order a child when to speak with its father: such restraint were fit only for slaves.

As a rule the larger number of the younger Chassidim were able to devote their whole time to religious exercises. It was the custom among the Jews in Eastern Europe for the young men to live at the expense of their own or their wives' parents, in order that they might give themselves up entirely to religious study. According to the old notions, this meant the study of the Talmud and its Commentaries; the Chassidim who cared little for the legal side of Jewish literature betook themselves to the literature of edification and mysticism. No small part of their time was taken up with endless conversations about the Zaddik, his piety, goodness, and self-sacrifice and the wonderful miracles which he had wrought. If a Zaddik was living in his own town, the youthful Chassid spent as many hours as he could in the Zaddik's company, in order to observe and study this embodied Torah as constantly as possible. Where no Zaddik was at hand, periodical pilgrimages were made to the town in which he lived, and endless were the tales which were afterwards repeated, to those who were obliged to stay at home, of the Zaddik's marvellous wisdom and extraordinary deeds. The last hours of the Sabbath day were looked upon as a special season of grace, and the Chassidim were therefore in the habit of collecting together in the waning of the Sabbath and celebrating the so-called "Supper of the Holy Queen." The meal was accompanied by the usual conversations as well as by hymns and prayers.

The Chassidim were second to no other sect in their loyalty and affection for each other. No sacrifice for a brother Chassid was too great. They knew no difference of rich and poor, old and young, wise and ignorant; for they all, with one accord, worshipped one common ideal, the Zaddik, who in his exalted position was equally raised above them all. Before him all minor differences of rank disappeared. When a Chassid travelled, he had no scruple in asking for lodging or entertainment in the house of any Chassid who could afford to give them. If he was in money difficulties the purse of his host was at his disposal. If that was not sufficient, it was supplemented by a grant from the fund of the community. These gifts were not looked upon in the light of charity either by giver or receiver; they were made to the Zaddik, to whom all Chassidim alike were debtors. It sometimes even happened that a Zaddik said that the son of some rich merchant was to marry the daughter of a poor schoolmaster, and both parties were equally delighted to fulfil the wish of their beloved chief.

It may easily be imagined that the innovations of the Chassidim provoked the wrath of the orthodox communities. But in their detestation of the Rabbis the Chassidim returned in full measure all the hatred they received. The Zaddik is the Moses of his age: the Rabbis its Korah and Abiram. Where the Chassidic party in any community gained the upper hand, the Rabbi was deposed and a Zaddik, if that was possible, elected in his place. The issue of these bitter attacks upon the old nobility of the Jewish race was a rigorous persecution. In many places the Chassidim were excommunicated, in others their leaders were publicly scourged and put into the stocks. Their books were burnt and their synagogues forcibly closed. But persecution produced only the usual result of increasing the popularity and the numbers of the sect. The devotion of the Chassidim to each other and to their common cause was increased a hundred-fold by suffering. In one case a distinguished Zaddik was accused of treason, before the Russian authorities, and was thrown into prison. In Russia, however, the power of money is considerable, and on payment of a large ransom not only was the beloved Zaddik released but as an obvious consequence his reputation greatly profited: the day of his release was celebrated as a yearly festival, while his sufferings were regarded by his followers as a sin-offering that atoned for the iniquities of his age. From this time the government maintained a purely neutral attitude towards the new sect, and ere long the persecution by the orthodox ceased.

The cessation of persecution may possibly be accounted for by the fact that Chassidism as a secession soon ceased to be formidable. There were early divisions within the sect. Even Beer's disciples began to quarrel over theological differences and to found separate communities. When once the course of corruption and spiritual decay had begun, it was the interest of the false Zaddikim to accentuate these differences. Each Zaddik sought to have a whole little sect to himself, from which to draw an undivided revenue. And each deluded little sect as it arose boasted of the exclusive possession of the true Zaddik.

It must not be supposed that these strictures apply to the whole class of Zaddikim. The greater number of Baalshem's leading disciples as well as Beer's were beyond question men of pure, unalloyed piety, who would have rejected with scorn any idea of making a trade of their sacred profession. Their motives and their zeal were alike ideal. Many gave up highly paid posts as Rabbis when they joined the new sect. Some emigrated to Palestine to lead a holy life on holy ground, others sought to become religious specialists, following out practically, although with some exaggeration, a favourite doctrine of the Founder, that he who observes but one commandment devotedly and lovingly, may reach the goal desired: the union with God. Thus one Zaddik made it his business never to tell the smallest falsehood, whatever the cost or the inconvenience of truth might be. It is related that the Russian Government, suspecting the Jews of his town of smuggling, consented to withdraw the charge if he declared his brethren innocent. Having no alternative but either to bring misfortune on his brethren or to tell an untruth, he prayed to God to save him from this dilemma by sending death upon him. And lo! when the officials came to fetch him before the law court they found him dead. Another, thinking that the commandment in Exodus xxiii. 3, relating to the help that should be given to a neighbour or enemy when "his ass is lying under its burden," was practically unobserved, devoted himself to its fulfillment. He was continually to be seen in the streets, helping one man to load his waggon, and another to drag his cart out of the mire. A third made the service of the oppressed his religious speciality. It is said that one day his wife, having had a quarrel with her maid, was setting out to the magistrate of the town to obtain satisfaction. Noticing that her husband was about to accompany her, she asked him whither he was bound. He replied, "to the magistrate." His wife declared that it was below his dignity to take any part in a quarrel with a servant. She could deal with the matter herself. The Zaddik replied, "That may be, but I intend to represent your maid, who when accused by my wife will find no one willing to take her part." And then, bursting into a passion of tears, he quoted Job xxxi. 13: "If I did despise the cause of my man-servant or of my maid-servant, when they contended with me, what shall I do when God riseth up?"

Several Zaddikim were learned men and thinkers of no ordinary kind. The works of Solomon Ladier or of Mendel Witipsker, read with attention and without Western preconceptions, certainly give the impression of both originality and depth of thought. But most characteristic of all is the passionate yearning of authors such as these towards the Divine. The reader is astonished and moved by the intense sincerity and ardour of their longing after God. But, despite the adherence of these worthy men, the fate of Chassidism, as a regenerative force, was sealed from the day when Zaddikism replaced the original doctrines of the sect.

For, apart from the obvious theological considerations already suggested, there are two points of inherent weakness in the cult of the Zaddik which naturally doomed it to perversion and failure. The necessary qualifications for "Zaddikship" are wholly undefined. We hear a great deal about what a Zaddik actually is, but we hear very little about what he should be. The Zaddik has many virtues, but we are nowhere told what are his indispensable qualifications. Moreover, the Zaddik is a being who can be comprehended by the understanding as little as an angel, or as God Himself. He is realised by faith, not conceived by thought. Hence there is no human test of a true Zaddik except the test of miracles; and every student of religious history knows the deceitful character of that test.

The second source of danger arose from the Chassidim holding it to be their sacred duty to provide for the Zaddik a life of comfort and ease. The Zaddik must pursue his divine avocations undisturbed by grosser cares. But what were the consequences? The Chassidim believed they could win the grace and blessing of the Zaddik by the richness and variety of their gifts. A Zaddik's career became a very profitable concern. The result of both defects was that not only was the opportunity given for every scheming charlatan to become a Zaddik, but inducements were offered to make the deception lucrative. Hence the anxiety of the false Zaddikim, already noticed, to found separate communities.

Among the Chassidim of to-day there is not one in ten thousand who has the faintest conception of those sublime ideas which inspired Baalshem and his immediate disciples. It is still the interest of the wretched ringleaders of a widely spread delusion to crush and keep down every trace of reflection and thought so that they may play at will with the conscience and purses of their adherents. The new scientific movement, inaugurated by such men as Krochmal, Zunz, and others who came under the influence of the German critical spirit, found in them its hottest and most fanatical opponents. That the cult of the Zaddikim has not led to still more disastrous consequences is solely due to the fact that the Chassidim in general have remained faithful to the Law. It is the Law, against the excessive study of which the original Chassidim protested, that has put limits to the license of its modern false prophets.

Amid much that is bad, the Chassidim have preserved through the whole movement a warm heart, and an ardent, sincere faith. There is a certain openness of character and a ready friendliness about even the modern Chassidim which are very attractive. Religion is still to them a matter of life and death. Their faith is still real enough to satisfy the demands of a Luther, but it is diverted and wasted upon unworthy objects. If Chassidism is to be reformed, its worship must no longer be of man; it must be brought back again to the source of all Beauty, all Wisdom, and all Goodness; it must be restored to God.

PART TWO: *Persons and Places*

7

NACHMANIDES [1]

R. CHAYIM VITAL, in his *Book of the Transmigrations of Souls,* gives the following bold characteristic of the two great teachers of Judaism, Maimonides and Nachmanides. Their souls both sprang forth from the head of Adam—it is a favourite idea of the Cabbalists to evolve the whole of ideal humanity from the archetype Adam—but the former, Maimonides, had his genius placed on the left curl of Adam, which is all judgment and severity, whilst that of the latter, Nachmanides, had its place on the right curl, which represents rather mercy and tenderness.

I start from these words in order to avoid disappointment. For Nachmanides was a great Talmudist, a great Bible student, a great philosopher, a great controversialist, and, perhaps, also a great physician; in one word, great in every respect, possessed of all the culture of his age. But, as I have already indicated by the passage quoted by way of introduction, it is not of Nachmanides in any of these excellent qualities that I wish to write here. For these aspects of his life and mind I must refer the reader to the works of Graetz, Weiss, Steinschneider, Perles, and others. I shall mostly confine myself to those features and peculiarities in his career

and works which will illustrate Nachmanides the tender and
compassionate, the Nachmanides who represented Judaism
from the side of emotion and feeling, as Maimonides did
from the side of reason and logic.

R. Moses ben Nachman, or Bonastruc de Portas, as he was
called by his fellow-countrymen, or Nachmanides, as he is
commonly called now, was born in Gerona about the year
1195. Gerona is a little town in the province of Catalonia in
Spain. But though in Spain, Gerona was not distinguished
for its philosophers or poets like Granada, Barcelona, or
Toledo. Situated as it was in the North of Spain, Gerona was
under the influence of Franco-Jewish sympathies, and thus
its boast lay in the great Talmudists that it produced. I shall
only mention the name of R. Zerahiah Hallevi Gerundi—so-
called after his native place—whose strictures on the Code of
R. Isaac Alfasi, which he began as a youth of nineteen years,
will always remain a marvel of critical insight and independent research. Nachmanides is supposed by some authors to
have been a descendant of R. Isaac ben Reuben of Barcelona,
whose hymns are still to be found in certain rituals. The
evidence for this is insufficient, but we know that he was a
cousin of R. Jonah Gerundi, not less famous for his Talmudic learning than for his saintliness and piety. Nachmanides thus belonged to the best Jewish families of Gerona.
Various great men are mentioned as his teachers, but we have
certainty only about two, namely R. Judah ben Yakar, the
commentator of the prayers, and R. Meir ben Nathan of
Trinquintaines. The mystic, R. Ezra (or Azriel), is indeed
alleged to have been his instructor in the Cabbalah, and this
is not impossible, as he also was an inhabitant of Gerona; but
it is more probable that Nachmanides was initiated into the
Cabbalah by the R. Judah just mentioned, who also belonged
to the mystical school.

Whoever his masters were, they must have been well satis-

fied with their promising pupil, for he undertook, at the age
of fifteen, to write supplements to the Code of R. Isaac Alfasi.
Nor was it at a much later date that he began to compose his
work, *The Wars of the Lord,* in which he defends this great
codifier against the strictures of R. Zerahiah, to which we
have referred above. I shall in the course of this essay have
further occasion to speak of this latter work; for the present
we will follow the career of its author.

Concerning the private life of Nachmanides very little has
come down to us. We only know that he had a family of sons
and daughters. He was not spared the greatest grief that can
befall a father, for he lost a son; it was on the day of the New
Year.[2] On the other hand, it must have been a great source
of joy to him when he married his son Solomon to the
daughter of R. Jonah, whom he revered as a saint and a man
of God. As a token of the admiration in which he held his
friend, the following incident may be mentioned. It seems
that it was the custom in Spain to name the first child in a
family after his paternal grandfather; but Nachmanides
ceded his right in behalf of his friend, and thus his daughter-
in-law's first son was named Jonah. Another son of Nachmanides whom we know of was Nachman, to whom his father
addressed his letters from Palestine, and who also wrote
Novellæ to the Talmud, still extant in MS. But the later
posterity of Nachmanides is better known to fame. R. Levi
ben Gershom was one of his descendants; so was also R.
Simeon Duran;[3] whilst R. Jacob Sasportas, in the eighteenth
century,[4] derived his pedigree from Nachmanides in the
eleventh generation.

As to his calling, he was occupied as Rabbi and teacher,
first in Gerona and afterwards in Barcelona. But this meant
as much as if we should say of a man that he is a philan-
thropist by profession, with the only difference that the treasures of which Nachmanides disposed were more of a spiritual

kind. For his livelihood he probably depended upon his medical practice.

I need hardly say that the life of Nachmanides, "whose words were held in Catalonia in almost as high authority as the Scriptures," was not without its great public events. At least we know of two.

The one was about the year 1232, on the occasion of the great struggle about Maimonides' *Guide of the Perplexed,* and the first book of his great Compendium of the Law. The Maimonists looked upon these works almost as a new revelation, whilst the Anti-Maimonists condemned both as heretical, or at least conducive to heresy.[5] It would be profitless to reproduce the details of this sad affair. The motives may have been pure and good, but the actions were decidedly bad. People denounced each other, excommunicated each other, and did not (from either side) spare even the dead from the most bitter calumnies. Nachmanides stood between two fires. The French Rabbis, from whom most of the Anti-Maimonists were recruited, he held in very high esteem and considered himself as their pupil. Some of the leaders of this party were also his relatives. He, too, had, as we shall see later on, a theory of his own about God and the world little in agreement with that of Maimonides. It is worth noting that Nachmanides objected to calling Maimonides "our teacher Moses" (Rabbenu Mosheh),[6] thinking it improper to confer upon him the title by which the Rabbis honoured the Master of the Prophets. The very fact, however, that he had some theory of the Universe shows that he had a problem to solve, whilst the real French Rabbis were hardly troubled by difficulties of a metaphysical character. Indeed, Nachmanides pays them the rather doubtful compliment that Maimonides' work was not intended for them, who were barricaded by their faith and happy in their belief, wanting no protection against the works of Aristotle and Galen, by whose philosophy others might be led astray. In other words, their strength lay in an ignorance of Greek philosophy, to which the cultivated Jews of Spain would not aspire. Nachmanides was also a great admirer of Maimonides, whose virtues and great merits in the service of Judaism he describes in his letter to the French Rabbis. Thus, the only way left open to him was to play the part of the conciliator. The course of this struggle is fully described in every Jewish history. It is sufficient to say that, in spite of his great authority, Nachmanides was not successful in his effort to moderate the violence of either party, and that the controversy was at last settled through the harsh interference of outsiders who well-nigh crushed Maimonists and Anti-Maimonists alike.

The second public event in the life of Nachmanides was his Disputation, held in Barcelona, at the Court and in the presence of King Jayme I, of Aragon, in the year 1263. It was the usual story. A convert to Christianity, named Pablo Christiani, who burned with zealous anxiety to see his former co-religionists saved, after many vain attempts in this direction, applied to the King of Aragon to order Nachmanides to take part in a public disputation. Pablo maintained that he could prove the justice of the Messianic claims of Jesus from the Talmud and other Rabbinic writings. If he could only succeed in convincing the great Rabbi of Spain of the truth of his argument, the bulk of the Jews was sure to follow. By the way, it was the same Talmud which some twenty years previously was, at the instance of another Jewish convert, burned in Paris, for containing passages against Christianity. Nachmanides had to conform with the command of the king, and, on the 21st of July, 1263, was begun the controversy, which lasted for four or five days.

I do not think that there is in the whole domain of literature less profitable reading than that of the controversies between Jews and Christians. These public disputations occasionally forced the Jews themselves to review their position towards their own literature, and led them to draw clearer distinctions between what they regarded as religion and what as folklore. But beyond this, the polemics between Jews and Christians were barren of good results. If you have read one you have read enough for all time. The same casuistry and the same disregard of history turn up again and again. Nervousness and humility are always on the side of the Jews, who know that, whatever the result may be, the end will be persecution; arrogance is always on the side of their antagonists, who are supported by a band of Knights of the Holy Cross, prepared to prove the soundness of their cause at the point of their daggers.

Besides, was there enough common ground between Judaism and thirteenth century Christianity to have justified the hope of a mutual understanding? The Old Testament was almost forgotten in the Church. The First Person in the Trinity was leading a sort of shadowy existence in art, which could only be the more repulsive to a Jew on that account. The largest part of Church worship was monopolised by devotion to the Virgin Mother, prayers to the saints, and kneeling before their relics. And a Jew may well be pardoned if he did not entertain higher views of this form of worship than Luther and Knox did at a later period. It will thus not be worth our while to dwell much on the matter of this controversy, in which the essence of the real dispute is scarcely touched. There are only two points in it which are worth noticing. The first is that Nachmanides declared the Agadoth[7] in the Talmud to be only a series of sermons (he uses this very word), expressing the individual opinions of the preacher, and thus possessing no authoritative weight. The convert Pablo is quite aghast at this statement, and accuses Nachmanides of heterodoxy.

Secondly—and here I take leave to complete the rather

obscure passage in the controversy by a parallel in his book, *The Date of Redemption*,[8] quoted by Azariah de Rossi— the question of the Messiah is not of that dogmatic importance to the Jews that Christians imagine. For even if Jews supposed their sins to be so great that they forfeited all the promises made to them in the Scriptures, or that, on some hidden ground, it would please the Almighty never to restore their national independence, this would in no way alter the obligations of Jews towards the Torah. Nor is the coming of the Messiah desired by Jews as an end in itself. For it is not the goal of their hopes that they shall be able again to eat of the fruit of Palestine, or enjoy other pleasures there; not even the chance of the restoration of sacrifices and the worship of the Temple is the greatest of Jewish expectations (connected with the appearance of the Messiah). What makes them long for his coming is the hope that they will then witness, in the company of the prophets and priests, a greater spread of purity and holiness than is now possible. In other words, the possibility for them to live a holy life after the will of God will be greater than now. But, on the other hand, considering that such a godly life under a Christian government requires greater sacrifices than it would under a Jewish king; and, considering again that the merits and rewards of a good act increase with the obstacles that are in the way of executing it —considering this, a Jew might even prefer to live under the King of Aragon than under the Messiah, where he would perforce act in accordance with the precepts of the Torah.

Now there is in this statement much that has only to be looked upon as a compliment to the government of Spain. I am inclined to think that if the alternative laid before Nachmanides had been a really practical one, he would have decided in favour of the clement rule of the Messiah in preference to that of the most cruel king on earth. But the fact that he repeats this statement in another place, where there was no occasion to be over polite to the Government, tends to show, as we have said, that the belief in the Messiah was not the basis on which Nachmanides' religion was built up.

The result of the controversy is contested by the different parties; the Christian writers claim the victory for Pablo, whilst the Jewish documents maintain that the issue was with Nachmanides. In any case, *"Der Jude wird verbrannt."* For in the next year (1264) all the books of the Jews in Aragon were confiscated and submitted to the censorship of a commission, of which the well-known author of the *Pugio Fidei,* Raymund Martini, was, perhaps, the most important member. The books were not burned this time, but had to suffer a severe mutilation; the anti-Christian passages, or such as were supposed to be so, were struck out or obliterated. Nachmanides' account of the controversy, which he probably published from a sense of duty towards those whom he represented, was declared to contain blasphemies against the dominant religion. The pamphlet was condemned to be burned publicly, whilst the author was, as it seems, punished with expulsion from his country. It is not reported where Nachmanides found a home during the next three years; probably he had to accept the hospitality of his friends, either in Castile or in the south of France; but we know that in the year 1267 he left Europe and emigrated to Palestine.

Nachmanides was, at this juncture of his life, already a man of about seventy. But it would seem as if the seven decades which he had spent in the Spanish Peninsula were only meant as a preparation for the three years which he was destined to live in the Holy Land, for it was during this stage of his life that the greatest part of his *Commentary on the Pentateuch* was written. In this work, as is agreed on all sides, his finest thoughts and noblest sentiments were put down.

Before proceeding to speak of his works, let us first cast a glance at his letters from Palestine, forming as they do a certain link between his former life and that which was to occupy him exclusively for the rest of his days. We have three letters, the first of which I shall translate here *in extenso.*

The letter was written soon after his arrival at Jerusalem in the year 1267. It was addressed to his son Nachman, and runs as follows:

The Lord shall bless thee, my son Nachman, and thou shalt see the good of Jerusalem. Yea, thou shalt see thy children's children (Ps. cxxviii), and thy table shall be like that of our father Abraham! [9] In Jerusalem, the Holy City, I write this letter. For, thanks and praise unto the rock of my salvation, I was thought worthy by God to arrive here safely on the 9th of the month of Elul, and I remained there till the day after the Day of Atonement. Now I intend going to Hebron, to the sepulchre of our ancestors, to prostrate myself, and there to dig my grave. But what am I to say to you with regard to the country? Great is the solitude and great the wastes, and, to characterise it in short, the more sacred the places, the greater their desolation! Jerusalem is more desolate than the rest of the country: Judæa more than Galilee. But even in this destruction it is a blessed land. It has about 2000 inhabitants, about 300 Christians live there who escaped the sword of the Sultan. There are no Jews. For since the arrival of the Tartars, some fled, others died by the sword. There are only two brothers, dyers by trade, who have to buy their ingredients from the government. There the Ten Men[10] meet, and on Sabbaths they hold service at their house. But we encouraged them, and we succeeded in finding a vacant house, built on pillars of marble with a beautiful arch. That we took for a synagogue. For the town is without a master, and whoever will take possession of the ruins can do so. We gave our offerings towards the repairs of the house. We have sent already to Shechem to fetch some scrolls of the Law from there which had been brought thither from Jerusalem at the invasion of the Tartars. Thus they will organise a synagogue and worship there. For continually people crowd to Jerusalem, men and women, from Damascus, Zobah (Aleppo),[11] and from all parts of the country to see the Sanctuary and to mourn over it. He who thought us worthy to let us see Jerusalem in her desertion, he shall bless us to behold her again, built and restored, when the glory of the Lord will return unto her. But you, my son, and your brothers and the whole of our family, you all shall live to see the salvation of Jerusalem and the comfort of Zion. These are the words of your father who is yearning and forgetting, who is seeing and enjoying, Moses ben Nachman. Give also my peace to my pupil Moses, the son of Solomon, the nephew of your mother. I wish to tell him . . . that there, facing the holy temple, I have read his verses, weeping bitterly over them. May he who caused his name to rest in the Holy Temple increase your peace together with the peace of the whole community.

This letter may be illustrated by a few parallels taken from the appendix to Nachmanides' *Commentary on the Pentateuch,* which contains some rather incoherent notes which the author seems to have jotted down when he arrived in Jerusalem. After a lengthy account of the material as well as the spiritual glories of the holy city in the past, he proceeds to say:

A mournful sight I have perceived in thee (Jerusalem); only one Jew is here, a dyer, persecuted, oppressed and despised. At his house gather great and small when they can get the Ten Men. They are wretched folk, without occupation and trade, consisting of a few pilgrims and beggars, though the fruit of the land is still magnificent and the harvests rich. Indeed, it is still a blessed country, flowing with milk and honey. . . . Oh! I am the man who saw affliction. I am banished from my table, far removed from friend and kinsman, and too long is the distance to meet again. . . . I left my family, I forsook my house. There with my sons and daughters, and with the sweet and dear children whom I have brought up on my knees, I left also my soul. My heart and my eyes will dwell with them for ever. . . . But the loss of all this and of every other glory my eyes saw is compensated by having now the joy of being a day in thy courts (O Jerusalem), visiting the ruins of the Temple and crying over the ruined Sanctuary; where I am permitted to caress thy stones, to fondle thy dust, and to weep over thy ruins. I wept bitterly, but I found joy in my tears. I tore my garments, but I felt relieved by it.

Of some later date is his letter from Acra, which may be considered as a sort of ethical will, and which has been justly characterised as a eulogy of humility. Here is an extract from it:

Accustom yourself to speak gently to all men at all times, and thus you will avoid anger, which leads to so much sin. . . . Humility is the first of virtues; for if you think how lowly is man, how great is God, you will fear Him and avoid sinfulness. On the humble man rests the divine glory; the man that is haughty to others denies God. Look not boldly at one whom you address. . . . Regard every one as greater than thyself. . . . Remember always that you stand before God, both when you pray and when you converse with others. . . . Think before you speak. . . . Act as I have bidden you, and your words, and deeds, and thoughts, will be honest, and your prayers pure and acceptable before God.

The third letter is addressed to his son (R. Solomon?) who was staying (in the service of the king) in Castile. It is in its chief content a eulogy of chastity.[12] Probably Nachmanides had some dread of the dangerous allurements of the court, and he begs his son never to do anything of which he knows that his father would not approve, and to keep his father's image always before his eyes.

As to his works, we may divide them into two classes. The one would contain those of a strictly legalistic (Halachic), whilst the other those of a more homiletic-exegetical and devotional character (Agadic). As already indicated in the preliminary lines of this paper, I cannot dwell long on the former class of our author's writings. It consists either of Glosses or Novellæ to the Talmud, in the style and manner of the French Rabbis, or of Compendia of certain parts of the Law after the model set by R. Isaac Alfasi or Maimonides, or in defences of the "Earlier Authorities" against the strictures made on them by a later generation. A few words must be said with regard to these defences; for they reveal that deep respect for authority which forms a special feature of Nachmanides' writings. His *Wars of the Lord,* in which he defends Alfasi against R. Zerahiah of Gerona, was undertaken when he was very young, whilst his defence of the author of the *Halachoth Gedoloth*[13] against the attacks of Maimonides, which he began at a much more mature age, shows the same deference "to the great ones of the past." Indeed, he says in one place, "We bow before them (the earlier authorities), and though their words are not quite evident to us we submit to them"; or, as he expresses himself elsewhere, "Only he who dips (deeply enough) in the wisdom of the 'ancient ones' will drink the pure (old) wine." But it would be unjust to the genius of Nachmanides to represent him as a blind worshipper of authority. Humble and generous in disposition, he certainly would bow before every recognised authority, and he would also think it his duty to take up the cudgels for him as long as there was even the least chance of making an honourable defence. But when this chance had gone, when Nachmanides was fully convinced that his hero was in the wrong, he followed no guide but truth. "Notwith-standing," he says in his introduction to the defences of the *Halachoth Gedoloth,* "my desire and delight to be the disciple of the Earlier Authorities, to maintain their views and to assert them, I do not consider myself a 'donkey carrying books.' I will explain their way and appreciate their value, but when their views are inconceivable to my thoughts, I will plead in all modesty, but shall judge according to the sight of my eyes. And when the meaning is clear I shall flatter none, for the Lord gives wisdom in all times and ages." But, on the other hand, there seems to have been a certain sort of literary agnosticism about Nachmanides which made it very difficult for him to find the "clear meaning." The passage in the *Wars of the Lord* to the effect "that there is in the art (of commenting) no such certain demonstration as in mathe-matics or astronomy," is well known and has often been quoted; but still more characteristic of this literary agnosti-cism is the first paragraph of the above-mentioned defences of the *Halachoth Gedoloth.* Whilst all his predecessors ac-cepted, on the authority of R. Simlai,[14] the number (613) of the commandments as an uncontested fact, and based their compositions on it, Nachmanides questions the whole matter, and shows that the passages relating to this enumeration of laws are only of a homiletical nature, and thus of little consequence. Nay, he goes so far as to say, "Indeed the system how to number the commandments is a matter in which I suspect all of us (are mistaken) and the truth must be left to him who will solve all doubts." We should thus be inclined to think that this adherence to the words of the earlier Authorities was at least as much due to this critical scepticism as to his conservative tendencies.

The space left to me I shall devote to the second class of his writings, in which Nachmanides worked less after given types. These reveal to us more of his inner being, and offer us some insight into his theological system.

The great problem which seems to have presented itself to Nachmanides' mind was less how to reconcile religion with reason than how to reconcile man with religion. What is man? The usual answer is not flattering. He is an animal that owes its existence to the same instinct that produces even the lower creatures, and he is condemned, like them, to go to a place of worm and maggot. But, may not one ask, why should a creature so lowly born, and doomed to so hapless a future, be burdened with the awful responsibility of knowing that he is destined "to give reckoning and judgment before the King of kings, the Holy One, blessed be He"? It is true that man is also endowed with a heavenly soul, but this only brings us back again to the antithesis of flesh and spirit which was the stumbling-block of many a theological system. Nor does it help us much towards the solution of the indicated difficulty; for what relation can there be between this *materia impura* of body and the pure intellect of soul? And again, must not the unfavourable condition in which the latter is placed through this uncongenial society heavily clog and suppress all aspiration for perfection? It is "a house divided against itself," doomed to an everlasting contest, without hope for co-operation or even of harmony.

The works *The Sacred Letter* and *The Law of Man* may

be considered as an attempt by Nachmanides, if not to remove, at least to relieve the harshness of this antithesis. The
former, in which he blames Maimonides for following
Aristotle in denouncing certain desires implanted in us by
nature as ignominious and unworthy of man, may, perhaps,
be characterised as a vindication of the flesh from a religious
point of view. The contempt in which "that Greek," as
Nachmanides terms Aristotle, held the flesh is inconsistent
with the theory of the religious man, who believes that everything (including the body, with all its functions) is created
by God, whose work is perfect and good, without impure or
inharmonious parts. It is only sin and neglect that disfigure
God's creations. I cannot enter into any further details of this
work, but I may be permitted to remark that there is a very
strong similarity between the tendency of the *Sacred Letter*
and certain leading ideas of Milton. Indeed, if the first two
chapters of the former were a little condensed and put into
English, they could not be better summarised than by the
famous lines in the *Paradise Lost:*

> Whatever hypocrites austerely talk
> Of purity, and place, and innocence,
> Defaming as impure what God declares
> Pure, and commands to some, leaves free to all,
> Our Maker bids increase; who bids abstain
> But our destroyer, foe to God and man?
> Hail, wedded love, mysterious law! . . .
> Far be it that I should write thee sin or blame
> Or think thee unbefitting holiest place,
> Perpetual fountain of domestic sweets.

The second of these two works, the *Law of Man,* may be
regarded as a sanctification of grief, and particularly of the
grief of griefs, death. The bulk of the book is legalistic,
treating of mourning rites, burial customs, and similar topics;
but there is much in the preface which bears on our subject.
For here again Nachmanides takes the opportunity of com-

bating a chilling philosophy, which tries to arm us against suffering by stifling our emotions. "My son," he says, "be not persuaded by certain propositions of the great philosophers who endeavour to harden our hearts and to deaden our sensations by their idle comfort, which consists in denying the past and despairing of the future. One of them has even declared that there is nothing in the world over the loss of which it is worth crying, and the possession of which would justify joy. This is an heretical view. Our perfect Torah bids us to be joyful in the day of prosperity and to shed tears in the day of misfortune. It in no way forbids crying or demands of us to suppress our grief. On the contrary, the Torah suggests to us that to mourn over heavy losses is equivalent to a service of God, leading us, as it does, to reflect on our end and ponder over our destiny."

This destiny, as well as Reward and Punishment in general, is treated in the concluding chapter of the *Law of Man*, which is known under the title of *The Gate of Reward*.[15] Nachmanides does not conceal from himself the difficulties besetting inquiries of this description. He knows well enough that in the last instance we must appeal to that implicit faith in the inscrutable justice of God with which the believer begins. Nevertheless he thinks that only the "despisers of wisdom" would fail to bring to this faith as full a conviction as possible, which latter is only to be gained by speculation. I shall have by and by occasion to refer to the results of this speculation. Here we must only notice the fact of Nachmanides insisting on the *bodily* resurrection which will take place after the coming of the Messiah, and will be followed by the *Olam Habba*[16] (the life in the world to come) of which the Rabbis spoke.

Irrational as this belief may look, it is only a consequence of his theory, which, as we have seen, assigns even to the flesh an almost spiritual importance. Indeed, he thinks that the soul may have such an influence on the body as to transform the latter into so pure an essence that it will become safe for eternity. For, as he hints in another place, by the continual practising of a thing the whole man, the body included, becomes so identified with the thing that we call him after it, just as the Holy Singer said: I am prayer,[17] so that

> Oft converse with heavenly habitants
> Begins to cast a beam on the outward shape,
> The unpolluted temple of the mind,
> And turns it by degrees to the soul's essence,
> Till all be made immortal.

But if even the body holds such a high position as to make all its instincts and functions, if properly regulated, a service of God, and to destine it for a glorious future of eternal bliss and rejoicing in God, we can easily imagine what a high place the soul must occupy in the system of Nachmanides. To be sure it is a much higher one than that to which philosophy would fain admit her. A beautiful parable of the Persian poet Yellaladeen (quoted by the late Mr. Lowell) narrates that "One knocked at the beloved's door, and a voice asked from within, 'Who is there?' and he answered, 'It is I.' Then the voice said, 'This house will not hold me and thee,' and the door was not opened. Then went the lover into the desert and fasted and prayed in solitude, and after a year he returned and knocked again at the door, and again the voice asked 'Who is there?' and he said 'It is thyself'; and the door was opened to him." This is also the difference between the two schools—the mystical and the philosophical—with regard to the soul. With the rationalist the soul is indeed a superior abstract intelligence created by God, but, like all His creations, has an existence of its own, and is thus separated from God. With the mystic, however, the soul is God, or a direct emanation from God. "For he who breathes into another thing (Gen. ii. 7) gives unto it something of his own breath (or soul)," and as it is said in Job xxxii. 8, "And the soul of the Almighty giveth them understanding." This emanation, or rather immanence—for Nachmanides insists in another place that the Hebrew term employed for it, *Aziluth*,[18] means a permanent dwelling with the thing emanating—which became manifest with the creation of man, must not be confounded with the moving soul (or the *Nephesh Chayah*),[19] which is common to man with all creatures.

It may be remarked here that Nachmanides endows all animals with a soul which is derived from the "Superior Powers," and its presence is proved by certain marks of intelligence which they show. By this fact he tries to account for the law prohibiting cruelty to animals, "all souls belonging to God." Their original disposition was, it would seem, according to Nachmanides, peaceful and harmless.

> About them frisking played
> All beasts of earth, since wild, and of all chace
> In wood or wilderness, forest or den.

It was only after man had sinned that war entered into creation, but with the coming of the Messiah, when sin will disappear, all the living beings will regain their primæval gentleness, and be reinstituted in their first rights.

The special soul of man, however, or rather the "over-soul," was pre-existent to the creation of the world, treasured up as a wave in the sea or fountain of souls—dwelling in the eternal light and holiness of God. There, in God, the soul abides in its ideal existence before it enters into its material life through the medium of man; though it must be noted that, according to Nachmanides' belief in the Transmigration of souls, it is not necessary to perceive in the soul of every new-born child, "a fresh message from heaven" coming directly from the fountainhead. Nachmanides finds this belief indicated in the commandment of levirate marriage, where the child born of the deceased brother's wife inherits not only the name of the brother of his actual father, but also his soul, and thus perpetuates his existence on earth. The fourth verse of Ecclesiastes ii Nachmanides seems to interpret to mean that the very generation which passes away comes up again, by which he tries to explain the difficulty of God's visiting the iniquity of the fathers on their children; the latter being the very fathers who committed the sins. However, whatever trials and changes the soul may have to pass through during its bodily existence, its origin is in God and thither it will return in the end, "just as the waters rise always to the same high level from which their source sprang forth."

It is for this man, with a body so superior, and a soul so sublime—more sublime than the angels—that the world was *created*. I emphasise the last word, for the belief in the creation of the world by God from nothing forms, according to Nachmanides, the first of the three fundamental dogmas of Judaism. The other two also refer to God's relation to the world and man. They are the belief in God's Providence and his *Yediah*.[20] Creation from nothing is for Nachmanides the keynote to his whole religion, since it is only by this fact, as he points out in many places, that God gains real dominion over nature. For, as he says, as soon as we admit the eternity of matter, we must (logically) deny God even "the power of enlarging the wing of a fly, or shortening the leg of an ant." But the whole Torah is nothing if not a record of God's mastery in and over the world, and of His miraculous deeds. One of the first proclamations of Abraham to his generation was that God is the Lord (or Master) of the world (Gen. xviii. 33). The injunction given to Abraham, and repeated afterwards to the whole of Israel (Gen. xvii. 2, and Deut. xviii. 13), to be perfect with God, Nachmanides numbers as one of the 613 commandments, and explains it to mean that man must have a whole belief in God without blemish or reservation, and acknowledge Him possessed of power over nature and the world, man and beast, devil and angel, power being attributable to Him alone. Indeed, when the angel said to Jacob, "Why dost thou ask after my name?" (Gen. xxxii. 29), he meant to indicate by his question the impotence of the heavenly host, so that there is no use in knowing their name, the power and might belonging only to God.

We may venture even a step further, and maintain that in Nachmanides' system there is hardly room left for such a thing as nature or "the order of the world." There are only two categories of miracles by which the world is governed, or in which God's Providence is seen. The one is the category of the manifest miracles, as the ten plagues in Egypt, or the crossing of the Red Sea; the other is that of the hidden miracles, which we do not perceive as such, because of their frequency and continuity. "No man," he declares, "can share in the Torah of our Teacher, Moses (that is, can be considered a follower of the Jewish religion), unless he believes that all our affairs and events, whether they concern the masses or the individual, are all miracles (worked by the direct will of God), attributing nothing to nature or to the order of the world." Under this second order he classes all the promises the Torah makes to the righteous, and the punishments with which evil-doers are threatened. For, as he points out in many places, there is nothing in the nature of the commandments themselves that would make their fulfilment necessarily prolong the life of man, and cause the skies to pour down rain, or, on the other hand, would associate disobedience to them with famine and death. All these results can, therefore, only be accomplished in a supernatural way by the direct workings of God.

Thus miracles are raised to a place in the regular scheme of things, and the difficulty regarding the possibility of God's

interferences with nature disappears by their very multi-
plication. But a still more important point is, that, by this
unbroken chain of miracles, which unconditionally implies
God's presence to perform them, Nachmanides arrives at a
theory establishing a closer contact between the Deity and
the world than that set forth by other thinkers. Thus, he
insists that the term *Shechinah,* or *Cabod* [21] (Glory of God),
must not be understood, with some Jewish philosophers, as
something separate from God, or as *glory created* by God.
"Were this the case," he proceeds to say, "we could not
possibly say, 'Blessed be the glory of the Lord from his place,
since every mark of worship to anything *created* involves
the sin of idolatry." Such terms as *Shechinah,* or *Cabod,*
can therefore only mean the immediate divine presence.
This proves, as may be noted in passing, how unphilosophical
the idea of those writers is who maintain that the rigid
monotheism of the Jews makes God so transcendental that
He is banished from the world. As we see, it is just this assertion of His absolute Unity which not only suffers no
substitute for God, but also removes every separation between Him and the world. Hence also Nachmanides insists
that the prophecy even of the successors of Moses was a direct
communion of God with the prophet, and not, as others
maintained, furnished through the medium of an angel.

The third fundamental dogma, *Yediah,* includes, according to Nachmanides, not only the omniscience of God—as
the term is usually translated—but also His recognition of
mankind and His special concern in them. Thus, he explains
the words in the Bible with regard to Abraham, "For I know
him" (Gen. xviii. 19), to indicate the special attachment of
God's Providence to the patriarch, which, on account of his
righteousness, was to be uninterrupted for ever; whilst in
other places we have to understand, under God's knowledge
of a thing, his determination to deal with it compassionately,

as, for instance, when Scripture says that God knew (Exod. ii. 25), it means that His relation to Israel emanated from His attribute of mercy and love. But just as God knows (which means loves) the world, He requires also to be recognised and known by it. "For this was the purpose of the whole creation, that man should recognise and know Him and give praise to His name," as it is said, "Everything that is called by my name (meaning, chosen to promulgate God's name), for my glory have I created it."

It is this fact which gives Israel their high prerogative, for by receiving the Torah they were the first to know God's name, to which they remained true in spite of all adversities; and thus accomplished God's intention in creating the world. It is, again, by this Torah that the whole of Israel not only succeeded in being real prophets (at the moment of the Revelation), but also became *Segulah*,[22] which indicates the inseparable attachment between God and His people, whilst the righteous who never disobey His will become the seat of His throne.

The position of the rest of humanity is also determined by their relation to the Torah. "It is," Nachmanides tells us, "a main principle to know that all that man contrives to possess of knowledge and wisdom is only the fruits of the Torah or the fruits of its fruits. But for this knowledge there would be no difference between man and the lower animated species. The existence of the civilised nations of the world does not disprove this rule "both Christians and Mahometans being also the heirs of the Torah. For when the Romans gained strength over Israel they made them translate the Torah which they studied, and they even accommodated some of their laws and institutions to those of the Bible." Those nations, however, who live far away from the centre of the world (the Holy Land) and never come into contact with Israel are outside the pale of civilisation, and can hardly be ranked together with the human species. "They are the isles afar off, that have not heard my fame, neither have seen my glory."

What Nachmanides meant by maintaining that all knowledge and wisdom were "the fruits of the Torah, or the fruits of these fruits," will be best seen from his *Commentary on the Pentateuch.* I have already made use of this Commentary in the preceding quotations, but, being the greatest of the works of Nachmanides, it calls for some special attention by itself. Its general purpose is edification, or as he says, "to appease the mind of the students (labouring under persecution and troubles) when they read the portion on Sabbaths and festivals, and to attract their heart by simple explanations and sweet words." The explanations occupy a considerable space. As Dr. Perles has shown in his able essay on this work of Nachmanides, our author neglected no resource of philology or archæology accessible in his age which could contribute to establish the "simple explanations" on a sound scientific basis. The prominent feature of this Commentary, however, is the "sweet words." Indeed, how sweet and soothing to his contemporaries must have been such words as we read at the end of the "Song of Moses" (Deut. xxxii.): "And behold there is nothing conditional in this Song. It is a charter testifying that we shall have to suffer heavily for our sins, but that, nevertheless, God will not destroy us, being reconciled to us (though we shall have no merits), and forgiving our sins for his name's sake alone. . . . And so our Rabbis said, Great is this song, embracing as it does both the past (of Israel) and the future, this world and the world to come. . . . And if this song were the composition of a mere astrologer we should be constrained to believe in it, considering that all its words were fulfilled. How much more have we to hope with all our hearts and to trust to the word of God, through the mouth of his prophet Moses, the faithful in all his house, like unto whom there was none, whether before him or after him." A part of these sweet words may also be seen in the numerous passages in which he attempts to account for various laws, and to detect their underlying principles.

For though "the Torah is the expression of God's simple and absolute will, which man has to follow without any consideration of reward," still this will is not arbitrary, and even that class of laws which are called *chukkim*[23] (which means, according to some Jewish commentators, motiveless decrees) have their good reasons, notwithstanding that they are unfathomable to us. "They are all meant for the good of man, either to keep aloof from us something hurtful, or to educate us in goodness, or to remove from us an evil belief and to make us know his name. This is what they (the Rabbis) meant by saying that commandments have a purifying purpose, namely, that man being purified and tried by them becomes as one without alloy of bad thoughts and unworthy qualities." Indeed, the soul of man is so sensitive to every impurity that it suffers a sort of infection even by an unintentional sin. Hence the injunction to bring a *Korban* (sacrifice) even in this case; the effect of the *Korban*, as its etymology (*Karab*)[24] indicates, is to bring man back to God, or rather to facilitate this approach. All this again is, as Nachmanides points out, only an affluence from God's mercy and love to mankind. God derives no benefit from it. "If he be righteous what can he give thee?" And even those laws and institutions which are intended to commemorate God's wonders and the creation of the world (for instance, the Passover festival and the Sabbath) are not meant for His glorification, or, as Heine maliciously expressed it:—

> Der Weltkapellenmeister hier oben
> Er selbst sogar hört gerne loben
> Gleichfalls seine Werke. . . .

"For all the honour (we give to Him), and the praising of His work are counted by Him less than nothing and as vanity to Him." What He desires is that we may know the truth, and be confirmed in it, for this makes us worthy of finding in Him "our Protector and King."

The lessons which Nachmanides draws from the various Biblical narratives also belong to these "sweet words." They are mostly of a typical character. For, true as all the stories in the Scriptures are, "the whole Torah is," as he tells us (with allusion to Gen. v. 1), "the book of the generations of Adam," or, as we should say, a history of humanity written in advance. Thus the account of the six days of the creation is turned into a prophecy of the most important events which would occur during the succeeding six thousand years, whilst the Sabbath is a forecast of the millennium in the seventh thousand, which will be the day of the Lord. Jacob and Esau are, as in the old Rabbinic homilies generally, the prototypes of Israel and Rome; and so is the battle of Moses and Joshua with Amalek indicative of the war which Elijah and the Messiah the son of Joseph will wage against Edom (the prototype of Rome), before the Redeemer from the house of David will appear.[25] Sometimes these stories convey both a moral and a pre-justification of what was destined to happen to Israel. So Nachmanides' remarks with reference to Sarah's treatment of Hagar (Gen. xvi. 6): "Our mother Sarah sinned greatly by inflicting this pain on Hagar, as did also Abraham, who allowed such a thing to pass; but God saw her affliction and rewarded her by a son (the ancestor of a wild race), who would inflict on the seed of Abraham and Sarah every sort of oppression." In this he alluded to the Islamic empires. Nor does he approve of Abraham's conduct on the occasion of his coming to Egypt, when he asked Sarah to pass as his sister (Gen. xii). "Unintentionally," Nachmanides says, "Abraham, under the fear of being murdered, committed a great sin

when he exposed his virtuous wife to such a temptation. For
he ought to have trusted that God would save both him and
his wife. . . . It is on account of this deed that his children
had to suffer exile under the rule of Pharaoh. There, where
the sin was committed, also the judgment took place." It is
also worth noticing that, in opposition to Maimonides, he
allows no apology for the attack of Simeon and Levi on the
population of Shechem (Gen. xxxiv. 25). It is true that they
were idolaters, immoral, and steeped in every abomination;
but Jacob and his sons were not commissioned with executing
justice on them. The people of Shechem trusted their word,
therefore they ought to have spared them. Hence Jacob's protest, and his curse against their wrath, which would have
been quite unjustified had he looked on the action of his
sons as a good work.

Besides these typical meanings, the matters of the Torah
have also their symbolical importance, which places them
almost above the sphere of human conception; they are
neither exactly what they seem to be nor entirely what their
name implies, but a reflex from things unseen, which makes
any human interference both preposterous and dangerous.
Of "the things *called* Tree of Life and Tree of Knowledge,"
Nachmanides tells us that their mystery is very great, reaching
into higher worlds. Otherwise, why should God, who is good
and the dispenser of good, have prevented Adam from eating
the fruit (of the latter), whilst in another place he says:
"And if thou wilt be worthy, and understand the mystery
of the word *Bereshith*[26] (with which the Torah begins), thou
wilt see that in truth the Scripture, though apparently speaking of matters here below (on earth), is always pointing to
things above (heaven)"; for "every glory and every wonder,
and every deep mystery, and all beautiful wisdom are hidden
in the Torah, sealed up in her treasures."

It is very characteristic of the bent of Nachmanides' mind,

that he is perhaps the first Jewish writer who mentions the apocryphal book *The Wisdom of Solomon,* which he knew from a Syriac version, and which he believed to be genuine. And when we read there (vii. 7-25), "Wherefore I prayed and understanding was given to me. I called upon God and the spirit of wisdom came upon me. . . . For God has given me unmistakable knowledge to know how the world was made, and the operations of the planets. The beginning, ending, and midst of the times, the alterations and the turnings of the sun, the changes of the seasons, the natures of the living creatures and the furies of the wild beasts, the force of the spirits and the reasonings of men, the diversities of plants and the virtues of the roots. All such things that are either secret or manifest, them I knew"—the wise king was, according to Nachmanides (who quotes the passages which I have just cited), speaking of the Torah, which is identical with this wisdom, a wisdom which existed before the creation, and by which God planned the world. Hence it bears the impression of all the universe, whilst on the other hand when it is said, "The king brought me into his chambers," those secret recesses of the Torah are meant in which all the great mysteries relating to Creation and to the Chariot (Ezekiel i) are hidden.

We must content ourselves with these few sparks struck from the glowing fires of these inner compartments, which, imperfectly luminous as my treatment has left them, may yet shed some light on the personality of Nachmanides, which is the main object of this essay. But I do not propose to accompany the mystic into the "chambers of the king," lest we may soon get into a labyrinth of obscure terms and strange ways of thinking for which the Ariadne thread is still wanting. We might also be confronted by the Fifty Gates of Understanding, the Thirty-Two Paths of Wisdom, and the Two Hundred and Thirty-One Permutations or Ciphers of the Alphabet, the key to which I do not hold. It is also questionable whether it would always be worth while to seek for it. When one, for instance, sees such a heaping on of nouns (with some Cabbalists) as the Land of Life, the Land of Promise, the Lord of the World, the Foundation Stone, Zion, Mother, Daughter, Sister, the Congregation of Israel, the Twin Roes, the Bride, Blue, End, Oral Law, Sea, Wisdom, etc., meant to represent the same thing or attribute, and to pass one into another, one cannot possibly help feeling some suspicion that one stands before a conglomerate of words run riot, over which the writer had lost all control.

Indeed Nachmanides himself, in the preface to the above-mentioned Commentary, gives us the kind advice not to meditate, or rather brood, over the mystical hints which are scattered over this work, "speculation being (in such matters) folly, and reasoning over them fraught with danger." Indeed, the danger is obvious. I have, to give one or two instances, already alluded to the theory which accepts the Torah or the Wisdom as an agent in the creation of the world. But the mystic pushes further, and asks for the Primal Being to which this Wisdom owes its origin. The answer given is from the great Nothing, as it is written, And the Wisdom shall be found from Nothing.[27] What is intended by this, if it means anything, is probably to divest the first cause of every possible quality which by its very qualifying nature must be limiting and exclusive. Hence, God becomes the Unknowable. But suppose a metaphysical Hamlet, who, handling words indelicately, should impetuously exclaim, To be or not to be, that is the question?—into what abyss of utter negations would he drag all those who despair, by his terrible Nothing.

On the other hand, into what gross anthropomorphisms may we be drawn by roughly handling certain metaphors which some Cabbalists have employed in their struggling after an adequate expression of God's manifestations in His attribute of love, if we forget for a single moment that they are only figures of speech, but liable to get defiled by the slightest touch of an unchaste thought.

But the greater the dangers that beset the path of mysticism, the deeper the interest which we feel in the mystic. In connection with the above-mentioned warning, Nachmanides cites the words from the Scriptures, "But let not the priests and the people break through to come up unto the Lord, lest he break forth upon them" (Exod. xix. 24). Nevertheless, when we read in the Talmud the famous story of the four Rabbis[28] who went up into the *Pardes*, or Garden of Mystical Contemplation, we do not withold our sympathy, either from Ben Azzai, who shot a glance and died, or from Ben Zoma, who shot a glance and was struck (in his mind). Nay, we feel the greatest admiration for these daring spirits, who, in their passionate attempt to "break through" the veil before the Infinite, hazarded their lives, and even that which is dearer than life, their minds, for a single glance. And did R. Meir deny his sympathies even to Other One or Elisha ben Abuyah, who "cut down the plants"? He is said to have heard a voice from heaven, "Return, oh backsliding children, except Other One," which prevented his repentance. Poor fallen Acher, he mistook hell for heaven. But do not the struggle and despair which led to this unfortunate confusion rather plead for our commiseration?

Nachmanides, however, in his gentle way, did not mean to storm heaven. Like R. Akiba, "he entered in peace, and departed in peace." And it was by this peacefulness of his nature that he gained an influence over posterity which is equalled only by that of Maimonides. "If he was not a profound thinker," like the author of the *Guide of the Perplexed*, he had that which is next best—"he felt profoundly." Some writers of a rather reactionary character even went so far as to assign to him a higher place than to Maimonides.

This is unjust. What a blank would there have been in Jewish thought but for Maimonides' great work, on which the noblest thinkers of Israel fed for centuries! As long as Job and Ecclesiastes hold their proper place in the Bible, and the Talmud contains hundreds of passages suggesting difficulties relating to such problems as the creation of the world, God's exact relation to it, the origin of evil, free will and predestination, none will persuade me that philosophy does not form an integral part of Jewish tradition, which, in its historical developments, took the shape which Maimonides and his successors gave to it. If Maimonides' *Guide,* which he considered as an interpretation of the Bible and of many strange sayings in the old Rabbinic homilies in the Talmud, is Aristotelian in its tone, so is tradition too; even the Talmud in many places betrays all sorts of foreign influences, and none would think of declaring it un-Jewish on this ground. I may also remark in passing that the certainty with which some writers deprecate the aids which religion may receive from philosophy is a little too hasty. For the question will always remain, What religion? The religion of R. Moses of Tachau or R. Joseph Jabez[29] would certainly have been greatly endangered by the slightest touch of speculation, while that of Bachya,[30] Maimonides, Jedaiah of Bedres, and Delmedigo undoubtedly received from philosophy its noblest support, and became intensified by the union.

But apart from that consideration, the sphere of the activity of these two leaders seems to have been so widely different that it is hardly just to consider them as antagonists, or at least to emphasise the antagonism too much. Maimonides wrote his chief work, the *Guide,* for the few elect, who, like Ibn Tibbon[31] for instance, would traverse whole continents if a single syllogism went wrong. And if he could be of use to one wise man of this stamp, Maimonides would do so at the risk of "saying things unsuitable for ten thousand fools." But with Nachmanides, it would seem, it was these ten thousand who formed the main object of his tender care. They are, as we have seen, cultivated men, indeed "students," having enjoyed a proper education; but the happy times of abstract thinking have gone, and being under a perpetual strain of persecutions and cares, they long for the Sabbath and Festivals, which would bring them both bodily and spiritual recreation. They find no fault with religion, a false syllogism does not jar on their ears; what they are afraid of is that, being engaged as they are, all the six days of work, in their domestic affairs, religion may be too good a thing for them. "To appease their minds," to edify them, to make life more sweet and death less terrible to them, and to show them that even their weaknesses, as far as they are conditioned by nature, are not irreconcilable with a holy life, was what Nachmanides strove after. Now and then he permits them a glance into the mystical world in which he himself loved to move, but he does not care to stifle their senses into an idle contemplation, and passes quickly to some more practical application. To be sure, the tabernacle is nothing but a complete map of the superlunar world; but nevertheless its rather minute description is meant to teach us "that God desires us to work."

This tendency toward being useful to the great majority of mankind may account for the want of consistency of which Nachmanides was so often accused. It is only the logician who can afford to be thoroughgoing in his theory, and even he would become most absurd and even dangerous but for the redeeming fact "that men are better than their principles." But with Nachmanides these "principles" would have proved even more fatal. Could he, for instance, have upset authority in the face of the ten thousand? They need to be guided rather than to guide. But he does not want them to follow either the Gaon or anybody else slavishly, "the gates of wisdom never having been shut," whilst on the other hand he hints to them that there is something divine in every man, which places him at least on the same high level with any authority. Take another instance—his wavering attitude between the Maimonists and the Anti-Maimonists, for which he was often censured. Apart from other reasons, to which I have pointed above, might he not have felt that, in spite of his personal admiration for Maimonides' genius, he had no right to put himself entirely on the side where there was little room for the ten thousand who were entrusted to his guidance, whilst the French Rabbis, with all their prejudices and intolerance, would never deny their sympathies to simple emotional folk?

This tender and absorbing care for the people in general may also account for the fact that we do not know of a single treatise by Nachmanides of a purely Cabbalistic character in the style of the *Book of Weight,* by Moses de Leon, or the *Orchard,* by R. Moses Cordovora, or the *Tree of Life* by R. Isaac Loria.[32] The story that attributes to him the discovery of the *Zohar* in a cave in Palestine, from whence he sent it to Catalonia, needs as little refutation as the other story connected with his conversion to the Cabbalah, which is even more silly and of such a nature as not to bear repetition. The *Lilac of Mysteries*[33] and other mystical works passed also for a long time under his name, but their claim to this honour has been entirely disproved by the bibliographers, and they rank now among the *pseudepigraphica.* It is true that R. Nissim, of Gerona, said of Nachmanides that he was too much addicted to the belief in the Cabbalah, and as a fellow-countryman he may have had some personal knowledge about the matter. But as far as his writings go, this belief finds expression only in incidental remarks and occasional citations from the *Bahir,*[34] which he never thrusts upon the reader. It was chiefly when philosophy called in question his deep sympathies with even lower humanity, and threatened to withdraw them from those ennobling influences under which he wanted to keep them, that he asserted his mystical theories.

Nachmanides' inconsistency has also proved beneficial in another respect. For mysticism has, by its over-emphasising of the divine in man, shown a strong tendency to remove God altogether and replace Him by the creature of His hands. Witness only the theological bubble of Shabbethai Tsebi—happily it burst quickly enough—which resulted in mere idolatry (in more polite language, Hero Worship) on the one side, and in the grossest antinomianism on the other. Nachmanides, however, with a happy inconsistency, combined with the belief of man's origin in God, a not less strong conviction of man's liability to sin, of the fact that he *does* sin—even the patriarchs were not free from it, as we have seen above—and that this sin *does* alienate man from God. This healthy control over man's extravagant idea of his own species was with Nachmanides also a fruit of the Torah, within the limits of which everything must move, the mystic and his aspirations included, whilst its fair admixture of 365 *Do not's* with 248 *Do's* preserved him from that "holy doing nothing" which so many mystics indulged in, and made his a most active life.

Much of this activity was displayed in Palestine, "the land to which the providence of God is especially attached," and which was, as with R. Judah Hallevi, always "his ideal home." There he not only completed his *Commentary on the Pentateuch,* but also erected synagogues, and engaged in organising communities, whose tone he tried to elevate both by his lectures and by his sermons. His career in Palestine was not a long one, for he lived there only about three years, and in 1270 he must already have been dead. A pretty legend narrates that when he emigrated to Palestine his pupils asked him to give them a sign enabling them to ascertain the day of his death. He answered them that on that day a rift in the shape of a lamp would be seen in the tombstone of his mother. After three years a pupil suddenly noticed this rift, when the mourning over the Rabbi began. Thus, stone, or anything else earthly, breaks finally, and the life of the master passes into light.

What life meant to him, how deeply he was convinced that there is no other life but that originating in God, how deeply stirred his soul was by the consciousness of sin, what agonies the thought of the alienation from God caused him, how he felt that there is nothing left to him but to throw himself upon the mercy of God, and how he rejoiced in the hope of a final reunion with Him—of all these sentiments we find the best expression in the following religious poem, with which this paper may conclude. Nachmanides composed it in Hebrew, and it is still preserved in some rituals as a hymn, recited on the Day of Atonement. It is here given in the English translation of Mrs. Henry Lucas.[35]

> Ere time began, ere age to age had thrilled,
> I waited in his storehouse, as he willed;
> He gave me being, but, my years fulfilled,
>   I shall be summoned back before the King.
>
> He called the hidden to the light of day,
> To right and left, each side the fountain lay,
> From out the stream and down the steps, the way
>   That led me to the garden of the King.
>
> Thou gavest me a light my path to guide,
> To prove my heart's recesses still untried;
> And as I went, thy voice in warning cried:
>   "Child! fear thou him who is thy God and King!"
>
> True weight and measure learned my heart from thee;
> If blessings follow, then what joy for me!
> If nought but sin, all mine the shame must be,
>   For that was not determined by the King.
>
> I hasten, trembling, to confess the whole
> Of my transgressions, ere I reach the goal

Where mine own words must witness 'gainst my soul,
    And who dares doubt the writing of the King?

Erring, I wandered in the wilderness,
In passion's grave nigh sinking powerless;
Now deeply I repent, in sore distress,
    That I kept not the statutes of the King!

With worldly longings was my bosom fraught,
Earth's idle toys and follies all I sought;
Ah! when he judges joys so dearly bought,
    How greatly shall I fear my Lord and King!

Now conscience-stricken, humbled to the dust,
Doubting himself, in thee alone his trust,
He shrinks in terror back, for God is just—
    How can a sinner hope to reach the King?

Oh, be thy mercy in the balance laid,
To hold thy servant's sins more lightly weighed,
When, his confession penitently made,
    He answers for his guilt before the King.

Thine is the love, O God, and thine the grace,
That folds the sinner in its mild embrace;
Thine the forgiveness, bridging o'er the space
    'Twixt man's works and the task set by the King.

Unheeding all my sins, I cling to thee;
I know that mercy shall thy footstool be:
Before I call, oh, do thou answer me,
    For nothing dare I claim of thee, my King!

O thou, who makest guilt to disappear,
My help, my hope, my rock, I will not fear;
Though thou the body hold in dungeon drear,
    The soul has found the palace of the King!

POSTSCRIPT

The third letter of Nachmanides to which I have alluded above, is embodied in the following will by R. Solomon, son of the martyr Isaac. Neither the date nor the country of the testator is known, but style and language make it probable that he was a Spanish Jew, and lived in the fourteenth century. I give here a translation from the whole document as it is to be found in the Manuscripts.

These are the regulations which I, Solomon, the son of the martyr, Rabbi Isaac, the son of R. Zadok, of blessed memory, draw up for myself. That as long as I am in good health, and free from accident, and think of it, I shall not eat before I have studied one page of the Talmud or of its commentaries. Should I transgress this rule intentionally, I must not drink wine on that day, or I shall pay half a *Zehub*[36] to charity. Again, that I shall every week read the Lesson twice in the Hebrew text, and once in the Aramaic version. Should I intentionally omit completing the Lesson as above, then I must pay two *Zehubs* to charity. Again, that I shall every Sabbath take three meals, consisting of bread or fruit. Should I omit to do so, I must give in charity half a *Zehub*. Again, in order to subdue my appetites, and not to enjoy in this world more than is necessary for the maintenance of my body, I must not eat at one meal more than one course of meat, and not more than two courses altogether; nor must I drink more than two cups of wine at one meal, apart from the blessing-cup (over which grace is said), except on Sabbath, Festivals, Chanukah (the Maccabean Dedication Feast), New Moon, and at other religious meals (for instance, wedding-dinners and similar festive occasions). Again, I must not have any regular meal on the day preceding Sabbath or Festivals. I must not have during the day more than one course, so that I shall enter upon the holy day with a good appetite. Should I transgress this resolve intentionally I shall have to fast a day, or to pay two *Zehubs*. Again, that I shall not eat the fish called *burbot*,[37] if I think of it. Again, even on the above-mentioned days, I must not eat more than three courses at a meal, nor drink more than three cups of wine, exclusive of the blessing-cup. Again, . . . I must not swear by God, nor mention the name of Heaven without a purpose, nor curse any man in the name of God. Should I, God forbid, transgress it, I must not drink more than one cup of wine on that day exclusive of the blessing-cup. Should I, however, transgress this after dinner, I must abstain from wine the following day. Should I transgress it, I have to pay half a *Zehub*. Again, that I shall get up every night to praise God, to supplicate for His mercy, and to confess. On those nights when confession is not to be said (Sabbaths and Festivals), I shall say hymns and psalms. This I shall do when I am in my house, and in good health, free from any accident. Should I transgress it, I shall drink not more than one cup of wine the following day, except the blessing-cup. I again take upon myself to give in charity the following proportion of my expenditure— from each dress which I shall have made for myself or for one member of my family, costing more than ten *Zehubs*, I must pay one *Pashut* [38] for each ten *Zehubs*. Again, if I should buy an animal, or a slave, or a female slave, or ground, that I shall also pay at the same rate. And if I shall buy clothes for sale, called *fashas*, I shall pay two *Pashuts* for each garment. As often as I have occasion to say the benediction of thanksgivings for having escaped danger I shall pay a *Zehub*, except when I am travelling [also involving danger in those times!], in which case I shall have to pay a *Zehub* on my arrival, and two *Pashuts* daily during the journey. Again, from every kind of fish bought for me, costing more than a *Zehub*, I shall pay a *Pashut* for each *Zehub*. And also, if I shall be deemed worthy by God to marry my children, and to be present at their wedding, to cause them to give to the poor from the dowry brought to them by their wives, whether in money or in kind, at the rate of one per cent. If God will find me worthy of having sons, I must give in charity according to my means at the time.

I shall also, between New Year and the Day of Atonement in each year, calculate my profits during the past year and (after deducting expenses) give a tithe thereof to the poor. Should I be unable to make an accurate calculation, then I shall give approximately. This tithe I shall put aside, together with the other money for religious (charitable) purpose, to dispose of it as I shall deem best. I also propose to have the liberty of employing the money in any profitable speculation with a view to augmenting it. But in respect of all I have written above I shall not hold myself guilty if I transgress, if such transgression be the result of forgetfulness; but in order to guard against it, I shall read this through weekly.

I also command my children to take upon themselves as many of the above regulations as may be in their power to observe, and also to bind them (*i.e.* the regulations), from generation to generation, upon their children. And he who carries them out, and even adds to them, at pain of discomfort to himself, shall merit a special blessing. And this is the text of the will which I, the above-mentioned Solomon, draw up for my children, may God preserve them. That they shall pray thrice daily, and endeavour always to utter their prayers with devotion. Again, that this prayer shall be said in the *Beth Hammidrash*, or in the synagogue together with the congregation. Again, that they shall apply all their powers to maintain the synagogues and the houses of study, which our ancestors have built, as well as to continue the endowments established by my ancestors and myself. They must always endeavour to imitate them, so that goodness shall never cease from among them. Again, that they shall always have a chair on which a volume of the Talmud, or some other Talmudical work, shall lie; so that they shall always open a book when they come home. At least, they shall read in any book they like four lines before taking their meal. Again, that they shall every week read the Lesson twice in the Hebrew text, and once in the Aramaic version. Again, to take three meals on the Sabbath. . . .

Again, that they shall be always modest, merciful, and charitable, for these are the qualities by which the children of Israel are known. Let also all their thoughts and meditations be always directed to the service of the Lord, and be as charitable and benevolent as possible, for this is all that remains to man of his labour. They shall also endeavour to regulate their diet according to the rules laid down by Rabbi Moses (b. Maimon, or Maimonides), so as to fulfil the words of Scripture: "The righteous eateth to the satisfying of his soul." And let them always be careful not to take the name of God in vain, to be honest in all business transactions, and let their yea be always yea. They shall always be under the obligation to train their children to the Study of the Torah, but one shall devote his life exclusively to the study thereof. And it shall be incumbent upon his brothers to support this one, and to invest his moneys, and to provide for him that he and his family may live respectably, so that he be not distracted by worldly cares from his studies. Let also the elder love the younger brothers as their own children, and the younger respect the elder as a parent. Thus they may always bear in mind that they are of a God-fearing family. Let them love and honour scholars, thus to merit the honour of having scholars for their sons and sons-in-law. This will they shall themselves read weekly, and shall also make it incumbent upon their children, from generation to generation, to read weekly, in order to fulfil what is written (Gen. xviii. 19), "For I know him that he will command his children," etc., and also the words of Isaiah (lix. 21), "And this is my covenant," etc. But as often as they shall read this will, they shall also read the two letters below written, which Rabbi Moses ben Nachman sent to his sons, with a view of being serviceable to them in many respects. Should, heaven forbid, they be by any sad accident prevented from fulfilling the injunctions above laid down, they must fine themselves by not drinking wine on that day, or by eating one course less at the dinner, or by giving some fine in charity. . . .

And this is the letter which the above-mentioned Rabbi sent from the Holy Land to Castile, when his son was staying before the king (in his service):

. . . May God bless you and preserve you from sin and punishment. Behold, our master, King David, had a son, wise and of an understanding heart, like unto whom there was never one before or after. Nevertheless he said to him (1 Kings ii. 2): "And keep the charge of the Lord thy God," etc. He also said to him: "And thou, my son, know the God of thy father" (1 Chron. xxviii. 9). Now, my son, if thou wilt measure thyself with Solomon, thou wilt find thyself a worm—not a man, merely an insect; nevertheless, if thou wilt seek God, he will make thee great; and if thou wilt forsake him, thou wilt be turned out and forsaken. My son, be careful that thou read the *Shema*[39] morning and evening, as well as that thou say the daily prayers. Have always with thee a Pentateuch written correctly, and read therein the Lesson for each Sabbath. . . . "Cast thy burden upon the Lord," for the thing which thou believest far from thee is often very near unto thee. Know, again, that thou art not master over thy words, nor hast power over thy hand; but everything is in the hand of the Lord, who formeth thy heart. . . . Be especially careful to keep aloof from the women [of the court?]. Know that our God hates immorality, and Balaam could in no other way injure Israel than by inciting them to unchastity. [Here come many quotations from Malachi and Ezra.] . . . My son, remember me always, and let the image of my countenance be never absent from before thine eyes. Love not that which I hate. . . . Let the words of the Psalmist be always upon thy lips, "I am a stranger in the earth: hide not thy commandments from me" (Ps. cxix. 19); and God, who is good and the dispenser of good, shall increase thy peace and prolong thy life in peace and happiness, and promote thy honour according to thy wish and the wish of thy father who begat thee, Moses ben Nachman.

8

SAFED IN THE SIXTEENTH CENTURY

A CITY OF LEGISTS AND MYSTICS

SAFED is a small city in Upper Galilee situated on a hill in a mountainous country, and forming part of the Holy Land assigned in the Scriptures to the tribe of Naphtali. Of the various cities of Palestine boasting of a large Jewish population it is relatively the most modern. Neither the Bible nor the Talmud has any definite reference to it, whilst the mention of a locality Zephed, by Kalir, is obscure, and can serve little for purposes of identification.[1]

Yet this was the spot of which R. Joseph Caro wrote in the sixteenth century: "After nearly fifteen hundred years of living in the exile and persecution, he (God) remembered unto his people his covenant with their fathers, and brought them back from their captivity, one of a city and two of a family, from the corners of the earth to the land of glory, and they settled in the city of Safed, the desire of all lands." [2]

The impulse under which the "one of a city and two of a family" acted when they preferred the "land of glory" to the great commercial centres of Europe was a religious one.

Samuel Usque, the famous author of the *"Consolacam as tribulacoes de Ysrael"* ("The Consolation and the Tribulations of Israel"), has the following passage in praise of the country in which most of his fellow-sufferers from the Pyrenean peninsula found an asylum: "Great Turkey, . . . there the gates of freedom and equal opportunity for the unhindered practice of Jewish worship are ever open to Israel; they are never closed against thee. There thou canst renew thy inward life, change thy condition, strip off thy habits, cast away erroneous teachings, recover thy ancient truths, and abandon the practices which, by the violence of the nations among which thou wast a pilgrim, thou wast forced to imitate. In this land thou receivest boundless grace from the Lord, since therein he granteth thee unlimited freedom to begin thy repentance." [3]

The inducement thus held out to the exiled from Spain and Portugal was not only that they would in the new country be allowed to serve their God, without let or hindrance, but also that an opportunity would be granted them of a total regeneration and renewal of heart.

The sense of sin apparently weighing so heavily on Usque may be detected also in other writers, as, for instance, Joseph Jabez, who depicted the spiritual condition of the Jews in Spain in the darkest colours, and describes the men who witnessed the expulsion as an "evil generation, increasing rebellions and transgressions without number." He declared that it was mainly the Spanish Jewesses who remained faithful, and who themselves suffered, and made their husbands suffer, martyrdom for the Sanctification of the Name.[4] Another instance is found in the chronicler Abraham ben Solomon, of Torrutiel in Spain, who says, "Our iniquities had increased over our heads, and our trespasses had grown up unto the heavens, seeing the evils and the sin and the terrible pride so rampant among the Jews in the kingdom of Spain." Jabez and Abraham ben Solomon belonged to the anti-rationalistic party of the Spanish Jews, and may have exaggerated the evils of the situation in their accusations, but their feelings were very likely shared, to some extent, by all other exiles.[5] Nathan Nata of Hanover, the well-known author of the *Yeven Mezulah,* concludes his account of the terrible suffering of the Jews during the Chmielnicki persecution with the words: "What shall we speak, or how shall we call ourselves? The Lord has found out our sins. Does God execute judgment without justice?" [6] The sufferers of Spain doubtless viewed their misfortunes from the same standpoint. And since these evils must have been in some way proportionate to the greatness of the catastrophe which had overtaken them, those of deeper religious sensitiveness must certainly have felt the need of a new life and a regeneration.

It is to this need that we have to attribute the fact that large numbers of the exiles were impelled to emigrate to the Holy Land, the country which, from the times of the prophets down to Judah Halevi in the twelfth century, and from the time of Judah Halevi down to the disciples of Elijah Wilna and Israel Baal Shem in the eighteenth and nineteenth centuries, was always considered a country of great "spiritual opportunities." As a Spanish Jew of the thirteenth century who took a vow to emigrate to the Holy Land expressed it, "There (in Jerusalem, or near it) is the place for fulfilling the commandments and receiving upon oneself the Kingdom of Heaven. Our worship there is acceptable, for there is the House of our God and the Gate of Heaven." [7]

Indeed, it may be stated without fear of contradiction, that there never was a time in which the Holy Land was not an object of attraction and deep longing for the pious Jew, even though he was not always able to gratify his longing in this respect. As we know now, there were for centuries after the destruction of the Holy Temple, every year during the Feast

of Tabernacles, large meetings on the Mount of Olives constituted of pilgrims from Palestine itself, Babylon, Egypt, and
perhaps also from Europe.[8]

These meetings were probably brought to an end in the
eleventh century through the troubles of the Crusades; but
the second decade of the thirteenth century witnessed the
famous pilgrimage of three hundred Rabbis from France,
England, and Spain to the Holy Land.[9] In the fourteenth
century the well-known traveller Pharchi explored the Holy
Land, and reported about different settlements in various
localities.[10] Emigration to Palestine assumed, however, larger
dimensions in the fifteenth and sixteenth centuries, caused by
the general distress of the Jews in almost all parts of Christendom. The majority of the refugees escaped to Turkey, but a
considerable minority, composed, as already indicated, of the
more spiritual-minded among them, directed their steps to
the Holy Land.

As hinted before, Safed has no Biblical nor even Talmudic
record. Its first appearance in Jewish history dates from about
the beginning of the thirteenth century, when the traveller
Samuel ben Shimshon reports the existence of a community
there of more than fifty members. Somewhat later it is mentioned in connexion with a document relating to the Maimonides controversy, which bears also the signatures of R.
Moses ben Judah and his colleagues, the Rabbis of Safed.[11]
R. Hananel Ibn Askara and R. Shem Tob Ibn Gaon, of
Spain, migrated to Safed in the same century;[12] whilst R.
Isaac ben Joseph Chelo, of Laresa in Spain, and Pharchi,
mentioned above, visited Safed in the fourteenth century
and speak of a large Jewish community dwelling there.[13]
Joseph Mantabia, who visited Safed in 1481, speaks of it
as a "fine" community, numbering about three hundred
families, including those living in the neighbouring villages.[14]

It is, however, not until the last decade of the fifteenth

century that Safed begins to be especially noted for the importance of its Jewish population. The man who was the most significant factor in the development of this Jewish settlement, which excelled Jerusalem not only in the size of its Jewish population but also in the number of great men it harboured, was R. Joseph Saragossi. Saragossi, hailing perhaps originally from Spain, was an exile from Sicily, and, after a residence in Beyrout and Sidon, finally settled in Safed, where he most likely established a school. He was of humble disposition, making peace between man and man, including non-Jews, and he probably did his best to blend the various elements of the new settlement, consisting of natives, of exiles from Spain, and of immigrants from the Barbary States, into one great community.[15]

The preference given to Safed, a non-Scriptural town, over Jerusalem, the historical metropolis of Palestine and the holiest city of the Holy Land, may be accounted for by the unfavourable conditions prevailing in Jerusalem at that time. As evidenced by certain contemporary documents, the administration of the Jewish community in Jerusalem was influenced by a rather ungenerous spirit, imposing heavy taxes on new arrivals, and making residence there a great hardship. The Mohammedan population seems also to have been hostile to the Jews, rapacious, and extortionate.[16] Safed, on the other hand, never having had before this time an important Jewish population, the community there had no occasion to make regulations calculated to exploit the foreigner, whilst the non-Jewish population seems to have been more kindly disposed toward the Jews, sparing them the heavy taxation which was the rule in Jerusalem. R. Obadiah of Bertinoro, who had no opportunity to visit the north, writes, in his famous letter dated 1489, that, according to report, the Jews of Safed and of other places in Galilee lived in peace and in quiet, not being exposed to persecution

on the part of the Mohammedans. He writes, "They are
mostly poor, spending their time in villages, going about
peddling in houses and on farms, asking for food." [17]

Another reason which may have been decisive in favour
of attracting immigrants to Safed was the simple life led by
the inhabitants of that city. The old saying, "Love work and
hate lordship" (in modern parlance, snobbery), was followed
by them to the letter. An anonymous traveller who passed
through Safed in the year 1496 writes of the learned Rabbi
Pharez Colobi, the head of the community, that he kept a
shop where articles of food were sold, by which he made a
living.[18] Shlomel of Moravia, the author of one of the
legendary biographies of Loria, writing from Safed in the
year 1607, says of its citizens that there were to be found
among them "great scholars, saints, and men of action, full
of Divine wisdom, so that they were worthy of the gift of the
Holy Spirit," but what he seemed to admire most was the
simplicity and the humility of spirit which they possessed.
"None among them," he writes, "is ashamed to go to the well
and draw water and carry home the pitcher on his shoulders,
or go to the market to buy bread, oil, and vegetables. All the
work in the house is done by themselves," without servants.
Shlomel's statement may be illustrated by the following story:
Once, R. Abraham Galanti, the leading disciple of Cordovero
and the author of many works, was carrying a sack of flour on
his shoulders from the market. But there came the famous
scholar R. Solomon Sagis (?) and snatched away the sack from
the shoulders of Galanti, and pronounced an oath, that no
man should be permitted to carry this sack of flour to its
destination except himself, who was so much younger and
stronger. On another occasion, Galanti was carrying a cask
of water on his shoulders from a village near Safed when the
Saint R. Misod met him and said, "Master, give me a drink,
as I am very thirsty." Whereupon Galanti offered him the

cask. R. Misod then snatched away the burden and carried it to Galanti's home in Safed.[19]

Thus material as well as spiritual considerations combined to make Safed the chosen city for the time being. The rapid growth of Safed may easily be seen by the fact that whilst, according to one account, Safed counted three synagogues in 1522, and could point perhaps to only one Talmudic college established by Saragossi, it could a few years later boast of being the centre of learning in Palestine, and, in 1603, according to Shlomel's letter of that year, it contained not less than eighteen Talmudic colleges and twenty-one synagogues, besides a large school for the children of the poor, with twenty teachers and four hundred pupils, maintained by wealthy Jews in Constantinople, who also provided the latter with clothes. The Jews in Turkey were particularly interested in maintaining the Safed schools, and special messengers were sent from this community to collect moneys. We even find mention of a single bequest for the Yeshiboth of Safed amounting to 100,000 *lebanim*.[20]

The history of the world, some maintain, is but the record of its great men. This is especially true of the history of Safed in the sixteenth century, which is essentially spiritual in its character, made and developed by men living lives purified by suffering, and hallowed by constant struggle after purification and holiness. The two figures standing out most prominently among these are R. Joseph Caro, the leading legist of the time, and his contemporary, R. Isaac Loria, the generally recognized head of the mystical school of Safed. It will, therefore, be advisable to group our remarks around these two heroes. From their eminence we shall be able to obtain a general view of the lives of the other mighty men in Israel engaged in the same general religious activities and pursuing the same spiritual ends, contributing their share to the fame which Safed has achieved in Jewish history.

R. Joseph Caro was born in the Pyrenean peninsula (probably Spain) in the year 1488, whence he emigrated as a boy of four, in the year 1492, with his father Ephraim, who was also his first teacher. After many wanderings and great suffering, they reached Nicopolis, in European Turkey, in which city the son Joseph remained until the year 1522.[21] He was advised there by his Maggid, a kind of Mentor-Angel (of whom more presently), to leave this place, whose inhabitants seem to have been rather close-fisted in their relations to the poor, and lacking in devotion to the Torah, and to move to Adrianople, in European Turkey, one of the various gathering points of the Spanish exiles.[22] There he remained for some years, serving in the capacity of the head of the Yeshibah, or Talmudic College. It was in this town that he began the composition of his work *Beth Joseph*, which occupied him for the next thirty years of his life (1522-1552).

The *Beth Joseph* is a gigantic work comprising four big folio volumes, the first edition of which appeared 1550-1559. It forms a sort of commentary to R. Jacob ben Asher's "Digest of the Law," *Arba Turim*, tracing each law to its original sources for nearly fifteen hundred years, pursuing it through its various stages of different interpreters and codifiers, giving in disputed cases the arguments on both sides, and bringing it down to his own time. It is hardly necessary to point to the tremendous learning and unsurpassed acquaintance with the Law in all its branches and ramifications displayed in the *Beth Joseph*. But what distinguishes it above other work of its kind is not only its comprehensiveness, covering as it does all the contents of the Oral Law which had not become obsolete by the destruction of the Holy Temple, but also the methodical treatment in which he was a master, and which enabled him to bring system and order into this chaos of argument, accumulated in every department of the Law, in its passage through the discussions of the schools for many centuries. Caro was by this work soon recognised as the greatest legist of his time, and was appealed to in matters of law even by his contemporaries, as the first Halachic authority.

Next to this in importance is his work *Shulchan Aruch,* which he finished in the year 1555. It forms only a sort of manual intended by Caro to serve chiefly as a repertory for his great book. The *Shulchan Aruch* soon proved to be the most popular code with students, both on account of its practical qualities and its close correspondence with the greater work of Caro, in which the origin of each law could be easily traced. It passed through several editions, and it is still consulted with profit by Rabbis engaged in giving ritual decisions according to the Law of Moses and the Talmud, even at this day representing the great bulk of the Jews— eleven millions and nine hundred thousand out of twelve millions. The *Shulchan Aruch* is disfigured by a few paragraphs expressing views incompatible with our present notions of tolerance. But there the discretion of the Rabbi comes in. By tacit consent these are considered obsolete by all Jewish students. Every Jewish scholar well knows that the fugitive from the tyranny of the pious royal couple, Ferdinand and Isabella of Spain, was not the person to make an effort to suppress intolerant matter. To meet intolerance with equal intolerance was considered a sort of self-defence. Nay, the student is even convinced that Caro himself would have hesitated to put such laws into practice. He would rather have followed the rule laid down by himself for himself, which was never to be betrayed into anger, even in matters of religion.

The other works of Caro published during his life or after his death add little to the greatness of Caro as a scholar, except, perhaps, certain portions of his *Keseph Mishneh,* forming a commentary to Maimonides' *Mishneh Torah,* and in his *Kelale ha-Talmud,* on the methodology of the Talmud, as well as certain Responsa embodied in various collections, in which Caro's passion for system and order and lucid and logical thinking is displayed even more clearly than in the works before named.

There is still one work to be considered, which brings us closer to Caro's personality, and that is the *Maggid Mesharim,* which appeared some thirty years after the death of its author.[23] The *Maggid Mesharim* is a long dream, lasting for nearly half a century. For, remarkable enough, the great legist and logical thinker was at the same time a dreamer of dreamers. Caro was passionately fond of the Mishnah, to which he is supposed to have written a commentary, lost to us, and its contents became so identified with his own self, that they shaped themselves into a species of Genius taking the form of a living reality personified in the Mentor-Angel above mentioned. This Mentor-Angel addresses him with such expressions as, "I am the Mishnah that speaketh through thy mouth; I am the soul of the Mishnah; I and the Mishnah and thou are united into one soul." [24]

As a rule, this *I-Mishnah* appeared to him in the depths of the night, after Caro had studied for some time one or more chapters of the Mishnah. Then the voice of his beloved, as Caro expressed himself, would begin to sound in his mouth, "singing of itself." [25] The voice was also audible to by-standers, as is clear from the famous letter of Alkabez, of whom I shall speak later, who was once fortunate enough to observe his friend Caro in such a fit of ecstasy, and who has left us a full account of the message delivered by the Mentor-Angel on that occasion.[26] From a description given by Caro himself of his prospects of being worthy one day to hold communion with the prophet Elijah, and the manner in which this communion will take place, we may also conclude that the listeners recognised in the strange sounds of the Mentor-Angel Caro's own voice, though to Caro himself these sounds appeared something alien, *not* himself. His other organs seem to have been at complete rest, which fact produced the impression in Caro that he served only as a sort of musical instrument to the sweet melody of the Mishnah. On the other hand, his mental faculties remained fairly unimpaired, as he retained complete recollection of all the Mentor-Angel revealed to him.

This recollection he wrote down in the *Maggid Mesharim,* which thus forms a mystical diary, recording the spiritual experience of a long lifetime. The fact that the book containing these recollections fills only a small volume proves nothing against this theory, as we possess it in a very defective state, whilst we also know that he did not always commit to writing the contents of his visions, for which neglect he is reproved by the Mentor-Angel.[27]

It must, however, not be thought that it is the explanation of obscure passages of the Mishnah that are revealed to Caro in his Mishnah visions. In the whole of the *Maggid Mesharim* there are only a few lines of a legal nature. Caro was sober enough not to allow his mystical proclivities to have a marked influence upon his judgment in matters of law. What occupied his thoughts in these moments of rapture was chiefly the mysteries of the Torah, as well as matters of conduct, falling under the heading of "superior holiness." I say "chiefly," for the "I," or Self, occasionally asserts itself and introduces matter which is rather of a private nature, as, for instance, his matrimonial affairs. From these we learn that he became a widower twice. His third wife, who brought him a large dowry, was the daughter of R. Zechariah Zechsel.[28] Caro also refers in a somewhat unkindly manner to certain great personalities. These reflections, which might have better been left unexpressed, were jotted down probably in moments of depression and resentment, for which we may not judge him too severely.[29] In the great majority of cases, however, Caro's Self was under the strict control of the Mishnah, or his ideal Mentor-Angel.

The Mentor-Angel is very exacting in his demands. "I am the mother that chastises her children," the Mishnah says to him, "be strong and cleave unto me." [30] This chastisement consisted partly in imposing upon Caro a number of regulations of an ascetic nature. He is bidden to fast on various occasions, and even on ordinary days his menu is prescribed for him, reduced to a minimum. He must not fully satisfy his desire for food and drink, not even in the first meal after a day of fasting.[31] Of course, he must not indulge in much wine, but he is at the same time rebuked by his Mentor-Angel for having allowed himself to be filled with water.[32] He is likewise warned against too much sleep, and when he married one of his daughters and, according to custom, spent much time at the banquet, so that he went to bed late and got up just one hour after the breaking of dawn, he was reproved for his slothful behaviour, and the Mentor-Angel tells him that it would only serve him right were he to abandon him, seeing that he separated his heart from the Torah for so long a time.[33] On another occasion, when Caro went to market to buy meat and poultry for Sabbath and failed in his errand, the Mentor-Angel declared himself responsible for this failure, proceeding to say that he wanted to show Caro that meat and wine are the habitation of the Evil One, that the Sabbath can be honoured without such luxuries, and concluding his admonition with the words, "Think about nothing but the Law of the Lord; thou art strictly observed in all thy actions, hence, be careful." [34]

Other instructions worth mentioning here are these: Be exceedingly lowly in spirit.—Never be betrayed into anger, not even in matters relating to Heaven.—Be chaste in thy behaviour.—Have always thy sins before thine eyes, and mourn over them.—Never speak an idle word.—Give a mild answer

to every man.—Never indulge in laughter and in scoffing.—
When thou readest the *Shema*, let thy thoughts be so single-
minded that they become the seat of the Divine Presence.[35]

He is also reminded by the Mentor-Angel of the necessity
of reading devotional books; among these the abridged version of Bachye's "Duties of the Heart" is especially recommended.[36] He is further bidden by the Mentor-Angel to devote himself more diligently to the study of the Cabbala,
which Caro seems to have neglected for a long time. "If thou
wilt have appointed times for the acquisition of the knowledge of the Cabbala, I will open thy heart so that thou shalt
receive the most hidden secrets unrevealed to man for many
years." [37]

The Mentor-Angel, however, was not always severe. His
motherly ways are not limited to chastisement. Thus he once
began his address, "Behold, I kiss thee the kiss of love; behold, I embrace thee." [38] Nor does he confine himself to re-
bukes and strictures. He also holds out hopes and promises.
These give us a fair insight into Caro's aspirations as a scholar
and a saint. They may, perhaps, be summed up in the following three points.

The first aspiration was that the books with which Caro
happened to be occupied, especially the *Beth Joseph,* should
be free from error, and after publication accepted as standard
works all over the Dispersion, whilst he himself should be
recognised as an authority of the first rank.[39] There is a
human touch in the fact, that notwithstanding this anxiety
Caro regards it as a joyful message when his Mentor-Angel
tells him that he will be blessed with a son who, besides being
one of the greatest mystics of the time, will also write strictures on his father's works.[40] Caro was especially anxious for
the privilege of spreading Torah in Israel, and had the repeated promise from his Mentor-Angel that he would be
worthy of presiding over the greatest gathering of disciples

in Israel, and that he would also receive sufficient material support for his college to enable his disciples to devote themselves entirely to the study of the Torah.[41]

As a mystic, all things on earth are to Caro only a reflex of some original in heaven, and thus in his capacity as the master of the greatest Torah-school here below, he is brought into communion with its prototype in the regions above. It is from there that his Mentor-Angel often brings him greetings in the typical expression, "Peace from the College of Heaven." [42] Sometimes the greeting begins with the words, "Behold the Holy One, blessed be he, and all the sons of the (heavenly) college, send unto thee peace, and are opening unto thee the gates of light." [43] Occasionally these greetings drift off into a string of solemn promises of the bliss and reward awaiting Caro in the world to come, where he will associate with all the heavenly hosts and the souls of the departed saints and scholars whose interpreter he was in this world.[44] It is interesting to see how the Mentor-Angel, with pedagogical insight, uses these very promises for a moral lesson. For instance, in one place where he gives him a full description of the glorious reception with which he will meet in the circle of the righteous, headed by the Divine Presence, and the fêtes which will be given in his honour, he winds up with the words: "Beloved, the Holy One and all the members of the Heavenly Academy send me to make thee acquainted with this secret, in order that thou mayest see thyself in this high degree, and thus thou wilt never come into the power of sin, not even by an evil thought. Should temptation become overpowering, rebuke it and say, 'Shall a man like me, whose future is meant for such glories, allow himself to sin, be it even only by an evil thought?' " [45] This is indeed one of the Mentor-Angel's pedagogical tactics, to impress Caro with his great importance, and at the same time show what duties such importance involves. By the very breath of his mouth when occupied with the uttering of the Mishnah, Caro creates whole hosts of angels, surrounding him as a suite surrounds a king. Every word of his, every thought, creates worlds; but so does it destroy worlds if it is of an unworthy and idle nature.[46]

The second aspiration of Caro was that he might be worthy to settle in the Holy Land.[47] This is a thought which probably occupied his mind for many years before he settled in Safed. The promise to help him realise that wish turns up again and again in the addresses of the Mentor-Angel. Solomon Alkabez, in the letter referred to above, reports how the Mentor-Angel said, "Lose no moment to go up to the Holy Land, for not all times are favourable. Regard not your stuff (i.e., household things). . . . I will maintain thee." It would seem that material considerations, at least for a time, prevented Caro from accomplishing the wish of his heart, for we find in another place, in which the Angel promises him that within a year he will be in Palestine, he says to him: "There is no need for thee to trouble thy mind; thou hast wanted nothing these last forty years, and thou wilt never know want. Thy income is prepared for thee. Thou hast seen this very moment that the Holy One, blessed be he, gave thee as much profit in two thousand Zuz as in five thousand." [48] When Caro tarries too long on his way, through war and other causes, the Mentor-Angel tells him that he may stay in certain cities, such as Salonica and others, for some time, but he must never settle anywhere until he reaches the Holy Land. Of course, with this aspiration is also connected his hope that he will be worthy of becoming the head of the Yeshibah and an elder of the Holy Land.[49]

His third aspiration was that he should die the death of a martyr at the stake. This is a wish which Caro cherished when he was still in Nicopolis, and which mingled with his dreams throughout his entire life.[50] Caro assures us that in visions without number he received the promise that he would be worthy to be burned for the sanctification of the Holy Name,[51] so that every taint of sin which may have cleaved unto him in his passage through this world would be removed, and his soul cleansed, and thus reach the degree of the holy and pure ones. Here again the Mentor-Angel employs this dearest wish of Caro's heart for his pedagogical purposes, as when he tells him: "Behold, I have singled thee out to be a burnt-offering, to be consumed in fire for the sake of the sanctification of the Name, but thou knowest that in the burnt-offering no blemish may be found, not even in thought. Hence, take care that all thy thoughts are absorbed by the Torah." [52] On the whole, the promises of the Mentor-Angel were fairly kept, except this. Turkey was perhaps at no time the country in which the crown of martyrdom could be easily gained. For this, one had to go to the lands of Christendom, where love was preached and murder acted. Caro showed no particular desire to return to Europe. In this connexion it is rather interesting to note that Caro was not quite free from anxiety, for he found it worth his while to write down the following apparently good message of his Mentor-Angel: "During the afternoon prayer, when the reader was chanting the portion from the scroll of the Law, I was told, 'Know, my beloved and dear Joseph, that the Sultan will win the battle in which he is now engaged against the King of Edom.' " [53]

The *Maggid Mesharim* occasionally contains references to different personages mentioned in Caro's other works. But whilst in these latter they are cited with their proper titles, as "Rabbi," "Master," or "the great Rabbi," in the *Maggid Mesharim,* as befitting a production of an angelic being, this official stiffness disappears. Titles are, for the most part, dropped, and they are introduced with such endearing epithets as "my chosen Moses" (Maimonides), "my saintly

Asher" (Rosh), "my God-fearing Jonah" (Rabbenu Jonah), "my dear Jacob" (Jacob ben Asher, the author of the *Turim*), "my modest Jeruham" (author of a well-known code of the Rabbinic Law). But the name which occurs most frequently is that of "my chosen Solomon." [54] This name is at most times used for Solomon Molko, but it is not impossible that in one or two places it refers to Solomon Alkabez, two beautiful souls who seem to have been the especial favourites of Caro.[55]

We must digress for a moment from Caro himself to consider the career of these two worthies. Solomon Molko deserves a monograph to himself. He would best form the subject of a great historical novel. If our novelists were somewhat less of realists, and would stop their eternal harping on the problem of mixed marriages, which is certainly no problem to those who begin to consider it in the light of a problem, and if they further possessed something of the sympathetic intuition of a Disraeli and the artistic insight into the past of a Sir Walter Scott or Charles Reade, they would find Molko the hero of one of the greatest historical romances ever written. For our purpose of presenting the friend of Caro a few data must suffice.[56]

Solomon Molko was born in Portugal about the year 1501, as a crypto-Jew, or Marrano, where he received the name Diogo Pires. He was endowed with all the graces of Nature calculated to make his personality both pleasing and impressive. He enjoyed an excellent education, and at a early age he was able to speak and write Latin, the learned language of the time. Like so many other Marranos, he received, in secret, instruction in Hebrew subjects, such as the Bible and the Talmud, and even the Cabbala, in which branches of study he acquired great proficiency. His various accomplishments secured for him rapid advancement in official circles. He was very young when he was appointed secretary at one of the high courts of justice in Lisbon. He was also a great favourite at the Court. But neither the duties of his office nor the diversions of Court life were sufficient to fill the vacuum he felt under the false life he led. His thoughts and his heart were with Judaism, over whose destiny and his part in it he constantly brooded. This brooding soon resulted in all sorts of visions and wild dreams, which visited him day and night. At the first impulse, supposed to have been given him by the famous adventurer David Reubeni, who was then travelling in Europe in the questionable capacity of an ambassador of the lost Ten Tribes, he was initiated into the covenant of Abraham, and became a Jew. This occurred about the year 1523. He then entered upon a course of ascetic practices, fasting for many days without interruption, depriving himself of sleep, and spending his time in prayer and meditation, which was naturally followed by more visions of an apocalyptic nature. The visions were manifested to him, as in the case of Caro, by a Maggid, who communed with him from heaven in dreams. In obedience to the command of this heavenly messenger, he left Portugal for Turkey, which was a safer place for men of Molko's cast of mind. There, as it would seem, he spent the next five or six years. The appearance of this enthusiastic, handsome young mystic made a deep impression upon the Jewish communities visited by him. Molko probably visited also Jerusalem and Safed in Palestine. There is no positive evidence for this fact, but it is hardly possible that he should have failed to explore the places which he saw with his spiritual eye in his mystic moments. Legend reports also that even after his death he would pay visits to his *fiancée* in Safed on every Friday evening, reading in her presence the Sanctification-Benediction over the cup of wine (*Kiddush*) with which the Sabbath is initiated. This would doubtless suggest that he had once been at this place.[57] The end of the year 1529 finds him at Ancona in Italy where he preached on the advent of the Messiah. His sermons seem to have made a great sensation, and were listened to by large crowds, both Jews and Christians, including some high dignitaries of the church. Some time after this he repaired to Rome, in which city he had again all sorts of visions and dreams. He soon gained access to the Pope, Clement VII, who felt rather attracted toward him, and together with certain cardinals, not less favourable to Molko than the Holy Father himself, protected him against the dangers threatening him from the Roman police as a renegade from the Christian faith. He predicted to the Pope the flood which was soon to come upon Rome, and went to Venice for a time. He returned to Rome and had several more conferences with the Pope and other high personages, all the time preaching publicly repentance as a preparation for the approaching advent of the Messiah, in which he was to play a conspicuous part, either as the forerunner of the Messiah or as the Messiah ben Joseph. But all the patronage he had did not protect him from the intrigues of his deadly enemy, the Jewish physician Jacob Mantino, who is not to be held entirely guiltless of his falling into the hands of the Emperor, Charles V. The latter, in turn, handed him over to the Inquisition. The end was that Molko was burned as a heretic in Mantua, in 1532. When approaching the stake, he was offered pardon in the name of the Emperor, if he would recant. Molko replied that he longed for the death of a martyr, to become "a burnt-offering of sweet savour unto the Lord; if he had anything to repent of, it was that he had been a Christian in his youth."

Caro's acquaintance with Molko must have been formed either in Adrianople or in Salonica, both of which cities were visited by the latter during his travels. The acquaintance grew into a strong attachment, at least on the part of Caro, who thought himself indebted to Molko for certain spiritual influences which he had on his life. Thus said the Mentor-Angel to Caro, "God brought thee together with my chosen Solomon to see whether thou wilt know him, and it was a merit (or rather, good fortune) that thou didst learn to know him and also didst learn from him to fear me." [58] It is, however, an exaggeration to think that it was Molko who converted Caro to his belief in the Cabbala, or that it was the martyr-death of Molko that incited in Caro the desire to end his life in a similar manner. Cabbala was in the air; the greatest men of Israel were committed to it, and it required no special agencies to make Caro one of its adherents. The fact is, that Molko was lovable, and Caro loved him. That the tragic death of Molko made a deep impression upon Caro, and mingled with his dreams and visions, only proves that the legalistic studies which formed the main occupation of Caro's life, do not incapacitate a man for the qualities of admiration and love. As to the longing of Caro for the death of a martyr, we have seen that he had the privilege of calls from the Mentor-Angel while he was still a resident of Nicopolis, and it was there that he received the promise of martyrdom for the first time from his heavenly messenger. This occurred about 1522, long before Caro even knew of the existence of such a person as Molko. It is to be noted that martyrdom in case of necessity is a regular command, forming one of the six hundred and thirteen laws. According to some authorities, the supreme act of martyrdom, like the fulfillment of any other command of the Law, should be preceded by a benediction, namely, "Blessed art thou, O Lord our God, King of the world, who hast sanctified us with thy commandments, and hast bidden us to hallow thy Name among the many." Now, if we consider how anxious a legist of Caro's frame of mind must have been to fulfil a command-

ment—the characteristic of the legalistic saints of every generation—no further explanation is needed for Caro's longing
for martyrdom. It was simply his desire to fulfil a commandment of the Torah. As one of the saints expresses it: If the
Heavenly Court were to decree hell punishment against him,
he would jump into the pit with all his might and without a
moment's delay, embracing with joy the opportunity to fulfil
a Divine command.[59]

Much less is known of the life of the second Solomon—
Solomon Halevi Alkabez. There are no records enabling us
to determine the place where he was born, nor the dates of
his birth and death. We know, however, that he flourished
about the first half of the sixteenth century, that he was the
disciple of Joseph Taytasak, Rabbi of Salonica, and that later
he became the master and brother-in-law of the famous Cabbalist Moses Cordovero. His acquaintance with Caro probably dates from the third decade of that century, he having
met him in Salonica or Adrianople. Alkabez was a scholar
and a poet. Of his books it suffices to mention here the
Manoth ha-Levi (Gifts of the Levite), a homiletical commentary on the Book of Esther, in which he showed his wide
acquaintance with Rabbinic literature, having had, as it
seems, access to manuscripts which he very judiciously used
in the said work. The story is that the title of the book was
suggested by the fact that it formed a present to his *fiancée*
on the occasion of the Purim festival. His father-in-law and
the girl, the tradition is, were more pleased with this gift than
with costly jewelry, which young men were then in the habit
of sending to their sweethearts on the day of Purim. But he
is best known by his poem, *Lechah Dodi,* "Come, my Beloved, etc.," with which he and his friends used to receive
Queen Sabbath. The Sabbath was to him a living reality to
be welcomed after a six days' absence with that expectant joy
and impatient love with which the groom meets his bride.

It is perhaps one of the finest pieces of religious poetry in existence, and has been translated by Herder and by Heine into German. Catholic Israel, whose love for Bride Sabbath and whose hope for final redemption it echoed so well, soon honoured Alkabez' poem with a prominent place in almost all its rituals; and the *Lechah Dodi* is now sung all over the world on Sabbath even, when Queen Sabbath holds her *levée* in the tents of Jacob.[60]

To return to Caro and Safed: When Caro arrived in Palestine, which could not well have been earlier than after the middle of the year 1536, Safed was already grown to the size of one thousand Jewish families. The additions to the community were mostly made up of Spanish and Portuguese exiles, who were soon in a position to build a second synagogue for the purpose of accommodating their newly-arrived countrymen.[61] Their numbers were so increased that they considered themselves strong enough to attempt to force their special usages with regard to the regulating of dowries upon other sections of the community. The Spanish language, the vernacular of the Sephardim, became soon the teaching medium in the schools, suppressing all other languages.[62] They quickly won, both by their numbers and by the distinction of their leaders, such an exceptional position that we find men of importance and standing among the native Jewish population vain enough to call themselves Sephardim, the name common to Jews hailing from Spain and Portugal.[63] There is reason to believe that at this time also a German Jewish community was established in Safed, perhaps presided over by the father-in-law of Caro. We have furthermore references to a Portuguese synagogue, an Italian synagogue, and a Greek synagogue, dating from about the same time.[64] The constitution of these communities seems to have been

strictly autonomous, each community having its own synagogue, its own preacher, and its own Yeshibah. They were
even, to a certain extent, jealous of every outside interference,
and it was expected that each new arrival would join the
congregation composed of his own fellow-countrymen.[65] On
the other hand, there is evidence that they had a *Beth ha-
Wa'ad* (meeting house), forming a sort of general board
consisting of the Rabbis of the various synagogues, to which
occasionally Rabbis attached to no congregation in particular
were invited. This board probably dealt only with matters
of grave importance and of general interest.[66]

The means of gaining a livelihood were various. The
natives, or, as they were called, the Moriscos, were probably
still engaged in peddling, as their ancestors had been.[67] There
is also evidence that they cultivated the ground in the neighbouring villages, producing wheat, barley, beans, cotton, oil,
wine, and figs. Those, again, who possessed some capital,
which was probably the case with many of the Spanish immigrants, were engaged in trading, exporting grain, wine,
and oil to Damascus and other places, and importing from
there articles for which there was a demand in Safed.[68] There
also grew up in Safed a large trade in the weaving of wool
and in the manufacturing of clothes; these trades were
entirely in the hands of the Jews.[69] Indeed, R. Levi ben
Chabib, of whom I shall speak presently, sarcastically asks
whether it was because of the large quantity of clothes manufactured there that Safed arrogated to itself the leadership
of Judaism.[70] Wealthy Jews in Constantinople and in Damascus would, as it seems, send ships laden with wool to
Safed for the purpose of encouraging the wool industry there
and giving employment to those engaged in it. About the
year 1600, such a ship, containing wool to the value of nearly
100,000 *Keseph* and 10,000 *Keseph* in cash for the desperate
poor, was wrecked on its voyage, which caused distress in

Safed.[71] There was also in Safed a great demand for such
artisans as weavers, smiths, tailors, tanners, wood-workers,
and builders. There was probably also some demand for men
connected with the printing trade, which was established in
Safed about the year 1653 by two German Jews. The first
book printed there was the commentary of R. Moses Alsheich
to Daniel, and was followed by several other works. "The
print of these books is excellent, and testifies to the good taste
and the prosperity of the Safed community at that time." [72]
The only profession for which there was not any room in
Safed was that of teacher, since the community was, we are
told, sufficiently provided with schools and instructors. Nor
was there any place for servants, as everybody, as we have
seen, attended to his own domestic work.[73] The prosperity
was so great that they were envied for it by their brethren
abroad. Thus a Roman Jew writes in 1543, "The good
message has come from the land of Desire (Palestine) that
the Lord remembered his people and his land and the
Children of Israel, granting to them wealth and honour in
most trades." [74]

However, men did not settle in Palestine for the purpose
of developing the natural resources of the country. What led
them there was, as indicated above, the spiritual wealth
which the Holy Land alone could afford. In such wealth,
Safed, at this period, was particularly rich. I have already
mentioned the letter of Shlomel, with its reference to the
population of Safed and the various Talmudical colleges
maintained there.[75] Though Shlomel writes at the beginning
of the seventeenth century, there is nothing to indicate that
the last decades of the sixteenth century witnessed a particular increase of immigration out of proportion to that
of the preceding decades. Indeed, we shall see later on that in
his time the glory of Safed was already on the wane. We have
the right to assume that the number of Rabbis of the six-

teenth century was at least not smaller than that of the seventeenth. Shlomel's statistics are, of course, like all statistics, not very reliable; indeed, the number three hundred occurs too frequently in the letters relating to Safed. It has also to be pointed out that the term "Rabbi" with Shlomel does not exactly mean the officiating minister, but simply a man who, both on account of his learning and his saintly life—two indispensable qualifications for a Rabbi in olden times— might easily perform the functions of a Rabbi. Still, there can be little doubt that no place in Jewish history since the destruction of the Holy Temple could point to so brilliant a gathering of men, so great in their respective branches, so diversified in the objects of their study, and so united by the dominant thought of religion, as were attracted to Safed during the greater part of the sixteenth century.

The fame of the "saints and men of action" must have spread "outside of the land" early in the sixteenth century, and it was probably the desire for their society which determined Caro in his choice of Safed. For such was the promise given him by the Mentor-Angel: "I will give thee places to walk among these that stand by" (Zech. 3: 7), "making thee worthy to go up to the land of Israel and join there my beloved Solomon and the Associates to learn and to teach." [76]

The most prominent among these was doubtless R. Jacob Berab.[77] Berab, who was an emigrant from Castile, Spain, and held the office of Rabbi in various Jewish communities, settled in Safed about the year 1535, where he soon became the recognised head of the Jewish community, which consisted at that time of at least seven congregations. It seems that he gathered around him some of the best minds of Safed, who acknowledged themselves as his disciples. Caro himself recognised him as an authority, quoting him as a rule with the epithet "our great master." Berab has left us a volume of Responsa, to which are appended commentaries on certain

portions of the Talmud, but he is best known to history by
his unsuccessful efforts to re-introduce the institution of
"Ordination" (*Semichah*) among the Jews. This attempt was
made in the year 1538, and bears evidence to the high
position held in Jewry by the sages of Safed, both by their
numbers and by the weight of their great learning: this fact
alone could have emboldened Berab and his friends to em-
bark upon their daring enterprise.[78] Ordination, as they
intended it, was not the mere ceremonious laying on of hands
in connexion with a candidate for Rabbinical office with some
solemn speech attendant thereon. What Berab aimed at, was
the re-establishment of the body of the Sanhedrin (that could
exist only in Palestine), which would wield supreme authority
over the whole of Israel in various ways, thus forming a new
Jewish spiritual centre. His great opponent in this matter
was R. Levi ben Chabib, a former resident of Safed, living
then at Jerusalem.

This is not the place to enter into the arguments of both
sides, which both parties drew from the Talmud. There may
have been also some petty personal jealousies; some of the
arguments are certainly of a rather petty character, particularly on Berab's side. Berab was something of what we might
call a strong man, of strenuous tendencies, and his treatment
of Ben Chabib was by no means tender. But there is no doubt
that Berab's aspirations were of great national importance,
and if realised would have served to strengthen the bonds
of union in Israel. The scholars of Safed worked in harmony
with Berab, twenty-five of their number signing the epistle
sent to the sages of Jerusalem that contained the resolution
of the former to re-introduce Ordination. The resolution was
soon translated into action, Berab ordaining four elders,
representing the flower of Safed's scholarship.[79] Caro, who
was one of the four, and apparently figured also among the

signatories of the correspondence with Jerusalem, is especially complimented by his Mentor-Angel for the zeal shown by him for the great cause. He must also have entertained the hope that he might succeed one day where Berab had failed; at least, he received the heavenly promise that he would be the instrument through which Ordination should be restored.[80] This is another of the Mentor-Angel's unfulfilled prophecies.

The excitement of the Ordination controversy subsided with the death of Berab, which occurred shortly after 1540. Caro, who devoted his time to lecturing to his disciples, writing his books, and attending to social work, or, as it is usually called in Hebrew literature, the "needs of the congregation," was constantly growing in influence and authority. He apparently felt trouble in his mind about this interference with his studies, for we find that the Mentor-Angel has to comfort him and make it clear that the social work in which he was engaged was also a part of his duties, which he had no right to ignore.[81]

His most formidable rival was R. Moses ben Joseph Trani, who settled in Safed in the year 1518, and became Rabbi of the Spanish congregation Beth Jacob, and the head of the Yeshibah connected with it, in 1521, which offices he retained until his death in 1580.[82] Like Caro, he was ordained by Berab, to whom he stood in the relation of a colleague-disciple, and he showed even more zeal for the honour of his master than Caro. Indeed, he resents in one place the indifference of Caro to the attacks made on Berab in connexion with certain legal decisions.[83] Trani wrote several works, one of which was of a semi-philosophical nature on doctrinal questions, but he is chiefly famous for the collection of his Responsa, which show him to have been a Talmudist of the first order and regarded as such by his contemporaries.

Though generally, like all other Rabbis of the place, confined in his jurisdiction to his own congregation, he seems to have been regarded by the whole community as a specialist in real estate questions. "I have," he says, "been one of the first in everything relating to the holiness of the land in the city of Safed since the year 5335. God put it in my heart to build up the desolate places thereof. I have watched over them in most of their building enterprises, that no man should encroach upon the property of his neighbour, and other matters relating to questions of surveying and ancient lights, even with regard to the synagogues which were built all these years, when (the worshippers) coming from Turkey and other places divided according to their languages." [84]

Several cases occurred in which Trani had the opportunity to clash with Caro's opinions; the most important of these seems to have been one in connexion with the observance of the Sabbatical Year, the laws in regard to which were not considered entirely obsolete in the Holy Land. The great majority of scholars, however, were in favour of Caro's opinion, to enforce it as the norm for the practice.[85] This case arose in the year 1574, a year before Caro's death, but his recognition as a master of the Holy Land or, as he expressed it somewhere else, "the great codifier of the Holy Land," came long before. In almost all the Opinions of that generation, Caro's signature appears first, and his Yeshibah had, according to tradition, a seating capacity of seven hundred students.[86] This is probably an exaggeration, but the attendance at his Yeshibah was undoubtedly very large, and included some of the greatest names of the time. As one of the Safed scholars expressed it, "We are all his disciples, drinking his waters, and bound to honour him." [87] Among these, Cordovero and Alsheich deserve special mention, both because of their connexion with the history of Safed and their influence on posterity.

R. Moses Cordovero was born in 1522 and died in 1570. Little is known about his private life except that he married a sister of Solomon Alkabez. In Talmud he was a disciple of Caro, who was apparently very proud of him and applied to him the verse, "My son, if thy heart be wise, my heart shall rejoice, even mine" (Prov. 23: 15). We know also that he acted as one of the Dayanim (Judges) of Safed and had a Yeshibah of his own. A Responsum of his incorporated in the Responsa Collection of Caro, testifies to his ability as a Rabbinical scholar, but his fame rests on his mystical work, in which he by far excelled all his predecessors.[88] At the early age of twenty, the Voice warned him to "heal the altar of the Lord which is broken down," under which he understood his neglect of a proper study of the mysteries of the Torah.[89] The "healing" came from his brother-in-law, Alkabez, in whom he perceived a holy angel come down from heaven, and who apparently figured at that period as the leading Cabbalist of Safed. Even Caro himself did not hesitate to seek instruction from Alkabez about a certain obscure passage in the Zohar.[90] At the age of twenty-six (1548), we find Cordovero in the company of the Associates (*Chaberim*). This was a society consisting of mystically-inclined students of Safed, apparently presided over by Alkabez. Very little has come down to us relative to the activity of this society, beyond the fact that its members used occasionally to undertake excursions to visit the graves of the ancient Rabbis supposed to be buried in the neighbourhood of Safed, on which occasions they would discuss mystical subjects.[91] But we possess in manuscript a list of moral precepts drawn up by Cordovero, of which there is good reason to assume that they were not meant exclusively for the guidance of their author, but formed a sort of hand-book for all the Associates. The following extracts will convey some idea of the frame of mind and the tender conscience of these men.

They are bidden not to divert their thoughts from the words of the Torah and things holy, so that their hearts become the abode of the *Shechinah;* not to be betrayed into anger, as anger delivers man into the power of sin; not to speak evil of any creature, including animals; never to curse any being, but to accustom oneself to bless even in moments of anger; never to take an oath, even on the truth; never to speak an untruth under any condition; to be careful not to be included among the four classes excluded from the Divine Presence, namely, the hypocrites, the liars, the scoffers, and the tale-bearers; not to indulge in banquets except on religious occasions. They are enjoined to mingle their minds with the minds of their fellow-men (that is, not to stand aloof from the world, but to share both in its joys and in its sorrows), and to behave in a kindly spirit toward their fellowmen, even though they be transgressors; to meet with one of the Associates for one or two hours every day for the purpose of discussing matters spiritual; to talk over with an Associate every Friday the deeds accomplished during the week, and then set out for the reception of Queen Sabbath; to pronounce Grace in a loud voice, letter by letter and word by word, so that the children at the table can repeat after the reader; to confess their sins before every meal and before going to sleep; to use the sacred language when speaking with the Associates, and to let this be always the language of conversation on Sabbath with other scholars as well. In another set of precepts drawn up by Alkabez, dating from this time and probably also meant for the guidance of these Associates, we have the ordinance that the students should rebuke or admonish each other, but the person admonished or rebuked must not make any reply in his defence before the lapse of three days.[92]

The most prominent among those for whose benefit these regulations were composed were the author himself, Cordovero, whose interviews with Alkabez seem to have been more frequent and of a more intimate nature than those of the other Associates. At a later period the relations of the latter to their master appear to have been almost forgotten, and they are quoted as the Associates of Cordovero. Indeed, it would seem that it was the great popularity achieved by the works of Cordovero that is responsible for the comparative oblivion into which the mystical writings of Alkabez fell, so that the greater part of them remained unpublished.[93]

Cordovero's *magnum opus* is the *Pardes* (the Garden), the clearest and most rational exposition of the Cabbala in existence, distinguished by the same qualities of methodical thought and logical argument which distinguished Caro's works in the department of things legal. The *Pardes* gave rise to a great number of works written by various mystics in Safed, in Italy, and in Germany.[94] The book is still considered a standard authority, even by modern scholars who have ever written anything worth reading about the Cabbala. Cordovero wrote besides this many other works, some of which are extant only in manuscript. The library of the Jewish Theological Seminary of America possesses a fine copy of his famous work *Alimah,* known from quotations by certain mystics. But these by no means fully represent his literary activity. R. Menahem Azariah, of Fano, in Italy, one of the greatest of Cordovero's students, states that the *Pardes,* in itself a big folio volume, forms only a thirtieth part of the works which Cordovero wrote, not counting many additions, appendixes, and a number of larger and smaller treatises which he composed.[95] His master, Caro, who survived him, gave the funeral oration at his death, in which he spoke of him as "the Holy Ark of the Torah, to be hidden away in the grave," whilst Loria is said to have seen two pillars of fire attending the hearse, a compliment shown by Heaven only to one or two men in a generation. Loria is also reported to have applied to him, in allusion to his name (Moses), the well-known phrase, "Moses is true, and his teaching is true." [96]

The second of the disciples of Caro deserving especial mention is R. Moses Alsheich, who survived his master for many years, being still alive in the year 1593. The master of his early youth was probably Joseph Taytasak. We possess from Alsheich a volume of Responsa in which his opinions in matters of the law were solicited by various Rabbis of repute. He also wrote Talmudical discourses and a commentary to the *Midrash Rabbah* lost to us. He lectured in two Yeshiboth in Safed (which Vital attended in the capacity of a pupil), and performed all the other functions of a Rabbi of that time. He is, however, best known by his homiletical Commentary on the Bible, which was studied both by preachers and laymen for centuries afterward, and is still popular with preachers in various countries. This Commentary is usually cited under the title, "the Holy Alsheich." Loria gave the testimony that most of his interpretations "hit the truth," though in spite of the efforts of Vital he did not admit him into his mystical circle.[97]

Besides these and other Rabbis known more or less to posterity, we have in the contemporary literature any number of references to sages and saints of Safed flourishing about this time, in addition to a goodly number of Rabbis and students whose spiritual pedigree cannot be easily determined. The influence of these scholars was not confined to the schools. A religious atmosphere seems to have pervaded all classes of the Jewish population, so that the impression the Safed of the sixteenth century leaves on us is that of a revival camp in permanence, constituted of penitents gathered from all parts of the world. Life practically meant for them an opportunity for worship, to be only occasionally interrupted by such minor considerations as the providing of a livelihood for their families and the procuring of the necessary taxes for the government. Prayer was the main and universal occupation. For this purpose special teachers were appointed to instruct women and children in the liturgy and in the prescribed benedictions.[98] But the regular order of the service, with its fixed hours, morning, afternoon, and evening, did not satisfy their longing for prayer. For them the day began in the middle of the night, when the "learned" and the "men of action" would repair to the synagogues dressed in black, seating themselves upon the floor and reading a special liturgy, the burden of which was mourning over the destruction of the Holy Temple and the downfall of the people of God, and which concluded with a confession of the sins of Israel delaying the redemption.[99] The example set by them seems soon to have infected the general Jewish public. The man who was especially distinguished for his religious activity among the masses was the mystic R. Abraham Halevi Beruchim. His main work was of a missionary nature. He was constantly preaching to the multitudes and exhorting Israel to repentance. In the middle of the night he would rise and walk through the Jewish quarter, exclaiming in tears, "My brethren of the House of Israel! Is it not known to you that our Strength, the very Divine Presence, is in exile because of our sins; that our Holy Temple is laid in ashes; that Israel is subjected to the most bitter persecutions, saintly men and women being daily martyred by sword and by fire . . . ? And ye, my brethren, allow yourselves to enjoy your sleep on your beds in quiet and rest. Come, my brethren; come, my friends! Rise, ye holy children, blessed by the Lord, and let us supplicate the Lord our God, the King who sitteth on the throne of Mercy." Thus he used to walk about, knocking on the doors, giving the inhabitants no rest until they rose and went to their places of worship, so that at one o'clock in the morning the voice of prayer or of the study of the Torah could be heard from all the synagogues. On Friday afternoon, again, he would go about in the market-place, in the high-roads, reminding the people to be prompt in their preparations for the coming day, so that they might not, by being late, become involved in the sin of the desecration of the Sabbath.[100] The eve of the New Moon offered another opportunity for an additional service, when all the people fasted, and "men, women, and students" would spend the day in supplications, confession of sin, and in various ascetic practices. The eve of the seventh day of Passover, of the first day of the Feast of Weeks, of the Day of Atonement, and of the seventh day of the Tabernacle Feast were also distinguished by special readings from the Scriptures and the chanting of hymns, lasting nearly the whole of the night.[101]

R. Abraham Halevi was probably assisted in his missionary work by certain "saints and men of action" of whom it is reported that they used, on certain occasions, to preach on the subjects of meekness, sin, and repentance. Possibly they were members of the society Tent of Peace (*Succath Shalom*), mentioned by R. Eliezer Azkari, for which he wrote his devotional treatise, *Sepher Charedim*. In this he tried to show how "those that tremble at the commandments of our God" (Ezra 10: 3) should consecrate the whole of man, in his various functions and different occupations, to the service of the Lord. The thought absorbing the minds of the "tremblers" and forming the object of their discussions at their meetings, was the delay of the advent of the Messiah, and the sins responsible for this delay, but it was also a part of their programme to cause "the many to turn away from sin" by lectures and exhortations. Like the Associates of Cordovero, the members of this society were also pledged to auricular confession, each of them giving at their weekly meetings a full and detailed account of his actions during the preceding week. The necessity of having to lay bare one's life before his fellow-men, and the shame following upon it in the case of an unworthy action would, so they thought, prove a preventive against sin. It should, however, be re-marked that Vital, notwithstanding all his other vagaries and ascetic tendencies, protested against this institution, and de-clined to follow his friends in its practice.[102]

Besides the Tent of Peace, we have also on record the existence of a Society of Penitents, especially distinguished for its ascetic practices, which were of a very severe nature. Some of its members, we are told, refrained from food and drink during the day, performed their afternoon devotions in tears, and put on sackcloth and ashes. Others, again, ob-served every week a fast extending over two or three days and nights in succession.[103] R. Elijah de Vidas, in his attempt to show how much one can accomplish in the ascetic line, points with evident pride to these Penitents, saying: "I saw many of them rise in the middle of the night, when they would commence to study, which occupied them until the morning, and then fast the whole of the day. All this they were able to accomplish by special Divine aid, for man does not live by bread alone." [104] Of the Associates of Cordovero we read that some among them used to observe a fast ex-tending over three or four days and nights, at the change of the four seasons of the year. It is further recorded that there were many pious scholars who refrained from wine and meat during week-days, whilst others observed on certain days of the year the same laws of levitical purity in respect to their food as the priests in olden times when eating the heave-offering and other sacrificial pieces.[105]

It should, however, be remarked that "doing penance" and chastisement of the flesh were not considered by them as synonymous with repentance. Repentance meant chiefly the absolute determination never to return to sin at the very risk of one's life, which must precede all regeneration of the heart. As Azkari himself expresses it, "Fasts and ascetic practices are vanity and the work of error without this preceding resolution," and he goes on to quote his contemporary, the Saint R. Jacob Gavinezo, who communicated to him the fact that a man committed a most atrocious crime after a continuous fast of three days. Like the sacrifice in the Temple, penance is only of value when preceded by purification of the heart, humility, and meekness.[106]

It is hardly needful to say that charity formed an important item in the Safed scheme of salvation. The injunction of the mystic is to give alms every day according to one's means.[107] This injunction, though originally intended for a small circle, was accepted by the general public, following the example of the saints of old, who used always to make some donation to the poor before beginning their prayers. The custom in Safed was to make a regular collection during the morning prayers in the synagogues. The men, however, with special aspirations to saintliness would tax themselves to the amount of twenty per cent of their income, and it is stated that even among the poor there were persons known to give two tithes. Others, again, would adopt boys and girls early orphaned, educating them in their own families, and bringing them into the holy state of matrimony when they approached the marriageable age.[108]

Yet Safed shows certain characteristics of its own which greatly redeem it from many an unpleasant feature which we are accustomed to associate with the modern revival camp. It is true that the strain was great, salvation being the absorbing topic of the community, and the terror of sin delaying this salvation ever present. No opportunity was allowed to pass for reminding men that Zion was still in ruins, and that man is a sinful creature and in need of grace, hence the injunction to confess sins before meals and before retiring to sleep, whilst the 137th Psalm, "By the rivers of Babylon we sat, etc.," was added to the Grace after meals.[109]

That this strain should produce certain psychological phenomena more interesting to the pathologist than to the theologian, is hardly necessary to state. The literature of the time, abounding in stories of all sorts of demoniacs, bears ample evidence to this fact.[110] We also have stories of men who through their importunate storming of Heaven for Salvation were, for some relapse from grace, suddenly hurled down to the very depths of hell, and doomed to perdition. The most tragic among these is the story of Joseph de la Reina, who flourished in Safed in the early decades of the sixteenth century. De la Reina is a sort of Jewish Faust, who, in his passion for salvation, did not hesitate to employ certain exorcisms and conjurations of a very daring nature. He succeeded in bringing the Evil One into his power, whose destruction is a preliminary condition to the advent of the Messiah. But in an unfortunate moment he was persuaded to show compassion to this fallen angel, allowing him to smell of the frankincense. The fiend then regained his former strength, and achieved full mastery over his captor, who, after realising his fall, abandoned himself to the most revolting immoralities, and ended his life by suicide.[111]

In spite of this strain, however, with all its hysteria and its dire results in some cases, it must not be thought that the Safed community was constantly on the mourning-bench and spent all its vitality in groaning and lamentations. Cordovero laid down the rule not to indulge in pretentious meals except on religious occasions, but these religious occasions were happily not infrequent, and the people were apparently not slow to avail themselves of the opportunities given to them. The Sabbath was such an opportunity, being held as a day of joy and recreation in every respect, physically and spiritually. Fasting was not only strictly prohibited on the Sabbath, but it was considered a religious work to partake of three meals, which, Caro's Mentor-Angel to the contrary notwithstanding, had to be distinguished by certain delicacies. Wine also was served at these meals, which even the Penitents would drink. The meals were further distinguished by a special set of hymns sung or chanted during the intervals between the various courses.[112] The prescribed ritual, again, in the synagogue was all joy and promise, containing no confession or the slightest reference to anything of a despondent nature. Indeed, the Sabbath should give man a foretaste of the blissful Messianic times when sin and sorrow shall have disappeared from the world.[113] Reluctant to part with these hours of serene peace and unalloyed joy, and anxious to prolong them as much as possible, the Sabbath received an extension both at the beginning and at the end. Thus they would, early Friday afternoon, dress in their best clothes and set out in groups to receive Queen Sabbath, with song and praise, reciting certain Psalms and singing certain hymns composed for the occasion. In like manner, they would refrain from work for several hours after the Sabbath sun had set, and spend them in chanting hymns and in feasting. They had even a special society whose members would meet to spend the end of the Sabbath, reaching way into the night, with song and dance. The New Moon was also observed as a partial holiday, affording an opportunity for relaxation and enjoyment, not to speak of festivals prescribed in the Bible, such as the Passover, the Pentecost, and the Feast of Tabernacles.[114]

All these things must have contributed more or less toward mitigating the evil effects of an exaggerated asceticism. Nor must it be forgotten that joy forms a prominent feature in the programme of the mystic. His maxim was: the Divine light reaching man through the fulfilment of the commandment is only in proportion to the joy expressed by him when performing a religious action.[115]

Moreover, it must be borne in mind that Safed was just as famous for its scholarship as for its piety. Most of the leaders of the ascetic and mystical movements were at the same time distinguished scholars. Ranting in such intellectual society was just as much out of place as idle brooding and unprofitable gloom. The study of the Torah, to which they were so much devoted, was always considered a joy, and the Safed of the sixteenth century must have been a veritable Paradise on earth to any man with a tendency toward intellectual pursuits. If his interests lay in the regions of the visible, he would attend the lectures of Caro, Trani, or Sagis, and various other Rabbis at the head of the great Yeshiboth of the place. If he were mystically inclined, he would attach himself to Alkabez or Cordovero; if he had a taste for homiletics, he would go to listen to the Biblical expositions of Alsheich, whilst he might also spare an hour for the lectures of R. Samuel de Useda on the Chapters of the Fathers (*Pirke Aboth*), whose work on this ethical tractate is still considered a standard commentary. He might besides this pay a visit with profit to the ancient R. David ben Zimra, who, though at the period of his second settlement in Safed, he must already have reached the age of ninety, was still a member of the General Board mentioned above, and interested in public affairs. An occasional walk with Vital might also have possessed its own attractions, for, besides being an adept in the Cabbala, he was, like so many devotees of nature-mysticism, likewise interested in alchemy, astronomy, astrology, magic, and all kinds of occult sciences. In the way of recreation one might attend recitals of the mystical bard, R. Israel Nagara, the author of the hymn book *Zemiroth Israel*, who, though somewhat "vividly erotic" in his metaphors, counted angels among his auditors, and probably came often to Safed on visits to his father, R. Joseph Nagara, a famous scribe of that city.[116]

Safed reached the zenith of its fame with the advent of Loria.[117] R. Isaac Loria was born in Jerusalem in the year 1534. He was a descendant of the famous German family Loria, on account of which fact he was also called Isaac Ashkenazi. It is not impossible that his ancestors came from the Rhine Provinces, from which most of the earlier scions of the Loria family hailed. Elijah Loanz (flourished about the end of the sixteenth century), who claimed some relationship with our Loria, was a native of Frankfort. One branch of this family settled in Poland, whilst the other seems to have emigrated to Palestine. The emigration of German Jews to Mohammedan countries was by no means confined to this case. The impulse to this expatriation from a land in which they had lived for many centuries and in which they had almost the claim of original settlers, came from the Epistle of a certain Joseph Zarphathi, whom fate drove from Germany to Turkey in his early youth. In this Epistle he described "the happy lot of the Jews under the Crescent as compared with their hard fate under the shadow of the Cross," and called upon them to escape from the German house of bondage and emigrate to Turkey. If the German Jews, he said, could realise but a tenth part of the prosperity awaiting them in Turkey, they would brave rain and snow, and would rest neither by day nor by night before reaching there. Another inducement that he offered them was that there is a route to the Holy Land lying open to them through Turkey. Though distance forbade emigration *en masse* from Germany, there can be no doubt that Zarphathi's Epistle was not quite without effect, for we soon find small congregations, both in Turkey and in Palestine, composed of Jewish emigrants from Germany. The Caraite Elijah Bashiatsi, of Adrianople, even complained of the bad influence of these newly-arrived Rabbinical students from Germany, alarming the community with their fringes and phylacteries, and their long gowns and their hoods, making themselves conspicuous and overawing the crowds.[118]

The birth of Loria was, as in the case of so many wonder-men, heralded to his father by the prophet Elijah, who said unto him: ". . . Be it known unto thee that the Holy One, blessed be he, sent me to bring thee the good message that thy wife will bear thee a son. Thou shalt name him Isaac; he will deliver Israel from the power of the Husks (that is, the powers of evil and contamination which are at war with the powers of the good and the holy, and obscure them); and he will redeem many souls that are undergoing the agony of transmigration, and through him shall be revealed the teaching of the Cabbala to the world." He was further bidden not to begin the initiation of his son into the covenant of Abraham until aware of the prophet's presence in the synagogue. The father did as he was bidden, and the boy proved indeed a wonder-child. At the tender age of eight he was considered to be a marvel of Rabbinical learning, so that none of the Jerusalem scholars could compete with him in a Talmudical discussion. Unfortunately, the father, Solomon, died about this time, and left his widow in such needy circumstances that she was not able even to procure the necessary books which her son required for his studies. There was nothing left for them to do but emigrate to Cairo, where her brother, the wealthy tax-farmer Mordecai Francis, resided. Mordecai received them kindly, and made generous provision for his sister and those dependent upon her. Her son Loria he adopted as his own, and placed him under the care of R. Bezaleel Ashkenazi, the famous author

of the *Shittah Mekubezeth,* under whose guidance he continued his Rabbinical studies until he reached the age of
fifteen, when he married the daughter of his benefactor.[119]
His introduction to the teaching of the Cabbala followed
some two years later. According to legend, it took place in
the following way: A stranger, whose business transactions
led him to Cairo, came one day to perform his devotions at
the synagogue in which Loria was in the habit of worshipping. It so happened that he took his seat opposite Loria and
ostensibly began to read his prayers from a written book
which he held in his hands. Loria, whose curiosity was evidently aroused by the sight of the manuscript, managed to
take a glance at the volume, and was surprised to see that its
contents embodied the great mysteries of the faith. Whereupon he approached the owner of the book and questioned
him as to his person and his profession, and also demanded
from him some information as to the contents of the manuscript. The owner, who felt embarrassed by Loria's importunate questioning, stated finally that he was a mere
Marrano, and even ignorant of the Hebrew letters of the
Torah, and confessed that he was only simulating the reading
of the volume in his hands out of sheer shame before the
other worshippers, who were all reading their prayers from
the prayer-books open before them. Loria then began to urge
him to sell him the manuscript, since it was of no real value
to its owner. This request was at first refused, but afterwards
our Marrano agreed to part with his treasure on condition
that Loria would employ his good offices with his father-in-
law, the tax-farmer, to have the duties upon the wares which
he was about to import to Egypt remitted for him.

The book, as it seems, proved to be the Book of Splendour,
or *Sepher ha-Zohar,* ascribed to R. Simon ben Yochai, of the
second century, and being, as is well known, the main classic
of the Cabbalists. Loria then, for eight years, abandoned

himself to the study of the Cabbala with all the energy and "fanatical enthusiasm" of which he was capable. The principal subject of his devotion was the Zohar, but it would seem that during the first six years of his study he did not always succeed in divining the real meaning of its supposed author, Simon ben Yochai. However, he received indications from "heaven" that to reach the desired end it would be necessary for him to submit to a more austere mode of living than had been his habit until then. He thereupon retired to a certain village, in the neighbourhood of Cairo, which belonged to his father-in-law, where he built for himself a cottage on the banks of the Nile. Here he lived during the whole week, returning to his family in the city only for the Sabbath. The other six days were spent in strict solitude, and in fasting, praying, and frequent ablutions, beside other kinds of voluntary self-chastisement. This continued for two years, when Loria, by reason of his holy life and complete absorption in meditation upon the holy mysteries, reached the degree of being worthy of the gift of the Holy Spirit, as well as of having communion with the prophet Elijah. Nothing is known of Loria's occupation during the next eight or ten years, preceding his emigration to Safed. We are told that this exodus was undertaken in obedience to a distinct command from Heaven, which announced to him that his tenure of life would be a short one, and ordered him, among other things, to leave the polluted land (Egypt) and go up to Safed in Upper Galilee.[120]

It will have been observed that no mention has been made of Loria's master in the department in which he was most to excel. Legend, which has served us as the source for the preceding description, is quite silent on this point. Nor was there any real need for a master in human shape. For, according to legend, it was the prophet Elijah himself who performed the functions of teacher in the case of Loria. It is further narrated that every night Loria's soul, released from all earthly ties, would ascend to heaven in the company of the "ministering angels," who watched over him until he reached the abode of the Celestials. Upon his arrival there, he would have his choice of attending any of the super-mundane academies, in which the souls of departed saints and great sages continue the occupations which formed their moments of bliss in the course of their earthly careers. But it may be humbly suggested also that Loria had, besides, a very fair library, in which, apart from the Zohar, were contained the works of various mystics who had preceded him. We know that he occasionally referred to them, assigning to each his proper place in the chain of mystical tradition. It is also possible that in the beginning he may have received some aid from R. David ben Zimra, at that time the Chief Rabbi of Cairo, who was also a great Cabbalist; as well as from his master, Bezaleel, who is recorded as having been learned in the mysteries of the Torah.[121]

More important is the indebtedness of Loria to Cordovero. This indebtedness is suggested by a passage in the "Writings" of Loria, in which Cordovero is cited as "our master and teacher." [122] The vagueness of the plural, however, as well as the uncertainty as to the genuineness of these "Writings," make it rather hazardous to base an important biographical fact upon them. But we are fully justified in doing so after the evidence of Sambari, who reports that "Cordovero was the master of Loria for a short time," whilst Conforte describes him as a disciple-colleague of Cordovero.[123] This evidence gathers strength from certain occasional remarks in a version of the life of Loria, in which the personal relations between the two masters are not entirely obliterated. Thus we learn that among the "men of wisdom and understanding whom Loria found in Safed upon his arrival there, were Caro, Cordovero, and R. Joseph Ashkenazi." The fact that these three sages were singled out by name, would suggest that Loria came into close relationship with them. From another place it is clear that it was practically Cordovero himself who designated Loria as his successor. Naturally, legend accounts for it by a miracle. Indeed, we are told that it was only to spare Cordovero's sensitiveness that Loria hesitated so long before revealing his greatness to the world.[124] But we may conclude that while Cordovero lived, Loria occupied the inferior position—that is, that of a disciple in the presence of his master.

I lay no claim to be initiated in the science of the invisible, and am thus unable to determine with any exactness how far this indebtedness of Loria to Cordovero extended. To cite a Biblical expression frequently used in such connexion, I am merely "looking through the lattice." And what one can perceive by means of such dim vision is that all the Cabbalists laboured under an awful alternative—the dread of confusing the creature with his Creator, and the dread not less keenly felt of the *horror vacui,* or a God-less world, in addition to the well-known metaphysical, or rather physical, difficulty of the possibility of evolving a finite world from the Infinite. This dread called into being a whole system of emanations and immanations, of straight rays and reflected lights, of radiations and beams, crossing each other and commingling, and forming endless combinations, creating universes. But these universes are, on the other hand, affected by a whole series of checks and balances, or defects and faults, disabling them from becoming identical with the life permeating them, but (just because of these defects) giving them tangible substance, by which process alone the creation of the world, as we see it, becomes possible. Still, this world, notwithstanding the endless gradations and disguises and husks, is not only reached by a Divine Essence, which created it, but is pervaded by it and is full of it. Cordovero's expression with regard to the first immanations, that they are identical and not identical, may be applied also to all other developments in the scale of the universes.[125] They are just effect enough not to be entirely confused with their cause, but in such close proximity or contiguity to the cause that they cannot be thought separated from the cause. Some mystics were bold enough to declare the world not only united with God, but one with God. Even the lowest worm in this scale becomes to a certain extent identical with all the causes of worlds or emanations preceding it. There is, accordingly, a constant blending of the temporal and the eternal. Indeed, the action of the first emanation, which assumes some room for immanation, became possible only by the process of the Divine Essence concentrating itself into itself, and thus making a place for a world or the possibility of emanations. This self-concentration of the Divine, creating space for the universes, or for ideas or attributes from which a universe might evolve, is counteracted by a process of expansion, or an outflow of the Divine Essence, thus making Creation God-full. The impossibility, however, on the part of the universes, or the "vessels," to become a real receptacle for the light emitted from Divine Grace, inasmuch as the receptacle cannot be identical with the thing received, caused a deterioration in the descending *scala* of universes or worlds, which brought about the condition of chaos, in which the origin of evil is to be sought. The chaos is so thorough and so complete that evil cannot be entirely without good, indeed, it would have no existence; whilst the good, in the lower worlds at least, is not entirely free from evil. This is especially the case with this world of ours, the most substantialised. It is the world of the Husks, of mere appearances or disguises, obscuring the real realities, and but for the "sparks," or beams, of the holy and pure scattered in it, it would disappear into nothingness, and be swallowed up by its own unredeemable darkness. The elimination of evil, and the restoration of the world to Divine goodness, is the great problem under which creation is labouring.

Loria is usually described as the author of this system of Concentration, called in Hebrew *Zimzum*. Now, it is true that Cordovero, as far as I could see, only once uses this term in his *Pardes*.[126] But it should be remarked that R. Sabbatai Horwitz, the author of the *Shepha Tal* (Abundance of Dew), an avowed disciple of Cordovero, and considered the best expounder of his system, is constantly operating with Zimzum, at the same time giving the most lucid expositions of the Concentration theory to be found in any Cabbalistic book; but he never so much as mentions Loria. However, I am prepared to accept in good faith the testimony of R. Menahem Azariah of Fano, mentioned above, who spent a large fortune in procuring the writings of Cordovero and in giving them wide circulation, but who subsequently declared that the system of Loria bears the same relation to that of Cordovero as the latter sustains to the Biblical commentaries of Kimchi, which give only the simple meaning of the Scriptures and never touch on the mysteries of the Torah.[127]

Some light perhaps may be thrown on this point by a remark ascribed by legend to Cordovero himself, to the effect that Cordovero on a certain occasion expressed his opinion that there was no real disagreement between his system and that of his successor (Loria); only whilst he himself dwelt more on the aspect of the *Sephiroth* (Emanations), his successor enlarged more on the *Parzuphim,* as they are to be found in the *Idras* of the Zohar.[128] Parzuphim, a Greek term, signifies, when occurring in the regular Rabbinical literature, faces, visages, forehead, and features. The mystic seemed to use the term in the wider sense of the "full stature," comprising all parts of the human body, allegorised, sublimised, to represent attributes and ideas. Starting from the favoured notion of the mystics, conceiving man as a microcosm (or the world in miniature), virtually connected with and focussing all the different orders of creation, and pressing (rather unduly) the logical consequence involved in the Scriptural statement, "So God created man in his own image" and similar verses, the mystic reverses the process, and if he does not exactly create God in the image of man, he conceives even in the ideal universe "man in enlargement," and looks to his image for the illustration of all Existence and Generation. His language then becomes less abstract and his metaphors much bolder. He imposes on himself, it is true, absolute silence with regard to the Infinite, or the Unknowable, or the Super-Essential, who is transcendentalised beyond language and beyond thought. But more intrepid grows his phraseology when he reaches the first manifestation of the Most Hidden of all Hidden, which he terms the Original Man, or the Ideal Man (*Adam Kadmon*), the archetype of creation, endowed with certain qualities making it possible to establish likeness "between the image and him who fashioned it." The danger of this system, with its bold negations on the one hand, and its hazardous "anthropology" on the other, is evident enough and needs no further explanation. It should, however, be remarked that no one felt this danger more deeply and warned against it more emphatically than the Cabbalists themselves. It is sufficient here to refer to the compiler of the Idras, which, as just indicated, were the main source of Loria's inspiration. The Idras may, perhaps, be characterised as the mystical anatomy of the "Original Man." They dilate, naturally, upon the corporeal expressions of the Bible in connexion with the Deity, but add to them also limbs and organs of the human body not occurring in the Scriptures, describing them minutely and explaining them in a theosophic and mystical manner. But this lengthy discourse (especially the so-called Great Idra, claiming to have been promulgated in the circle of the ancient Rabbis) is prefaced by a solemn warning by R. Simon ben Yochai, the alleged hero of this gathering, not to take these metaphors and terms literally. He enjoins them to rise and lift their hands when he pronounces the anathema over those not heeding his warning, with the Scriptural words, "Cursed be the man that maketh any graven or molten image an abomination unto the Lord, the work of the hands of the craftsman, and putteth it in a secret place. And all the people shall answer, and say Amen" (Deut. 27: 15).

Loria was apparently more given to this branch of the Cabbala than to any other. This is, at least, the impression one receives on examining the works or the hymns attributed to him. There the anthropomorphistic element is more conspicuous, and the terminology more concrete than in the works of his predecessors, and it is not impossible that it was just this novel feature in his teaching which proved attractive to the more daring spirits. But there must have been, besides, something great and attractive about Loria's personality that gave him this overwhelming influence in a city so abounding in great scholars and great mystics as was Safed. This will be more clearly seen if we follow his career in his new home.

The whole ministry of Loria in Safed lasted at the utmost six years.[129] With the exception of R. David ben Zimra, whom he had known in Cairo, there is nothing on record to show that he had any connexion with the leading spirits of Safed before his settling in this city. But we find him soon, as shown before, in the society of Caro and Cordovero, the recognised heads of the Talmudic and mystical schools respectively. His relation to Cordovero was that, as we have already pointed out, of a disciple or disciple-colleague to his master. As to Caro, we are in possession of a Responsum showing that Loria solicited his advice in the decision of a civil case, which suggests a certain subordination on the part of Loria in purely Rabbinic matters. But this did not prevent Caro from being counted, according to legend, among the greatest admirers of Loria. Their relations must have grown more intimate when Loria's son became engaged to a daughter of Caro. Shlomel, to whom we owe the knowledge of this fact, reports in this connexion, in the name of Caro's widow, that when her husband came home from the banquet given in honour of this betrothal, he said to her, "My wife, I can hardly describe to you how much I profited in my knowledge of the secrets of the Torah coming from the mouth of Loria at this banquet. Not even an angel is in possession of such heavenly lore as he displayed this night, his soul being that of an ancient prophet." It should, however, be noted that Shlomel naïvely proceeds to say that Loria rather discouraged Caro in his efforts to become his disciple in the Cabbala, maintaining that Caro's soul was only fit to receive wisdom on the plane of Cordovero. As a proof of this, Loria is supposed to have given fact, that as often as he began to reveal some great mystery to Caro, the latter would fall asleep, so that Caro himself became convinced that he was not sufficiently prepared for the revelations of Loria.[130]

The ascendency of Loria probably dated from the year 1570, when he succeeded Cordovero as the head of the mystical school. But whilst Cordovero was admired and revered as a saint and a scholar, Loria was looked upon as one of those superhuman beings who, by a special act of Providence, are permitted to visit us mortals for the especial purpose of our salvation. Their real home is heaven, and they come to us only on leave of absence. According to his biographers, his face was shining like the sun, and his thoughts were chaste and holy. In his knowledge of the Divine there was none like him since the glorious days of R. Simon ben Yochai. He was, moreover, master of all the sciences. He knew physiognomy and chiromancy, and understood the conversation of the trees, and the language of the birds, and the speech of the angels. Looking at the forehead of a man he could tell at a glance from what particular source his soul was derived, and the processes of transmigration through which it had passed, and what its present mission was on earth. He also could discern the souls of the wicked which (as a punishment) had taken up their abode in woods and in stone quarries, in the beasts of the field, in insects and unclean birds. He was able to tell men their past as well as predict their future, and to prescribe for them the rules of conduct calculated to make amends for their shortcomings in a previous existence.[131]

The name under which Loria usually appears in this new hagiology is ARI (Lion), forming the anagram of the Hebrew words signifying "the Divine Rabbi Isaac," whilst his disciples and other enthusiastic followers are termed "the Lion-Whelps." Probably they included among their number several of the old Associates of Cordovero who, indeed, under the leadership of Loria seem to have become more consolidated and to have figured more prominently as a compact body than in former days. It is true that we have indications that some of the disciples of Cordovero hesitated for some time in their recognition of the new master, putting him to the test in various ways. But all opposition seems soon to have ceased, so that Loria maintained the field.[132]

The most important acquisition to the Lion-Whelps was R. Chayim Vital who, it seems, had until then pursued his

mystical studies entirely independent of the Cabbalists of
Safed. At the time of Loria's appearance on the stage, Vital
was living in Damascus, occupied in writing a commentary
on the Zohar. He paid little attention to the rumours reaching him from Safed, that a great new master had arisen in
Israel. These rumours, however, were strengthened by visions
in dreams of the night, which, according to legend, Vital
could no longer disregard, so that he determined to go to
Safed and meet Loria. They had hardly met before Vital had
occasion to learn that at last he had found a master. He soon
became the most devoted member of Loria's school and the
most active in the propagation of his teaching.[133]

The text-book of the school was the Zohar, which Loria
would expound to his disciples after due preparation for it on
their part. The Idra, referred to above, seems to have been
the object of their particular inquiry and curiosity. But it
must be remarked that even in the narrow circle of his
trusted pupils, Loria was not very communicative in the
revelation of what he considered to be the "mystery of
mysteries." The few revelations he did make were made,
according to the testimony of his disciples, only under protest, at their urgent solicitation and at the very risk of the
life of the master, he having been apparently unwilling to
reveal such great secrets to insignificant mortals. But even his
disciples could not prevail upon him to give a presentation
of his system in a book for the benefit of posterity. Nay, even
the permission to take down notes of his lectures was given
only grudgingly and, as it seems, was withdrawn subsequently.[134]

Next to the mysteries of the Torah, it was apparently the
personality of Loria himself which exercised their minds.
Loria, it is true, was vaguely known to the general population
of Safed as "the Holy Man" and "the Divine Cabbalist." Occasionally he gave an edifying lecture in some synagogue.

There is also a tradition that he was a member of the Board of Censors in Safed, composed of various Rabbis who were responsible for the morals of the city, and that he distinguished himself there by defending the honour of a woman who lay under grave suspicion.[135] According to another account, he came also in contact with the world through his business relations, to which he gave up three days of the week.[136] I do not think that this report is correct. It is more probable that he had some competency granted to him by his rich uncle and father-in-law. Be this as it may, there is no doubt that he was best known to the Associates, numbering ten or twelve, who constituted the inner circle of Loria's acquaintance and converted themselves into as many Boswells. None of his movements escaped them. They watched to see how he rose from his bed and when; how he washed his hands, how he cut his nails, how he read his prayers, how he ate his meals, and more often, how he fasted and when; how he said Grace after meals, how he addressed himself to his fellow-men, and what his relations to them were; how he prepared himself for the Sabbath, and how many garments he wore on that day; what songs he intoned during the meal, and how he cut the bread, and what shape the table had at which these meals were served. This fitted in well with their system, in which man, as already hinted, plays the important part, especially the "superman," surrounded by that Divine halo which makes him, to use a Talmudical expression, a partner of the Holy One, blessed be he, in the creation of the world.[137] In the Talmud, this distinction of creating worlds is bestowed on the man who administers justice.[138] In the Cabbala, this function of creating worlds, and not less of destroying worlds (in the case of evil-doers), is extended to all the actions of man by reason of his soul being the *plexus* of the whole scale of worlds. This makes a whole universe sensitive to all his motions. In the case of Loria arose a whole literature, dealing with what is called Attentions, or Devotions, including the rules of conduct observed by Loria. The Attentions are for the most part of a mystical nature, bearing upon Loria's interpretation of the contents of the ritual and the mystical meaning which he divined in the performance of every commandment; but there are also Attentions of more general interest.[139]

Loria's first care was naturally for the young "Lions," or the Associates, who were apparently in need of a little taming and discipline, to effect which he erected for them an "enclosure," or rather, square, a block of buildings, providing chambers also for their wives and children. Isolation from the world, though living in the world, forms a part of the programme of every mystic. But the experiment was not successful. After a few months had passed, the women began to quarrel, and imparted their grievances to their husbands, leading to unpleasantness among the Associates. This mortified Loria very deeply.[140]

The Associates were divided into two classes, probably in accordance with their knowledge of mystical lore, but this did not prevent Loria from considering them as one body in the fullest sense of the word, each of the Associates being held only as a member or a joint of the body, so that in loving himself he loved the whole organism. Loria further bade them to pray constantly one for the other, and especially to feel the distress of each other in the case of sickness and misfortune. The love of the organism, however, extended to the whole of Israel, and Loria prescribed, that before beginning prayers man should receive upon himself the affirmative commandment, "And thou shalt love thy neighbour as thyself" (Lev. 19: 17), so that he may pray for Israel, in Israel, and with Israel. And it was this overwhelming sense of his solidarity with Israel which urged him to read the Confession prescribed for Yom Kippur (Day of Atonement) in all its fullest details, explaining that though there may be sins which he himself had not committed, he felt himself to be a member of the great body of Israel whose individual members form only one great unit of souls.[141] Vital, the favourite pupil of Loria, prescribes as one of the conditions for the acquiring of the gift of the Holy Spirit, "Love all creatures, including non-Jews." [142] Loria himself was careful not to kill any living creature, be it even an insect or a worm. This was probably a result of his belief in the teaching of Metempsychosis, so prominent in Loria's system, which peopled for him the animate world with the souls of a fallen humanity, now appearing in the shapes of lower creation.[143]

Prayer, as may be expected, was to Loria one of the main functions of life, there being, according to him, no prayer in which man, by reason of his close communion with God, does not become the receptacle of new Divine light and a new outflow of Divine mercy. Every word of the ritual, every letter in it, had, besides its literal meaning, also its awful mysteries, occupying a most prominent place in the writings attributed to him or to his disciples. He saw in the lack of proper devotion during prayer the great obstacle in the way of the redemption of Israel.[144] It is hardly to be wondered at that such sublime prayer, accompanied by all the "Attentions" as Loria prescribed them, should be preceded by a series of ablutions, forming a part of the mystical programme at all times. It is reported that Loria said that physical purity, obtained by such ablutions, is greatly helpful to man, and he would perform them in the severest cold. On the other hand, it is recorded that when his mother objected to them on account of his delicate health, he would defer to her wishes cheerfully.[145]

This trait of considerateness was an essential feature of his character. He led, as we can imagine, a very simple life, dressing very plainly and spending little on himself, but he would accept the budget of his wife without a protest, and grant all the expense she considered fit.[146] It was also his custom to pay for any object required for religious purposes the amount asked, whatever it might be. Anger he declared to be the source of all evil, considering it as a sort of spiritual suicide, and though he was very tender in the treatment of his disciples, he once rebuked one of the Associates who showed too much resentment against his brother for not being sufficiently attentive to his studies.[147] The man who is betrayed into anger puts up a strange god in his heart, which is a sanctuary, and where the Divine Presence should dwell. Hence, let no man be betrayed into anger, either against a Gentile or a Jew, not even in the case when he has been robbed or insulted, but let always his mind remain calm. "The Lord, his God, is with him, and the shout of the King is in him." It is reported that the Loria Associates made it a rule not to initiate anyone into the mysteries of the Cabbala who was by temperament inclined to anger.[148] There is also a story about Loria that he would, on his walks, usually place himself behind a certain student of Safed. It seems that his disciples rather resented this humility of their master, and expostulated with him. His answer was to the effect that he could see that the student felt especially honoured by walking before him; since this was his desire, Loria thought it his duty to satisfy it; just as we, according to the Rabbinic law, are bound to provide a proper escort for the poor of noble descent, if they have been accustomed to it all their lives.[149]

It is hardly necessary to say that Loria was charitable; he had appointed times every day when he gave a certain amount of alms to the treasurer of his synagogue, but he further considered it as a solemn act, and would, as in the most important prayers, stand on his feet when he gave his

Perutah. Often he would give all the money in his possession, not looking to see whether anything remained in his pocket.[150] This is certainly against all the rules of scientific charity. I hope that we shall overlook this defect in his character when we remember the remark of a French philosopher of the eighteenth century, who said that "magnanimity owes no account of its motives to prudence."

He was especially strict in the fulfilment of the command bidding us to pay the workman his wages on the very day on which he has performed his labour (Deut. 24: 15), and it went so far with him that he would not allow himself to read the afternoon prayer before getting the necessary money to pay off debts of this kind, saying, "How dare I approach my Maker when such a commandment came within my reach and I did not accomplish it?"[151]

In this connexion, the following story may be reproduced: As we have seen, many Jews in Safed were engaged in the clothing trade. Among these was R. Abraham Galanti, referred to above. One day Galanti came to Loria asking him, as the phrase was, to "give an improvement to his soul"— that is, to tell him whether Loria had not detected that he was backward in the fulfilment of one of the commandments. Loria at first declined to comply with his wish, as Galanti was one of the scholars and saints of Safed; but after much urging, he fixed his eyes on Galanti's forehead and said to him, "that he was defective in the commandment 'Thou shalt not defraud they neighbour, neither rob him'" (Lev. 1: 913). The mystical notion is that sin and passion leave their impression on the face of man, and disfigure the image of God. Galanti went home trembling in every limb, and deeply mortified that he should have disgraced himself so far as to be involved in the sin of dishonesty. He put on sackcloth and spread ashes on his head in accordance with the usage of penitents, and called a meeting of all the hands engaged in his factory. When they arrived, he said to them: "Know ye not that I am only flesh and blood, and therefore subject to error? Accordingly, I must ask that you should examine most carefully your accounts with me, to see that I do you no wrong." Their answer was: "We have no account against you. Since we have been in the master's employ we are wanting in nothing, and the Lord has sent us his blessing. There is none among us who would think of making a bill of his demands." Thereupon the Rabbi said: "It is through your negligence in this respect that I have become the victim of sin. I will, therefore, put money before you; take what you desire, and forgive any claims you may have against me." But they would not touch the money, except one woman, who stretched out her hands and took two *Perutoth*. Galanti then went to Loria, who said, as he came out to meet him, "Why did you feel so mortified?" Galanti answered, "Is it a small matter that I should feel that I may possibly have robbed somebody? Now, if I have found grace in your eyes, tell me if the mark of this sin is still upon my forehead?" Loria answered, "No sign of sin is visible any longer," and revealed to him that the mistake consisted in the fact that this woman who had taken two *Perutoth* was one of the best weavers in his factory, and should have been better paid than the other employees. "But they are very particular in heaven about such things," said Loria, "hence the ugly mark which I perceived on you." [152]

Sabbath was the day of days with Loria and the Associates, new heavenly light reaching our sublunar regions on that day. The preparation for the Sabbath began Friday morning, when Loria would read the portion of the week from a scroll of the Pentateuch. Then would come dressing the hair, ablutions, and arraying himself in white garments in honour of the Sabbath. Early in the afternoon, Loria would form a

procession, together with the Associates, to the fields to receive there Queen Sabbath with the song, "Come, my Beloved." [153] It was on such occasions that Loria, who was
otherwise, as we have seen, rather reserved in revealing the
mysteries of the Torah, would become communicative and
uncover Divine secrets which no ear had been worthy enough
to listen to before. And not only would the living profit by
this hour of grace, but also the souls of the departed would
benefit, wandering about for eternities, and taking up their
abodes in the different kingdoms, the mineral, the vegetable,
and the animal. These would on such occasions come to
Loria, asking for his prayers to lift them up into the higher
regions. "He saw spirits everywhere, and heard their whispers
in the rushing of the water, in the movements of the trees
and grass, in the song or twittering of the birds, even in the
flickering of flames." [154] The neighbourhood of Safed, to
which legend, long before this period, had transferred from
Judæa the earthly remains of prophets and ancient sages,
became to Loria, who saw their souls hovering on the graves,
a veritable Valley of Jehoshaphat in the hour of resurrection.
He held intercourse with them, and united, in "concentrated
prayer," his soul with theirs.[155] But, above all, it was contemporary humanity which harboured these souls, if such
an expression be permissible with Loria. Indeed, recognising
as Loria did, by the process of metempsychosis, in every person he met old acquaintances from history, with whom he
had associated in a former existence, and believing further,
as he did, that it was only with the advent of the Messiah
that this transmigration of souls would cease, all limits of
space and time practically disappeared for him. To him the
"generations past and the generations to come formed with
those who are alive one single whole." All souls were evolved
from the "original soul" of Adam, derived from the dif-

ferent parts of his body, and they suffered by his Fall. All live eternally, and are swayed by almost the same passions and by the same ideals as they were before. A certain neighbour of Loria, of a quarrelsome disposition, was none else to him than Korah of old, whilst Loria himself was a spark of the soul of Moses.[156] R. Abraham Halevi, referred to above, was reported by legend to have perceived the Divine Glory during his prayers at the Holy Wall in Jerusalem. Loria thereupon discovered in him a spark of the soul of the prophet Jeremiah, who, according to a Rabbinical legend, had a similar vision on the same consecrated spot.[157] R. Moses Alsheich, again, famous, as noted above, for his homiletical works, was pregnant with the soul of R. Samuel ben Nachmani, the famous Agadist of the fourth century.[158] Loria himself and the Associates, in their present capacity as mystics, represented the reincarnation of the supposed heroes of the Zohar, headed by R. Simon ben Yochai and his son R. Eleazar.[159] Men were not to him what they were, but what they had been once, and it was their former existence which determined his relations to them. Thus it is reported that one morning his disciple R. Samuel de Useda entered the house of Loria, who was lecturing to the Associates. Loria, upon perceiving him, at once arose before him and greeted him with the words, "Blessed be he that cometh," took him by the hand, placed him at his right side, and had a long conversation with him. Vital, who was present, was curious to know why his master showed this young man so much honour, and asked him the reason. He said: It was not before him that I arose, but before the soul of R. Phinehas ben Jair, who lived some eight hundred years ago, and was especially distinguished by his acts of charity and lovingkindness. Of this soul the young man became possessed to-day. Upon inquiry, Useda confessed that that morning, on his way to the synagogue, he had passed by a house from which the voice of lamentation and crying reached his ears. When he went in, he found the tenants all naked, robbers having taken away their clothes. He at once gave them all the raiment he had on, and returned home, where he clad himself in his Sabbath garments.[160]

Such things Loria saw best on the eve of the Sabbath by the aid of the Divine light radiating from the holiness of the day to come. When the prayers and the songs in the fields were over, Loria would return home, where he would be met by his mother, whom he kissed on entering the house. As it would seem, he was accompanied by Vital, who used to spend the Sabbath with him. Then would begin, as we can imagine, the *Kiddush* (Sanctification of the day over the cup of wine), and the meal, at which any number of concentrated "Attentions" were observed. We are also in possession of three mystical songs composed by Loria himself, sung at the three meals by which the Sabbath day was distinguished.[161]

The Sabbath emitted its rays, lighting up the whole week, sanctifying even such moments of human life as those in which material needs and common passions are very little favourable to spirituality. Loria, in common with other mystics, succeeded in spiritualising the whole life of man, just as the legalist finds nothing in human affairs which is either above or below the Torah. De Vidas, referred to before, the favourite pupil of Cordovero, wrote a book, *Reshith Chochmah,* dealing with such topics as the fear of God, the love of God, holiness, humility, sin, reward and punishment, and repentance, but he did not disdain to devote whole pages to such subjects as the intimate relations or intercourse between the sexes, commerce and trade, good manners and social etiquette, all of which form a part of the sacred life.

The same thing may be observed of the pupils of Loria. The book, *Ez ha-Chayim* (The Tree of Life), ascribed to Vital and supposed to represent a compilation of the most important of Loria's teachings, is prefaced among others by this motto, "Depart from evil and do good" (Psalms 34: 14). It is followed by a number of rules, some of which we have already met with in the preceding remarks. The first of them impresses upon the mystic the necessity of the strict fulfilment of the Law in all its minutiæ, whether Scriptural or traditional.[162] "The Gates of Holiness," by Vital, gives a set of rules for those who are in search of eternal perfection, the absorption in the Divine, and is pervaded by the same spirit of loyalty to the Law, both in its ceremonial and moral parts.

Thus the Safed of the sixteenth century, at least, is free from all antinominian tendencies, which are the supposed inevitable consequences of mysticism. The Safed Jew of that period saw no antagonism of principle between Caro and Loria. Caro was for him the authority, Loria the model. But just as Loria was amenable to the discipline of the Law, so was Caro not unresponsive to the finer impulses of love and admiration.

Loria died in the year 1572 (according to some, in 1574) after a short illness of three days.[163] Vital took over the leadership, and it was under his direction that various writings and works were soon compiled and put into circulation, claiming the authority of Loria. How far Loria would have felt himself responsible for all that was then written and said in his name, is a question not to be easily decided. Probably he would have disowned a great deal of what was afterwards known as the writings of Loria. I have already referred to his hesitation in giving publicity to what he considered to be the secrets of the Torah, but he must also have felt that his highly-coloured metaphors and rich imagery might become a stumbling-block to those who had not passed through all the grades of holiness, and were not satisfied with being brought near God on the "religious-fatigue" system, but preferred to have God brought down to them. We have it also on good authority that before his death he said to his disciples, "Know for a truth that you have not a single Proposition (of the mystical lore expounded by Loria) that can be considered complete." When they said to him, "Not even R. Chayim Vital?" he answered: "Perhaps he knows a little more than you, but not much." [164]

The Propositions, however, concerned only a few exalted personages among the mystics, who made them the special subject of their studies and further development. What filtered through these Propositions and reached those who laid no claim to this title, "was not metaphysic but moral, not immanence but sin," or rather the fear of sin. The Propositions placed man, as already hinted at, upon a pedestal, the eminence of which caused giddiness to many an exalted personage, who, deeming himself a god or a demi-god, lost his balance and fell beyond hope of redemption. The great majority of Israel remained mindful of the old warning, "Be not rash with thy mouth, and let not thine heart be hasty to utter anything before God: for God is in heaven, and thou upon earth: therefore let thy words be few" (Eccles. 5:2). Haste and rashness became especially discredited after the bursting of that theological bubble known in history as the Pseudo-Messianic claims of Sabbatai Zebi. The Propositions, with the over-emphasis of the God-likeness of man, were only allowed to stand so far as God-likeness demanded superior holiness on the part of man. With a proper instinct the people at large left the *Ez ha-Chayim* by Vital, with its Propositions, to the few, and it lasted nearly two centuries till it first appeared in print; but his book "The Gates of Holiness," with its deeply ethical contents, became at once a popular tract, and passed through many editions. Likewise, the Jewish public took but little notice of R. Moses Chayim Luzzatto's "One Hundred and Thirty-Eight Doors of Wisdom," but it did appreciate at once his noble "Path of the Upright," preaching morality and holiness. The book is constantly going through new editions, and in certain parts of the East there are special "Path of the Upright Societies" devoted to the study of this book. The Safed influence is especially marked on the devotional works of R. Isaiah Horwitz, R. Aaron Kaydanower, and R. Elijah Cohen, which works became the common spiritual good of the people. Their morality is austere, their tone sombre, and their demands on man's religious capabilities exacting. All this is traceable enough in the work of the Safed penitents. They certainly have not erred on the line of self-complacency and self-righteousness. They warn man not to behave "as so many fools do," who are so over-confident of their salvation because they are engaged in their trade the whole day, recite punctually the three prescribed prayers for the day, and neither steal nor rob nor commit any other acts of gross immorality, and harm nobody. These are cheap virtues, according to our moralists, of which even the Gentiles are not devoid, and which one's neighbours from motives of self-preservation would compel one to observe. What justifies man to entertain exalted hopes of the "world to come" is, according to the stern moralists, the minute observance of the Law in all its details "in great love," the constant increasing in the quality of saintliness, the possession of the quality to please God and man, and the readiness to give up his life in perfect joy for the sake of the love of God. On the other hand, they have, as indicated above, retained enough of the Safed emphasis of the God-likeness of man to disregard in the end the dualism of flesh and spirit, a conception un-Jewish in its origin, and now revived only under a mistaken notion of "spirituality." In spite of the ascetic teachings, with their depreciation of the "turbid body," to be threatened by the terrors of hell and cajoled by the joys of paradise, they were thus able to insist upon the holiness of the flesh (*Kedushath ha-Guph*) and upon its purity as much as upon that of the soul, as well as to accord to the flesh a share in the bliss to come, held out to man as a consequence of a holy and religious life, which a supercilious philosophy entirely denied.[165]

Caro passed away in 1575, Trani five years later (1580). The decline of Safed soon set in. Samson Bak, who travelled in Palestine in 1588, was compelled to leave Safed for Jerusalem on account of the distress which had overtaken the former city at that period. R. Isaiah Horwitz, who settled in Palestine soon after the beginning of the seventeenth century, describes the Jerusalem population as richer in numbers than that of Safed.[166]

The men who succeeded Caro and Loria were, for the most part, their disciples. R. Moses Galanti, an ordained disciple of Caro and an adherent of Loria, R. Yomtob Zahalon, described as the head of the city of Safed and of the Yeshibah, and R. Joseph Trani, the son of R. Moses Trani, who obtained in later life even more distinction than his famous father, seem to be the most prominent names of this period. At least this is the impression we receive from their Responsa collections, in which they figure as men of weight and authority. They still meet in the general board; and in a document giving the minutes of such a meeting dating from the first decade of the seventeenth century, we have the signatures of not less than twenty Rabbis, with some of whom he made acquaintance in the former pages. Mention is also made of a Rabbi Joshua ben Nun, who is described as the Chief Rabbi and the head of all the heads of the colleges, and who was, besides, the administrator of all the charities of the city. The old devotion to the study of the Torah and the occupation with mystical literature are still continued. After they finished their prayers, the whole congregation formed themselves into groups, listening to lectures on such subjects as Bible, Halachah, Hagadah, or the Zohar, so that none left the Synagogue to go to business before he gave some time to study. The fifh day in the week (Thursday) seems to have been a special day of devotion, when they would all gather in one big synagogue to pray for Israel and to bless those who sent support for the poor of the Holy Land. The service would conclude with a sermon by Galanti and other men distinguished for their humility and saintliness. It is not impossible that this synagogue was the one built by a wealthy man in Constantinople in memory of Loria, and richly endowed by him.[167] None, however, was sufficiently great to make his authority felt in such a way as to give him any real prominence over his contemporaries. Even Vital's authority does not seem to have been quite undisputed. He afterwards left Safed and died in Damascus in 1620, and the sons of Caro and Trani emigrated to Turkey. The Chmielnicki persecutions of the middle of the seventeenth century, which must have taxed the resources of Jewry to its utmost, probably withdrew a good deal of the support which Safed had received till then for its Talmudical Colleges; whilst the excesses of certain Cabbalists about the same period, who joined pseudo-Messiah movements, must have put a damper upon the zeal of the mystics and the study of mysticism which was the special glory of Safed.

Safed thus ceases to be a centre of attraction. It decays slowly, and Jerusalem comes to its rights. It lives on the past, profiting by the glory of Caro, Trani, Loria, and Cordovero. Even to-day the Synagogue of Caro and the Synagogue of Loria form the main sights in Safed. But it is not any longer the Safed of the sixteenth century.

9

RABBI ELIJAH WILNA, GAON

THE three great stars of German literature are usually characterised by German scholars in the following way: Goethe
they say represents the beautiful, Schiller the ideal, while
Lessing represents truth. I think that we may apply the
same characteristics to the three great luminaries, with which
the Jewish middle ages ceased—for as Zunz somewhere
remarked, the Jewish middle ages lasted till the beginning
of the eighteenth century—and the modern age of Judaism
opened. I am thinking of Mendelssohn in Germany, Israel
Baalshem, the founder of the sect of the Chassidim in
Podolia, and Elijah Wilna, or as he is more frequently called,
the Gaon,[1] the Great One, in Lithuania.

As to Mendelssohn, enough, and perhaps more than
enough, has already been written and spoken about his
merits in awakening the sense for the beautiful and the
harmonious which was almost entirely dormant among the
Jews of his age. In regard to the second, namely, Israel
Baalshem, I have only to refer the reader to the sixth essay
in this volume. The subject of the present essay will be R.
Elijah Wilna, who, among the Jews, as Lessing among the

Germans, represented truth, both by his life and by his literary activity.

I say that the Gaon represented truth, but these words must be taken *cum grano salis*. For I do not mean at all to say that he was in possession of the whole truth, still less in *exclusive* possession of it. It is true as we shall learn in the course of this essay, that the Gaon was a genius of the first order. But there are matters of truth, the obtaining of which cannot be accomplished by genius alone. R. Elijah Wilna did not know any other language than Hebrew. Truths, therefore, which are only to be reached through the medium of other languages, remained a secret to him. Again, records of ancient times which are buried in the shelves of remote libraries or under the ruins of past civilisations are not always a matter of intuition. Even the most gifted of men have to wait patiently till these are brought to light by the aid of spade and shovel, or the pen of some obscure copyist. But R. Elijah lived at a time when excavation had as yet done very little for Semitic studies, and when a Jew scarcely got admittance into the great libraries of Europe. Thus much truth which we get now in a very easy way was beyond this seer's eye.

But even if all the libraries on earth had been at his disposal, even if he had read all the cuneiform writings which ornament the British Museum, and had deciphered all the Hieroglyphics which the Louvre possesses, even in that case we should not be justified in terming him a representative of the truth, without qualifying our words.

"Truth," said the old Rabbis, "is the Seal of the Holy One, praised be He." But Heaven has no Lord Chancellor. Neither men nor angels are trusted with the great Seal. They are only allowed to catch a glimpse of it, or rather to long after this glimpse. However, even the longing and effort for this glimpse will bring man into communion with God, and make his life divine. And the life of the Gaon was, as we shall see, one long effort and unceasing longing after the truth.

Again, if I say that the Gaon represented truth, you must not think that he lacked the two other qualities. A life entirely devoted to such a great cause as that of seeking the truth is, *ipso facto,* ideal and harmonious. It is only in his influence on Judaism—more particularly on the Jews in the North of Europe—that this feature in his life becomes more prominent than his other admirable qualities.

In what this truth consisted, how the Gaon arrived at it, and by what means he conveyed it to others, we shall see in the course of this essay.

R. Elijah was born at Wilna in the year 1720. His father, Solomon Wilna, is called by his biographers the great Rabbi Solomon, and is said to have been the descendant of R. Moses Rivkas, the author of a learned work, containing notes to the Code of the Law by R. Joseph Caro.[2]

Having quoted the biographers, I must point out that there are only two biographies of the Gaon: the one by Finn, in his book *Faithful City,*[3] on the celebrities of Wilna, the other by Nachman of Horodna, in his book *Ascension of Elijah.*[4] The former is a very honest account of the Gaon's life, but a little too short. The latter is too long, or rather too much intermixed with that sort of absurd legend, the authors of which are incapable of marking the line which separates the monster from the hero.

Even in the region of imagination we must not for a moment forget the good advice given to us by one of our greatest scholars who had to deal with a kindred subject: "He," says this scholar, "who banishes the thought of higher and lower from his study, degrades it into a mere means of gratifying his curiosity, and disqualifies it for the lofty task which it is called upon to perform for modern society." We shall thus cling to the higher and stop at the hero.

Our hero was the first-born of five brothers. They were all famous men in their little world. According to the tradition in Wilna, Elijah was a lovely child, with beautiful eyes, and goodly to look at, or as it is expressed in another place, "as beautiful as an angel!" The tradition, or rather the legend, relates that as a child of six years he was already the pupil of R. Moses Margalith, the famous author of a commentary on the Talmud of Jerusalem. At the age of seven years he is said to have already perplexed the Chief Rabbi of his native town by his controversial skill in Talmudical subjects. At the early age of nine he was acquainted with the contents of the Bible, the Mishnah, the Talmud and its ancient commentaries; and even the Cabbalistic works of R. Isaac Loria were no secret to the youthful scholar.[5] At the age of twelve years he is said to have acquired the seven liberal arts, and to have puzzled the scholars of Wilna by his astronomical knowledge. At thirteen, when according to Jewish law he attained his majority, he was already the accomplished or "the great one" (Gaon); so far tradition. I am afraid that tradition is here, against all experience, too exact in its dates. But we may learn from it that the child Elijah showed many signs of the future Gaon, and was therefore considered as the prodigy of his age. Again it is likewise pretty certain that no man could boast of having been the master of Elijah. He was not the product of any school, nor was he biassed by the many prejudices of his time. He was allowed to walk his own way in his struggle after truth.

It is rather an unfortunate thing that history is so much made up of parallels and contrasts that the historian or even the biographer cannot possibly point out the greatness of some men without touching, however slightly, on the smallness of others. It is only natural that every strong shining object should push the minor lights of its surroundings into the background and darken them. Thus, when we are speaking of the superiority of the Gaon, we cannot escape hinting at least at the shortcomings of his contemporaries, as well as of his predecessors.

To indicate briefly in what this superiority consisted, I will premise here a few words from a Responsum by one of his great predecessors, the Gaon Rabbi Hai.[6] Consulted by a student as to the meaning of certain mystical passages in the tractate *Chagigah*,[7] Rabbi Hai, in warning his correspondent not to expect from him a long philosophical dissertation, writes as follows: "Know that it never was our business to palliate matters and explain them in a way of which the author never could have thought. This is fashionable with other people, but our method is to explain the words of this or that authority in accordance with his own meaning. We do not pledge ourselves that this meaning is 'right rule' in itself, for there *do* exist statements made by the old authorities that cannot be accepted as norm." Thus far the words of the Gaon of the tenth century, which speak volumes. The Gaon of the eighteenth century followed the same course. All his efforts were directed to this point; namely, to find out the true meaning of the Mishnah, the true meaning of the Gemara,[8] the true meaning of the Gaonim, the true meaning of the great codifiers, and the true meaning of the commentators on the ancient Rabbinical literature. Whether this meaning would be acceptable to us mattered very little to him. His only object was to understand the words of his predecessors, and this he obtained, as we shall soon see, by the best critical means. This was the method of the Gaon; that of other scholars (at least of the great majority) was dictated by entirely different considerations. They would not suffer the idea that the great man could be wrong at times. To them, all that he said was "right rule." Now suppose a great author like Maimonides had overlooked an important passage in the Talmud or any other statement by a great authority, the alternative remaining to them was either to explain away the passage of the Talmud or to give the words of Maimonides a strange meaning. This led originally to the famous method of the *Pilpul* (casuistry), a kind of spiritual gymnastic, which R. Liva of Prague in the sixteenth century, and many others condemned as most pernicious to Judaism and leading to the decay of the study of the Torah.

Now it is beyond doubt that the method of the two Gaonim is the only right one. But, in justice to the casuistic school, which includes many a great name, it is only right to remember that this impartiality towards acknowledged authorities as maintained by our hero is not at all such an easy matter as we imagine. We quote often with great satisfaction the famous saying, *Amicus Plato, amicus Socrates, sed magis amica veritas,* "Plato is our friend, so is Socrates, but Truth is, or rather ought to be, our greatest friend." This sounds very nicely, but let us only realise what difficulties it involves. To be a friend of Socrates or Plato means to know them, or in other words to have a thorough knowledge of the writings of the one and the recorded utterances of the other. But such a knowledge can with most men only be obtained by devoting one's *whole* life to the study of their works, so that there is not left much time for new friendships. And the few who are able to save a few years after long wanderings with these Greek philosophers, seldom see the necessity of new friendships. For what else did those long courtships of Plato or Aristotle mean except that those who conducted them thought that thereby they would wed Truth?

This impartiality is the more difficult when these friends are invested with a kind of religious authority where humility and submission are most important factors. The history of Lanfranc, the predecessor of Anselm of Canterbury, gives a striking example of what this submission meant in the Middle Ages. One day, we are told, when he was still an ordinary monk, he was reading at the table and pronounced a word as it ought to be pronounced, but not as seemed right to the person presiding, who bade him say it differently; "as if he had said *docēre*, with the middle syllable long, as is right, and the other had corrected it into *docĕre*, with the middle short, which is wrong; for that Prior was not a scholar. But the wise man, knowing that he owed obedience rather to Christ than to Donatus, the grammarian, gave up his pronunciation, and said what he was wrongly told to say; for to make a short syllable long, or a long one short, he knew to be no deadly sin, but not to obey one set over him in God's behalf was no light transgression." [9]

But this admiration—and here we turn again to the Gaon—must not prevent us from believing that Providence is not confined to such ungrammatical Priors, and that the men who are really working on behalf of God are those who teach us to pronounce rightly, and to think rightly, and to take matters as they are, not as we desire them to be on account of our friends.

As for the critical means to which I have alluded, the Gaon himself said somewhere that simplicity is the best criterion of truth, and this is the most characteristic feature of all his literary career. The Gaon studied Hebrew grammar in order to obtain a clear notion of the language in which the Scriptures are written. He tried to attain to the knowledge of the Bible by reading the Bible itself; and was not satisfied to become acquainted with its contents from the numerous quotations which are made from it in Rabbinical literature. Again, he studied mathematics, astronomy, and philosophy, as far as they could be found in Hebrew books. Certainly the Gaon did not study these subjects for their own sake, and they were considered by him only as a means to the end, or as the phrase goes, as the "hand-maidens" of Theology, the queen of all sciences. But it may be looked upon as a mark of great progress in an age when Queen Theology had become rather sulky, continually finding fault with her hand-maidens, and stigmatising every attention paid to them as conducive to disloyalty. To these accusations the Gaon answered that Queen Theology does not study her own interests. Knowledge of all arts and sciences, the Gaon maintained, is necessary for the real understanding of the Torah which embraces the whole of them. From his own writings it is evident that he himself was familiar with Euclid, and his *Ayil Meshulash* contains several original developments of Euclid. It was at his suggestion that a certain Baruch of Sclow translated Euclid into the Hebrew language.

Another way which led the Gaon to the discovery of many truths was his study of the pre-Talmudic literature, and of the Jerusalem Talmud. By some accident or other it came to pass that only the Babylonian Talmud was recognised as a guide *in the practices of religious life*. As the great teachers and their pupils cared more for satisfying the religious wants of their flocks than for theoretic researches, the consequence was that a most important part of the ancient Rabbinic literature was almost entirely neglected by them for many centuries. And it was certainly no exaggeration, when R. Elijah said that even the Gaonim and Maimonides, occupied as they were with the practical part of the law, did not pay sufficient attention to the Talmud of Jerusalem and the Tosephta.[10] The Gaon was no official head of any Jewish community, and was but little troubled by decisions of questions which concern daily life. He was thus in a position to leave for a little while the Babylonian Talmud and to become acquainted with the guides of the guide. I refer to Siphra, Siphré, Mechilta, Tosephta, the *Seder Olam*,[11] the Minor Tractates,[12] and above all the Talmud of Jerusalem, which, regarded from an historical and critical point of view, is even of more importance than its Babylonian twin-brother. But by this means there came a new light upon the whole of ancient Rabbinic literature. The words of the Torah, the Midrash says, are poor in one place, but we shall find them rich in another place. The Gaon by his acquaintance with the *whole* of the Torah had no difficulty whatever in discovering the rich places. If there was a difficult passage in this or that Tractate, he showed, by giving a reference to some other place, that it was wanting in some words or lines. Obscure passages in the Mishnah he tried to elucidate by parallel passages in the Tosephta. The too complicated controversies of the Babylonian Talmud he tried to explain by comparing them with the more ancient and more simple Talmud of Jerusalem.

There is little to be told of the Gaon's private affairs. Even the date of his marriage with a certain Miss Anna of Kaidon is not mentioned by his biographers. But it may be taken for granted that, in accordance with the custom in Poland, he married at a very early age, say about eighteen years. It was also when a young man that he travelled for some years through Poland and Germany. It is rather difficult to say what his object may have been in making these travels —for the Gaon was not the man to travel for pleasure's sake. Perhaps it was to become acquainted with the great Rabbis of these countries. It is also possible, as others maintain, that the Gaon considered the many privations which a traveller had to endure a hundred and fifty years ago, as an atonement for his imaginary sins. Indeed we find in many ascetic books that travelling, or as they term it "receiving upon oneself to be banished into the exile," [13] is recommended as a very successful substitute for penance. At least it seems that the coachmen whom the Gaon employed on his journeys looked at it from this point of view. One of them went so far in adding to the privations of the Gaon as to run away with his carriage when the Rabbi alighted from it in order to read his prayers. But the reading of the Eighteen Benedictions[14] must not be interrupted excepting in the case of danger; and the Gaon did not consider it very dangerous to be left without money and without luggage.

These travels ended in the year 1745. The Gaon left Wilna again at a later date with the purpose of going to Palestine and settling there. But he found so many obstacles on his way that he was soon compelled to give up his favourite plan and to return to his native town. It is not known whether he left Wilna again.

The position which the Gaon occupied in Wilna was, as already hinted, that of a private man. He could never be prevailed upon to accept the post of Rabbi or any other office in a Jewish community. I am unable to give the reason for his declining all the offers made to him in this direction. But it may be suggested here that it was in the time of the Gaon that there arose a bitter struggle between the Rabbi and the Jewish wardens of his native town, which ended in the abolition of the office of Rabbi. The history of the struggle is the more irritating, as it arose from the pettiest reasons imaginable. People actually discovered that there was no light in the house of the Rabbi after the middle of the night, which fact might lead to the conclusion that he did not study later than twelve o'clock P.M. What an idle man! And this idleness was the less pardonable in the eyes of the community, as the Rabbi's wife was so unfortunate as not to have been polite enough to some Mrs. Warden. Under such circumstances we must not wonder if the Gaon did not find it very desirable to meddle with congregational affairs in an official capacity. The relation of the Gaon to his contemporaries resembles rather the position in the olden times of a Tanna or Amora,[15] who neither enjoyed the title of Nasin or that of Ab Beth Din.[16] Like R. Akiba, or Mar Samuel, the Gaon became influential among his contemporaries only by his teaching and his exemplary life.

It must be said in praise of the Jews of Wilna that, notwithstanding their petty behavior towards their ecclesiastical chief, they willingly submitted to the authority of the Gaon (who was devoid of all official authority). They revered him as a saint. To converse with the Gaon was considered as a happy event in the life of a Jew in Wilna, to be of any use to him as the greatest distinction a man could attain on earth. But what is remarkable is the readiness with which even scholars acknowledged the authority of the Gaon. Scholars are usually more slow in recognising greatness than simple mortals. Every new luminary does not only outshine their minor lights and thus hurt their personal vanity, but it threatens also sometimes to obscure certain traditions which they wish to keep prominently in view. But the literary genius of the Gaon was too great to be opposed with success, and his piety and devotion to religion far above suspicion. Thus the Gaon was very soon recognised by his contemporaries as their master and guide; not only in literary questions, but also in matters of belief and conduct.

It would lead me too far to name here all the Gaon's disciples. It seems as if all the great scholars in his country considered themselves to be more or less his pupils. The Gaon used to give in the Beth Hammidrash, which he founded, public lectures on various subjects, and the students who attended these lectures also claimed the honour of being called his pupils. I shall mention here only his greatest disciple, R. Chayim Walosin, who, after the Gaon, influenced his countrymen more than any other scholar of that time. This R. Chayim also did not occupy any official post among his brethren. He was a cloth manufacturer by profession, and was very prosperous in his business. But it did not prevent him from being devoted to Hebrew literature, and he enjoyed a wide-spread fame as a great scholar. But as soon as the fame of the Gaon reached him, he left cloth manufactory and scholarship behind, and went to Wilna to "learn Torah" from the mouth of the great master. It must be noticed that even the giving up of his claim to scholarship was no little sacrifice. All our learning, said some scholar in Wilna, disappeared as soon as we crossed the threshold of the Gaon's house. He made every disciple who came into close contact with him begin at the beginning. He taught them Hebrew grammar, Bible, Mishnah, and many other subjects, which were, as already mentioned, very often neglected by the Talmudists of that time. R. Chayim had also to go through all this course. Some would have considered such treatment a degradation. R. Chayim, however, became the more attached to his master for it.

In such a way the life of the Gaon was spent, studying by himself or teaching his pupils. It must be understood that to learn Torah meant for the Gaon more than mere brain work for the purpose of gaining knowledge. To him it was a kind of service to God. Contemporaries who watched him when he was studying the Torah observed that the effect wrought on the personality of the Gaon was the same as when he was praying. With every word his countenance flushed with joy; with every line he was gaining strength for proceeding further. Only by looking at matters from this point of view shall we be able to understand the devotion and the love of the Gaon for study.

There has been, no doubt, among the Russian Jews a strong tendency to exaggerate the intellectual qualities of the Gaon. But one can readily excuse such a tendency. He was gifted by nature with such a wonderful memory that, having read a book once, he was able to recite it by heart for the rest of his life. Not less admirable was his sure grasp.

The most complicated controversies in the Talmud, into which other scholars would require whole days and weeks to find their way, the Gaon was able to read by a glance at the pages. Already as a boy he is said to have gone through in a single night the tractates *Zebachim* and *Menachoth*,[17] containing not less than two hundred and thirty pages, the contents of which are sometimes so difficult as to make even an aged scholar despair of understanding them. Again, he possessed so much common-sense that all the intellectual tricks of the casuistic schools did not exist for him. And nevertheless his biographers tell us that he was so much occupied by his studies, that he could not spare more than one hour and a half for sleep out of twenty-four hours. This is, no doubt, an exaggeration. But let us say five hours a day. He had not time to take his meals regularly. He used also, according to tradition, to repeat every chapter in the Bible, every passage in the Talmud, hundreds of times, even if they presented no difficulty at all. But it was, as already said, a matter of love for the Gaon; of love, not of passing affection.

Nothing on earth could be more despicable to the Gaon than amateurs who dabble with ancient literature. To understand a thing clearly made him happy. He is said to have spent more than six months on a single Mishnah in the tractate *Kilayim*,[18] and felt himself the happiest man when he succeeded in grasping its real meaning. Not to be able to go into the depth of a subject, to miss the truth embedded in a single passage, caused him the most bitter grief. A story told by his pupil, R. Chayim, may illustrate this fact. One Friday, narrates R. Chayim, the servant of the Gaon came to him with the message that his master wanted to see him as soon as possible. R. Chayim went instantly. When he came into the house, he found the Gaon lying in bed with a bandage on his head and looking very ill. The wife of the Gaon also reported to him that it was more than three days since her husband had taken any food, and that he had hardly enjoyed any sleep all this time. All this misery was caused by reason of not having been able to understand some difficult passages in the Talmud of Jerusalem. The Gaon now asked his disciples to resume with him their researches. Heaven, he said, might have mercy upon them and open their eyes, for it is written, "Two are better than one": and lo! Heaven did have mercy on them; they succeeded in getting the true meaning of the passage. The Gaon recovered instantly, and master and disciple had a very joyful Sabbath.

He is also reported to have said on one occasion, he would not like to have an angel for his teacher who would reveal to him all the mysteries of the Torah. Such a condition is only befitting the world to come, but in *this* world only things which are acquired by hard labour and great struggle are of any value. The German representative of truth expressed the same thought in other words, which are well worth repeating here: "Did the Almighty," says Lessing, "holding in His right hand Truth and in His left Search after Truth, deign to tender me the one I might prefer, in all humility and without hesitation I should select Search after Truth."

This absorption of all his being in the study of the Torah may also, I think, account for the fact that his biographers have so little to say about the family of the Gaon. Of his wife, we know only that she died in the year 1783. Not much fuller is our knowledge about his children. The biographers speak of them as of the family "which the Lord has blessed," referring to his two sons, Rabbi Aryeh Leb and Rabbi Abraham, who were known as great scholars and very pious men. The latter one is best known by his edition of a collection of smaller Midrashim. Mention is also made of the Gaon's sons-in-law, especially one Rabbi Moses of Pinsk. But this is all, and we are told nothing either about their lives or their callings. From his famous letter which he sent to his family when on his way to Palestine, we see that he was rather what one may call a severe father. He bids his wife punish his children most severely for swearing, scolding, and speaking untruth. He also advises her to live as retired a life as possible. Retirement he considers as a condition *sine qua non* for a religious life. He even advises his daughter to read her prayers at home, for in the synagogue she may get envious of the finer dresses of her friends, which is a most terrible sin. The only tender feature in this letter is perhaps where he implores his wife to be kind to his mother on account of her being a widow, and it were a great sin to cause her the least annoyance. From other passages we may gather that his family had at times to suffer hunger and cold by the excessive occupation of their father with the study of the Torah and other religious works. In short, the Gaon was a one-sided, severe ascetic, and would never have deserved the title of a good father, a good husband, an amiable man or any other appellation derived from those ordinary "household decencies" which, as Macaulay informs us, half of the tombstones claim for those who lie behind them. But I am very much afraid that many a great man who has made his mark in history could never claim these household virtues as his own. I do not want to enter here into the question whether Judaism be an ascetic religion or not. But even those who think Judaism identical with what is called "making the best of this life," will not dispute the fact that Jewish literature contains within it enough ascetic elements to justify the conduct of our greatest men whose lives were one long-continued self-denial and privation. "The Torah," says the Talmud, "cannot be obtained unless a man is prepared to give his life for it," or as the Talmud puts it, in another place, "if it be thy desire not to die, cease to live before thou diest." This was the principle by which the Gaon's life was actuated. And as he did not spare himself, he could not spare others. We could not expect him to act differently. The Scriptures tell us: "Thou shalt love thy neighbour as thyself." But how is it with the man who never loved himself, who never gave a thought to himself, who never lived for himself, but only for what he considered to be his duty and his mission from God on earth? Such a man we cannot expect to spend his time on coaxing and caressing us. As to the charge of one-sidedness at which I have hinted, if the giving up of everything else for the purpose of devoting oneself to a scholarly and saintly life is one-sidedness, the Gaon must certainly bear this charge; but in a world where there are so many on the other side, we ought, I think, to be only too grateful to Providence for sending us from time to time great and strong one-sided men, who, by their counterbalancing influence, bring God's spoilt world to a certain equilibrium again. To appease my more tender readers, I should like only to say that there is no occasion at all for pitying Mrs. Gaon. It would be a miserable world indeed if a good digestion and stupidity were, as a certain author maintained, the only conditions of happiness. Saints are happy in their sufferings, and noble souls find their happiness in sacrificing themselves for these sufferers.

Another severe feature in the life of the Gaon showed itself in his dispute with the Chassidim. I regret not to be able to enter here even into a brief account of the history of this struggle. I shall only take leave to say that I am afraid each party was right, the Gaon as well as the Chassidim; the latter, in attacking the Rabbis of their time, who mostly belonged to the casuistic schools, and in their intellectual pursuits almost entirely neglected the emotional side of religion; but none the less was the Gaon right in opposing a system which, as I have shown above, involved the danger of leading to a worship of men.

Excepting this incident, the Gaon never meddled with public affairs. He lived in retirement, always occupied with his own education and that of his disciples and friends. It is most remarkable that, in spite of his hard work and the many privations he had to endure, he enjoyed good health almost all his life. He never consulted a doctor. It was not until the year 1791, in the seventieth year of his life, that he began to feel the decline of his health. But he was not much interrupted by the failure of his powers. As a means of recovery, he esteemed very highly the conversation of the preacher Jacob of Dubna, better known as the Dubna Maggid,[19] whose parables and sallies of wit the Gaon used to enjoy very much. On the eve of the Day of Atonement in the year 1797, he fell very ill and gave his blessing to his children. He died on the third day of the Feast of Tabernacles, with the branch of the Lulab[20] in his hands. The Feast of Joy, relates a contemporary, was turned into days of mourning. In all the streets of Wilna were heard only lamenting and crying voices. The funeral orations delivered on this occasion in Wilna, as well as in other Jewish communities, would form a small library. His disciples wept for their master, the people of Wilna for the ornament of their native town, and the feeling of the Jews in general was that "the Ark of God was taken away."

After the foregoing sketch, the reader will hardly expect me to give an account of the Gaon's literary productions. The results of so long a life and such powers of mind devoted to one cause with such zeal and fervour, would furnish by themselves the subject of a whole series of essays. The tombstone set on his grave by his pious admirers bears the inscription, "The Gaon gave heed and sought and set in order" —that is to say, he wrote commentaries or notes on—"the Bible, the Mishnah, both Talmuds, the *Siphré, Siphra*, the *Zohar,* and many other works." Inscriptions on tombstones are proverbial for exaggeration, and we all know the saying, "as mendacious as an epitaph." But a glance at the catalogue of the British Museum under the heading of Elijah Wilna, will show that this inscription makes a praiseworthy exception. We will find that this list might be lengthened by many other works of great importance for Jewish life and thought. His commentary to the Code of R. Joseph Caro, in which one will find that in many cases he knew the sources of the religious customs and usages, put together in this work, better than its compiler himself, would have been sufficient to place him at the head of Halachic scholarship, whilst his notes and textual emendations to the *Tosephta* and *Seder Olam,* to the restoration of which he contributed so much, would have sufficed to establish his fame as a critic of the first order. And this is the more astonishing when we consider that all this was done without manuscripts or any other aid, and by mere intuition. We cannot wonder that scholars who had the opportunity of visiting great libraries and saw how the emendations of the Gaon agreed sometimes with the readings given in the best manuscripts exclaimed very often: "Only by inspiration could he have found out these secrets." We have no need to go so far; we shall simply say with the Talmud, "The powers of the real sage surpass those of the prophet." Nay, even had we possessed only his *Gleanings,* which form a kind of *obiter dicta* on various topics of Jewish literature, the Gaon would have remained a model of clear thinking and real ingenuity for all future generations.

However, a real appreciation of the Gaon's greatness as a scholar would only be possible either by a thorough study of his works, to which I have alluded, or by giving many specimens of them. The short space I am limited to makes such an undertaking impossible. I shall therefore use what remains to me to say a few words on the salutary influence the Gaon had on his countrymen, the Russian Jews.

The Russian Jew is still a riddle to us. We know this strange being only from the Reports of the Board of Guardians or from bombastic phrases in public speeches; for he has always been the victim of platform orators,

> So over violent or over civil,
> That every man with them is God or Devil.

From all, however, that I can gather from the best Jewish writers in Russia, I can only judge that the Russian Jew, when transplanted to a foreign soil, where he is cut off from the past and uncertain of his future, is for the time at least in a position in which his true character cannot be truly estimated. His real life is to be sought in his own country. There, amidst his friends and kinsmen who are all animated by the same ideals, attached to the same traditions, and proud of the same religious and charitable institutions, everything is full of life and meaning to him. Thus, a certain Russian writer addresses his younger colleagues who find so much fault with the bygone world: "Go and see how rich we always were in excellent men. In every town and every village you would find scholars, saints, and philanthropists. Their merits could sustain worlds, and each of them was an ornament of Israel." And he proceeds to give dozens of names of such excellent men, who are not all indeed known to us, but with whom the Russian Jew connects many noble and pious reminiscences of real greatness and heroic self-denial, and of whom he is justly proud.

The focus, however, of all this spiritual life is the Yeshibah (Talmudical College)[21] in Walosin. I hope that a glance at its history and constitution will not be found uninteresting. The intellectual originator of this institution which bears the name *Yeshibah Ets Chayim* (Tree of Life College),[22] was the Gaon himself. Being convinced that the study of the Torah is the very life of Judaism, but that this study must be

conducted in a scientific, not in a scholastic way, he bade his
chief disciple, the R. Chayim already mentioned, to found a
college in which Rabbinical literature should be taught according to his own true method. It would seem that, as long
as the Gaon was alive, R. Chayim preferred to be a pupil
rather than a teacher. When, however, the Gaon died, R.
Chayim did not rest till he had carried out the command
of his master, and in the year 1803 the College was opened in
Walosin. The cloth manufacturer and disciple now became
Rabbi and master. He began on a small scale, teaching at first
only a few pupils. But even for the sustenance of a small
number he had not sufficient means, and his pious wife sold
her jewellery to help him in accomplishing his favourite
plan. This is the best refutation of the French proverb *avare
comme une Rabbine.* The number, however, increased daily,
and before he died (1828), he was fortunate enough to lecture
to a hundred students. The number of students in the year
1888 amounted to 400, and the Russian Jews are thus right in
asserting that they have the greatest Talmudical College in
the world. It is evident that no private charity by a single
man, however great, could suffice to maintain such large
numbers. Thus R. Chayim was already compelled to appeal
to the liberality of his Russian brethren. The name of R.
Chayim, and the still greater name of his master, were recom-
mendation enough, and besides private offerings, many communities promised large sums towards supporting the students in Walosin. From time to time also messengers are sent
out by the committee to promote the interests of the Yeshibah. The writers to whom I owe these data tell us that these
messengers travel to all parts of the world to collect offerings
for Walosin: so that it is a standing joke with the students
that the existence of the mythical river Sambatyon[23] may be
questioned after all, otherwise it must long have been discovered by these messengers who explore the whole world in

their journeys. But it would seem that this world is only a
very small one. For the whole income of the Yeshibah has
never exceeded the sum of about £1800. Of this a certain part
is spent in providing the salaries of the teaching staff and
proctors, and on the repairs of the building; whilst the rest
is distributed amongst the students. Considering that no
scholarship exceeds £13—it is only the forty immortals of
Walosin who receive such high stipends—considering again
that the great majority of the students belong to the poorer
classes and thus receive no remittance from their parents,
we may be sure that the words of the Talmud: "This is the
way to study the Torah; eat bread and salt, drink water by
measure, sleep on the earth, and live a life of care," are
carried out by them literally. But it would seem that the
less they eat and the less they sleep, the more they work.
Indeed the industry and the enthusiasm of these Bachurim
(*alumni*)[24] in the study of the Torah is almost unsurpassable.
The official hours alone extend from nine in the morning
until ten in the evening, while many of the students volunteer to continue their studies till the middle of the night, or
to begin the day at three in the morning.

As to the subject of these studies, it is confined, as may
be imagined, to the exploration of the old Rabbinic literature
in all its branches. But it would be a mistake to think that
the modern spirit has left Walosin quite untouched. It would
be impossible that among 400 thinking heads there should
not be a few who are interested in mathematics, others again
in philosophy or history, while yet others would conjugate
the irregular verbs of some classical language when moving to
and fro over their Talmud folios and pretending to "*learn.*"
Indeed, almost all the writers who demand that these subjects
should be introduced as obligatory into the programme of
Walosin, belonged themselves to this Yeshibah. And it is
these writers who betray the secret how secular knowledge is

now invading the precincts of Walosin, as well as of other Talmudical Colleges in spite of all obstacles and prohibitions. In conquering these difficulties seem to consist the pleasures of life of many Bachurim at Walosin. Look only at that undergraduate, how, after a heavy day's work he is standing there in the street reading Buckle's *History of Civilisation* in the moonlight! Poor man, he is not so romantic as to prefer the moonlight to a cheerful, warm room, with the more prosaic light of a candle, but he has got tired of knocking at the door, for his landlady, to whom he has neglected to pay rent for the last three terms, made up her mind to let him freeze to-night. But still more cruel to him is his fellow-sufferer, who is also wandering in the streets with an overloaded brain and empty stomach; he roughly shakes him out of his dreams by telling him that Buckle is long ago antiquated, and that he had better study the works of Herbert Spencer, who has spoken the last word on every vital subject in the world. Still these two starving and freezing representatives of English thought in Walosin form only an exception. The general favourites are the representatives of Jewish thought. That such books as the *Guide of the Perplexed,* by Maimonides, the Metaphysical Researches of Levi b. Gershom,[25] and other philosophical works of the Spanish school are read by the Walosin students it is needless to say. These books now form a part of the Rabbinic literature, and it would be almost unorthodox to suspect their readers. But it is worth noticing that even the productions of the modern historico-critical school, such as the works of Zunz, Frankel, Graetz, Weiss, are very popular with the Bachurim, being much read and discussed by them.

Thus Walosin deserves rightly to be considered as the centre of Jewish thought in Russia, in which the spirit of the Gaon is still working.

I have very often, however, heard doubts expressed as to

the continuance of this spirit when, as it is to be hoped, better times come for the Jews in Russia. Is it not to be feared that liberty and emancipation will render untenable ideas and notions which arose under entirely different circumstances? There is no need of entertaining such fears. Rabbi Jedaiah of Bedres[26] concludes his philosophical work *Examination of the World*, with the following words: "The conclusion of the whole matter is, go either to the right, my heart, or go to the left, but believe all that R. Moses ben Maimon (Maimonides) has believed, the last of the Gaonim by time, but the first in rank." About five hundred years have passed away since these lines were written. Time, as we have seen, has brought another Gaon, and probably Time will favour us in future with still another. But times have also altered. The rebellious hearts of a liberal age are not likely to obey always the command, "Believe all that the Gaon said." But the heart of man will in all ages retain idealism enough to love and revere the greatest of men and to follow what was best in them.

10

NACHMAN KROCHMAL AND THE PER-PLEXITIES OF THE TIME

IN her good-natured panegyric of mediocrity which is known under the title of *Scenes of Clerical Life,* George Eliot remarked: "Let us hope that there is a saving ignorance."

Strange as this demand may sound, the wish of the great novelist to see her favoured mediocrities "saved," has been shared by the great majority of mankind. I know that I, at least, echo that desire with all my heart. And I am afraid that I am prompted by some rather selfish reasons. It would be somewhat hard, when one is born with small abilities, but a great desire for being saved, to be deprived of the hope held out by the author of *Adam Bede.*

But there are some, I am afraid, who are not satisfied with this dictum of George Eliot. They show a strong tendency to make salvation a monopoly of ignorance. This is a little too selfish. With all due respect to every form of ignorance, sacred as well as profane, we ought, I think, to believe that there is also such a thing as a saving knowledge. Nay, we might go even farther. There may be certain epochs in history when there is hardly any other path to salvation than knowledge, and the deep search after truth.

We all know the words of the Psalmist, "The Lord preserveth the simple." But as there are periods in the life of the individual when naïveté has to give way to sagacity and reflection, so there are times in history at which Providence does not choose to leave men in simplicity. At such times doubts arise, as though of themselves; questions suddenly become open when they had been supposed solved for centuries; and the human mind is stirred by a sceptical breeze of which no man can tell whence it came. One may under those circumstances be indifferent, but one can be simple no more.

Even in such cases, however, man has no cause to despair. When our dearest beliefs are shaken by all kinds of doubts, Providence sends us also great thinkers, earnest lovers of truth, who devote their lives to enlightening our puzzled minds. Not that these men try to answer all the questions by which we feel perplexed. They endeavour to satisfy us, partly by showing that many of our difficulties are not difficulties at all, but merely arise from superficiality, and partly by proving that the great cause about which we feel so much anxiety does not exactly depend on the solution of the questions that are troubling us. They give to the things which are dearer to us than our life a fresh aspect, which enables us to remain attached to them with the same devotion and love as before. To speak again in the words of the Psalmist: "Thou sendest forth Thy Spirit, and they are created, and Thou renewest the face of the earth."

This spirit that renews the face of things is what I understand by "saving knowledge." As men of that saving knowledge we may regard Rabban Johanan ben Zaccai[1] and his disciples, who made it possible for Judaism to survive the destruction of the Temple, which some believed to involve the end of the religion. As such men we may look upon R. Saadiah Gaon and his followers, who worked at a time when

Judaism was menaced in its inner life, namely in the tradition, by the attempts of the narrow-minded Caraites to convert it into a bookish religion.[2] Such men were Maimonides and his successors, who came to the aid of religion when it had got into dogmatic troubles by reason of its coming into contact with various philosophical systems. And in order to approach the subject of the present essay, I venture to say that a man of such saving knowledge was also Nachman Krochmal, who lived and laboured in the first half of the present century, when Judaism had been terribly shaken by the scepticism of Voltaire, and the platitudes of the so-called Mendelssohnian school.

Nachman Krochmal was born on the 17th of February in the year 1785. His father, Solomon Krochmal, was a merchant of Brody, a commercial frontier town in the north-east of Galicia in Austria. In his early years Solomon often used to visit Berlin for business purposes. He is said to have seen Mendelssohn there on one occasion, and to have learned greatly to revere the Jewish sage. And it is not unlikely that Nachman's subsequent admiration for Mendelssohn was partly due to his father's influence.

Solomon was a man of considerable wealth, and he, therefore, endeavoured to give his son the best possible education. But as a respectable member of a Polish community a hundred years ago, Solomon had to follow the fashion adopted by his neighbours, and the best possible education consisted in affording the child an opportunity to study the Talmud and other Rabbinical works. All other languages and their literatures were sealed books to the child—a very absurd and regrettable fashion indeed. But let us not be too hard on Polish Jews. I have been told that there are countries on our globe where people have been driven by the force of fashion into the opposite extreme; where, with few exceptions, they

think that the Talmud, as well as the whole Hebrew literature, must needs be excluded from the programme of a
gentleman's education.

Happily, or the reverse, Krochmal's childhood did not last
long, for in the year 1798 we find that Nachman, a boy
of fourteen, was already married to a Miss Haberman in
Zolkiew. As a result of this foolish custom of marrying at so
very early an age, Nachman was hardly ever a boy; we have
at once to deal with him as a man.

It was then customary in Poland, and perhaps is so still,
for the father of the bride to provide for the support of the
young couple for some years after their marriage. In order
to reduce the expense of this arrangement, the bridegroom
had to reside in the same house as his father-in-law. Thus we
see Krochmal removing from Brody to Zolkiew, the native
town of his wife. Here Krochmal lived in the house of her
father for many years, entirely devoted to his studies; and he
certainly needed all his time for them. For he now began to
expand the sphere of his education, to embrace subjects quite
new to him. By his marriage Nachman seems to have gained
a certain amount of independence, and the first use he made
of it was to study the *Guide of the Perplexed*[3] of Maimonides, the *Commentaries* of Ibn Ezra on the Bible,[4] and
other more or less philosophical works written in the Hebrew
language. His next step was to learn German; but, as his
biographers inform us, he was not able to follow this course
without undergoing many struggles, and overcoming many
obstacles.

It would lead us too far to give a full account of the difficulties which the young scholar had to conquer while
pursuing his new studies. They will be sufficiently characterised by the following extract from a Hebrew letter of his
disciple, Solomon Leb Rapoport, who, writing in 1841 concerning his master and friend, remarks: "Consider this, ye

inhabitants of Germany"—and, I may add, ye inhabitants of England—"and you will be astounded. It is easy for you to avoid being one-sided, and to study different sciences, for you possess many schools and teachers from every branch of learning. It is not so in Poland and Russia even at present, much less was it so forty years ago. There is no teacher, no guide, no supporter, for the Jew who desires any sort of improvement. The Jew who wishes to enter on a new path of learning has to prepare the road for himself. And when he has entered on it, his friend will come to him and ask, 'Is it true that you have got scientific books in your house? Mind you do not mention it to any one. There are enough bigots in the town to persecute you and all your family if they get scent of it.' " It was under these conditions that Krochmal pursued his studies, which were by no means few or easy, for he was not content with a knowledge of only the lighter portions of German literature. He soon began to read the works of Lessing, Mendelssohn, and more especially of Kant, who always remained his favourite philosopher. In his later years he also became acquainted with the writings of Fichte, Schelling, and Hegel. But to the last he could not console himself for having missed the advantages of a systematic university education.

After having learned German, Krochmal proceeded to acquire a knowledge of Latin and French, and to read the best books written in those languages. To deepen his knowledge of Hebrew, he studied Arabic and Syriac, but we are unable to say how far he succeeded in mastering these languages. With these studies, which appear to have occupied our philosopher for an interval of ten years after his marriage, the first period of his life seems also to end. But the hard work of ten years did not pass over the delicate youth without undermining his health for ever. At the age of twenty-four, Krochmal fell sick of an illness which compelled him to interrupt his work. He was forced to go to Lemberg to consult the doctors of that town, and he had to remain there for a long time. And now began Krochmal's career as a teacher. For during his stay at Lemberg there gathered round him a band of young scholars whom Krochmal's fame had already reached. It is useless to enumerate the names of all these students. Among them figured Isaac Erter, Samson Bloch, A. Bodek, and many others. The most gifted of them was undoubtedly Rapoport, who afterwards became even more famous than his master Krochmal. It is not easy to define accurately the relation that subsisted between these two men. Graetz, in his history, calls Rapoport a disciple of Krochmal. Rapoport himself, in his memoir of Krochmal, describes the latter as a dear friend with whom he was wont to discuss literary topics. Zunz does not mention Rapoport at all in his account of our author. It seems to me that this relation may be most aptly defined by the Talmudic term "Talmid-Chaber," [5] "disciple-colleague."

Indeed, Krochmal's whole method of teaching was rather that of a companion than of a professor. He gave no set lectures on particular subjects, but conveyed his instruction rather by means of suggestive conversations with his younger friends. His usual habit was to walk with his pupils in the neighbourhood of the town, and to try to influence their minds each in accordance with its bent. If any of his disciples showed an inclination for poetry, Krochmal sought to refine his taste by directing his attention to the best works in Hebrew and German literature. To another, whose fancy strayed into mysticism, he recommended the writings of Philo and Ibn Ezra, at the same time suggesting how the works of the latter should be interpreted. A third who, like Rapoport, was interested in historical researches, Krochmal instructed in the methods of critical inquiry.

There must have been some fascinating charm in Nachman's personality, which made him irresistible to all who came into contact with him. Rapoport has described his first interview with Krochmal. "It is more than thirty years since I first made his acquaintance, and beheld the glory of his presence. Though he was in weak health, still his soul was strong; and as soon as I conversed with him there came over me a spirit of judgment and knowledge. I felt almost transformed into another man." Elsewhere the same writer says: "Oh, how sweet to me were these walks with Krochmal—sweeter than all the pleasures of this world. I could never have enough of his wisdom; with his every word he conveyed a new lesson."

After a lengthy stay at Lemberg, Krochmal partially, though not entirely, recovered from his severe illness; he remained weak and pale for the rest of his days. His antagonists, the Chassidim, believed him to be possessed by a demon who could find no better dwelling-place than in the person of this arch-heretic. Had it been in their power they would probably have dragged him to some exorcist for the purpose of driving out his German, French, Latin, and other symptoms of demoniacal heresy. Happily the orthodox were powerless to do this, so Krochmal was left unmolested, and was allowed to resume his walks and studies. It may be here remarked that Krochmal in general avoided giving the Chassidim any cause for reasonable complaint. Rapoport asserts that his master was "deeply religious and a strict observer of the law. He was zealously anxious to perform every ordinance, Biblical or Rabbinical." The only liberty that Krochmal claimed for himself and his disciples was the right to study what they thought best and in the way they thought best. When this liberty was attacked, he showed a firmness and resolution which would hardly have been expected from this quiet and gentle man. To one of his pupils, who made concessions to the Chassidim and their Zaddikim worship,

Krochmal wrote: "Be firm in this matter unless you wish to earn the contempt of every honest man. One who is afraid of these people, and debases himself before them bears a mean soul that was born to slavery. The man that wishes to rise above the mob, with its confused notions and corrupt morality, must be courageous as a lion in conquering the obstacles that beset his path. Consideration of what people will say, what bigots will whisper, what crafty enemies will scheme—questions such as these can have but one effect,— to darken the intellect and confuse the faculty of judgment."

So Krochmal continued his studies without interruption till 1814, when the death of his wife's mother brought his period of ease and comfort to an end. His father-in-law seems to have died some time before, and Krochmal was forced to seek his own living. He became a merchant, but it is to be regretted that he did not prove as successful a man of business as he was a man of letters. He found it a hard struggle to earn a living. But the severest trial which he had to undergo was the death of his wife in 1826. In a letter, dating from about this time, to a friend who had asked him for assistance in his philosophical inquiries, Krochmal wrote —"How can I help you now? I am already an old man; my head is gray, and my health is broken. In the last three years I have met with many misfortunes. My beloved wife died after a long illness. My daughter will soon leave me to get married, my elder son will depart to seek his livelihood, and I shall be left alone with only a child of ten years, the son of my old age. I will lift up mine eyes unto the hills: From whence shall my help come?"

Nachman was evidently in very low spirits at this time, but he was in too true a sense a philosopher to despair. He turned for comfort to his studies, and at this dark epoch of his life he first became acquainted with the Philosophy of

Hegel, whose system he was wont to call the "Philosophy of Philosophies."

For the next ten years the works of Hegel and inquiries into Jewish history appear to have absorbed all the leisure that his mercantile occupation left him. We shall presently see what the result of these studies was. No fresh subjects were undertaken by Krochmal in the last years of his life; he had already acquired a fund of knowledge vast enough to engage all his thoughts. There are, however, some remaining points in his private circumstances which it may not be un-interesting to mention.

Krochmal, as has been already related, was not prosperous in his business. Things went from bad to worse, and he was compelled in 1836 to seek a situation. "There ought to be literary men poor," some writer has maintained, "to show whether they are genuine or not." This test Krochmal success-fully passed through. Even as a young man Nachman's strength of character was admired by his contemporaries not less than his rare learning. In his subsequent distress, he gave evidence of the truth of this judgment. Despite his poverty, his friends could not prevail upon him to accept the post of Rabbi in any Jewish community. "I am unwilling," he wrote to a friend, "to be the cause of dissensions in any Jewish congregation. I should prefer to die of hunger rather than become a Rabbi under present circumstances." He ex-pressed his views on this subject even more decidedly on a later occasion when the Berlin congregation offered him the post of Chief Rabbi in that town. In a letter, conveying his refusal of this honourable office, he says: "I never thought of becoming the Conscience-counsellor (*Gewissensrath*) of men. My line of studies was not directed to that end, nor would it accord with my disposition and sentiments. The only post that I should care to accept would be that of teacher in the Jewish Theological Seminary, which, as I was informed, you were thinking of establishing in Berlin." The plan to found such an institution was not realised till forty years later, and in the interval Nachman had to look for his living in other regions than Jewish theology. Being in poor circumstances, and as his children and friends had left him, he felt very lonely at Zolkiew. "Nobody cares for me here," he writes, "and I am equally indifferent." His one desire was to obtain a situation at Brody, possibly as book-keeper with a salary of some thirty pounds a year, on condition that he would be expected to devote only half the day to his business duties, thus securing for himself leisure for philosophical studies.

His terms were accepted, and he obtained the humble post he sought. He remained in Brody for the next two years, 1836-8, but at the end of 1838 he fell so dangerously ill that he could no longer resist the pressing request of his daughter to live with her at Tarnopol. She had urged him to take this step even previous to his removal to Brody, but he had declined on the plea that he preferred to live by the labour of his hands. Now, however, he yielded to her wish, and betook himself to Tarnopol, where for two years longer he lived affectionately tended by his children and respected by all who knew him. In May 1840, Krochmal's illness began to develop fatal symptoms, and he died in the arms of his daughter on the 31st of July (the first of Ab), at the age of fifty-five. As Zunz happily remarked: "This great man was born on the 7th of Adar, the birthday of Moses (according to Jewish tradition), and died on the first of Ab, the anniversary of the death of Aaron, the High Priest."

I have tried in the foregoing remarks to give a short sketch of our Rabbi's life according to the accounts of Zunz, Rapoport, and Letteris. There is one other point to which I must allude, as it involves a consideration on which Letteris seems

to lay much stress. This biographer appears to think that
Krochmal was in his youth greatly influenced by the society
in which he moved, consisting as it did of many learned and
enlightened men. There is, too, the oft-quoted saying of
Goethe:

> Wer den Dichter will verstehen
> Muss in Dichters Lande gehen.

And I am probably expected to give some account of the
state of society in which Nachman grew up. I regret that I
must ask to be excused from doing so. I cannot consent to
take the reader to Krochmal's land. And if I might venture
to give him my humble advice, I should only say, "By all
means stop at home." Goethe may be right about the poet,
but his remark does not apply to the case of the scholar. It
may be true, as some think, that every great man is the
product of his time, but it certainly does not follow that he is
the product of his country. Nor could I name any other
country of which Krochmal was the product. Many a city
no doubt boasted itself a town full of *"Chakhamim* and
Sopherim" [6] as the Hebrew phrase is, or, as we would express
it, "a seat of learning," full of scholars of the ancient and
modern schools. But neither these ancient scholars nor the
modern were of a kind to produce a real scholar and an enlightened thinker like Krochmal. There were many men who
knew by heart the whole of the Halachic works of Maimonides, the Mishnah, and even the whole of the Babylonian
Talmud. This is very imposing. But if you look a little closer,
you will find that with a few exceptions—such as the school
of R. Elijah Wilna—these men, generally speaking, hardly
deserve the name of scholars at all. They were rather a sort
of studying engines. The steam-engine passes over a continent, here through romantic scenery, there in the midst
of arid deserts, by stream and mountain and valley, always

with the same monotonous hum and shriek. So these scholars went through the Talmud with never changing feelings. They did not rejoice at the dscription which is given in tractate *Biccurim*[7] of the procession formed when the first-fruits were brought into the Holy Temple. They were not much saddened when reading in tractate *Taanith*[8] of the unhappy days so recurrent in Jewish history. They were not delighted by the wisdom of *Seder Nezikin*,[9] which deals with civil law; nor were they vexed by *Seder Taharoth*,[10] which treats of the laws of cleanliness and uncleanliness, that by their exaggeration gave cause to much dissension in the time of the Temple. The pre-Talmudic literature, such as the *Siphra, Siphré,* and *Mechilta*[11]—the only existing means of obtaining an insight into the Talmud—were altogether neglected. All that these readers cared for was to push on to the end, and the prayer recited at the close was of more importance to them than the treatise they had perused.

Not less melancholy was the spectacle presented by the so-called men of "Enlightenment" (*Aufklärung*). They belonged chiefly to the rationalistic school of Mendelssohn, but they equalled their master neither in knowledge nor in moral character. It was an enlightenment without foundation in real scholarship, and did not lead to an ideal life, though again I must add that there were exceptions. These men were rather what Germans would term *Schöngeister,* a set of dilettanti who cared to study as little as possible, and to write as much as possible. They wrote bad grammars, superficial commentaries on the Bible, and terribly dull poems. Of this literature, with the exception of Erter's *Watchman*,[12] there is scarcely a work that one would care to read twice. Most of them despised Rabbinism, but without understanding its noblest forms as they are to be traced in the Talmud and later Hebrew literature. They did not dislike Judaism, but the only Judaism they affected was one "which does not oppose itself to anything in particular"; or, as Heine would have described it, *"Eine reinliche Religion."* In one respect these little men were great: in mutual admiration, which reached such a pitch that such titles as "Great Luminary," "World-famed Sage," were considered altogether too insignificant and commonplace.

I will now pass to the writings of Krochmal. It must be premised that Krochmal was not a voluminous author. All his writings, including a few letters which were published in various Hebrew periodicals, would scarcely occupy four hundred pages. Krochmal used to call himself *"der ewige Student"* (the perpetual pupil). He did not read books, nor study philosophical systems, with the object of writing books of his own on them. He read and studied in order that he might become a better and a wiser man. Besides, he did not think himself competent to judge on grave subjects, nor did he consider his judgment, even if he formed one, worthy of publication. He counselled his friends to be equally slow in publishing their views to the world. "Be not," he wrote to a correspondent—"be not hasty in forming your opinions before you have studied the literature of the subject with care and devotion. This is no easy matter, for no man can obtain any real knowledge of the Torah and philosophy unless he is prepared to give himself up in single-hearted devotion to his studies." Severe though he was to his friends, he was still more severe to himself. Though he had been collecting materials on subjects of Jewish history and philosophy from his early youth, it was not until he had endured much persuasion and pressure from his friends that he began to write down his thoughts in a connected form. We thus possess only one work from the pen of this author; but that work is the *Guide of the Perplexed of the Time,*[13] a posthumous book published in 1851, eleven years after Krochmal's death. His work had been much interrupted by illness during the last years of his life, and as a necessary consequence many parts of his treatise finally remained in an unfinished state. Krochmal commissioned his children to hand over his papers to Zunz, who was to arrange and edit them as best he might. Zunz, who in his reverence for Krochmal went so far as to call him the man of God, gladly accepted the task, in which he was aided by Steinschneider. Unfortunately, the work was published in Lemberg, a place famous for spoiling books. Even the skill of these two great masters did not suffice to save Krochmal's work from the fate to which all the books printed in Lemberg seem inevitably doomed. Thus Krochmal's work is printed on bad paper, and with faint ink; it is full of misprints and the text is sometimes confused with the notes. A second edition appeared in Lemberg in 1863; but, it is scarcely necessary to add, the reprint is even worse than the original issue.

The work occupies some 350 pages, and is divided into seventeen chapters. The opening six treat of Religion in general. The author first indicates the opposite dangers to which men are liable. On the one hand, men are exposed to extravagant phantasy (*Schwärmerei*), superstition and ceremonialism (*Werkheiligkeit*). Some, on the other hand, in their endeavour to avoid this danger, fall into the opposite extreme, materialism, unbelief, and moral degeneracy as a consequence of their neglect of all law. He proceeds to say: Even in the ritual part of religion, such as the regulations of the Sabbath, the dietary laws and so forth, we find abstract definitions necessary, and differences of opinions prevalent. In the dogmatic aspects of religion, dealing as they do with the grave subjects of metaphysics, the mystery of life and death, the destiny of man, his relation to God, reward and punishment, the inner meaning of the laws—in these spiritual matters, the difficulty of accurate definition must be far greater and the opportunities for difference of opinion more frequent and important. What guide are we to follow, seeing that every error involves the most dangerous consequences? Shall we abandon altogether the effort of thinking on these grave subjects? Such a course is impossible. Do not believe, says Krochmal, that there ever was a time when the religious man was entirely satisfied by deeds of righteousness, as some people maintain. On the contrary, every man, whether an independent thinker or a simple believer, always feels the weight of these questions upon him. Every man desires to have some ideal basis for his actions which must constitute his real life in its noblest moments. Krochmal here quotes a famous passage from the Midrash.[14] The Torah, according to one of our ancient sages, may be compared to two paths, the one burning with fire, the other covered with snow. If a man enters on the former path he will die by the heat; if he walks by the latter path he will be frozen by the snow. What, then, must he do? He must walk in the middle, or, as we should say, he must choose the golden mean. But, as Krochmal suggests, the middle way in historical and philosophical doubts does not consist, as some idle heads suppose, in a kind of compromise between two opposing views. If one of two contending parties declares that twice two make six, while his opponent asserts that twice two make eight, a sort of compromise might be arrived at by conceding that twice two make seven. But such a compromise would be as false as either extreme; and the seeker after the truth must revert to that mean which is the heart of all things, independently of all factions, placing himself above them.

Having dealt with the arguments relating to the existence of God as elaborated in the philosophical systems of his time, Krochmal leads up to his treatment of the History of Israel by a chapter on the ideal gifts bestowed upon the various ancient nations, which, possessed by them through many centuries, were lost when their nationality ceased. We next come, in Chapter VII, to the ideal gifts of Israel. These are the religious gift and the faculty and desire for seeking the ideal of all ideals, namely, God. But Israel, whose mission it was to propagate this ideal, was, even as other nations, subject to natural laws; and its history presents progress and reaction, rise and decline. Krochmal devotes his next three chapters to showing how, in the history of Israel, as in other histories, may be detected a triple process. These three stages are the budding, the period of maturity, and the decay. As the history of Israel is more a history of religion than of politics and battles, its rise and decline correspond more or less with Israel's attachment to God, and its falling away from Him. The decay would be associated with the adoption of either of the extremes, the dangerous effects of which have been already mentioned. But "through progress and backsliding, amid infectious contact with idolatry, amid survival of old growths of superstition, of the crude practices of the past; amid the solicitation of new aspects of life; in material prosperity and in material ruin," Israel was never wholly detached from God. In the worst times it had its judges or its prophets, its heroes or its sages, its Rabbis or its philosophers, who strove to bring Israel back to its mission, and who succeeded in their efforts to do so. Even in its decay traces of the Divine spirit made themselves felt, and revived the nation, which entered again on a triple course and repeated its three phases. The first of these three-fold epochs began, according to Krochmal's eighth chapter, with the times of the Patriarchs, and ended with the death of Gedaliah after the destruction of the first Temple. Next, in the following two chapters, Krochmal finds the second triple movement in the interval between the prophets of the exile in Babylon and the death of Bar-Cochba about 135 A.C. The author also hints at the existence of a third such epoch beginning with R. Judah the Patriarch, the compiler of the Mishnah (220

A.C.),[15] and ending with the expulsion of the Jews from Spain (1492). This idea is not further developed by Krochmal; but it would be interesting to ask, by the way, in which phase of the three-fold process—rise, maturity, or decay—are we at the present time?

The next five chapters may be regarded as an excursus on the preceding two. Krochmal discusses the Biblical books which belong to the period of the Exile and of the Second Temple, such as the Second Isaiah, certain Exilic and Maccabean psalms, Ecclesiastes, certain Apocryphal books, and the work of the Men of the Great Synagogue. They contain, again, researches on the various sects, such as the Assideans, Sadducees, Pharisees, Essenes, the Gnostics, the Cabbalists and their relation to the latter, and the Minim,[16] who are mentioned in the Talmud. In another part of this excursus Krochmal describes the systems of the Alexandrian Jewish philosophers, such as Philo and Aristobulus, and discusses their relation to certain theosophic ideas in various Midrash-collections. The author also attempts to prove the necessity of Tradition; he shows its first traces in the Bible, and explains the term Sopherim (scribes); and he points out the meaning of the phrase "A law unto Moses from Mount Sinai," [17] and similar expressions. He gives a summary of the development of the Halachah in its different stages, the criteria by which the older Halachahs may be discriminated; he seeks to arrive at the origin of the Mishnah, and deals with various cognate topics. In another discourse Krochmal endeavours to explain the term Agadah,[18] its origin and development; the different kinds of Agadah and their relative value. Chapter XVI contains the Prolegomena to a philosophy of the Jewish religion in accordance with the principles laid down by Hegel. In the seventeenth and last chapter the author gives a general introduction to the Philosophy of Ibn Ezra, and quotes illustrative extracts.

The space of an essay does not permit me to give further details of Krochmal's book. I am conscious that the preceding outline is deficient in quality as well as in quantity. Yet, even from this meagre abstract, the reader will gather that Krochmal reviews many of the great problems which concern religion in general and Judaism in particular. Zunz somewhere remarks that Krochmal was inspired in his work by the study of Hegel, just as Maimonides had been by the study of Aristotle. I give this statement solely on the authority of Zunz, as I myself have never made a study of the works of the German philosopher, and am therefore unable to express an opinion on the question.

Now there is no doubt that Krochmal's book is not without defects. The materials are not always well arranged, there is at times a want of proportion in the length at which the various points are treated, and the author occasionally seems to wander from the subject in hand. But we shall be better able to account for these and similar technical faults, as well as to appreciate the real value of the author's work, if we consider the following fact. Nachman Krochmal's object was to elaborate a philosophy of Jewish history, to trace the leading ideas that ran through it, and the ultimate causes that led to its various phases. But, unfortunately, at the time when Krochmal began to write, there did not exist a Jewish history at all. The labours of Zunz were conducted in an altogether different field. Not to mention the names of the younger scholars then unborn, Graetz, the author of the *History of the Jews,* and Weiss, who wrote a history of the Tradition, were still studying at college. Frankel's masterly essays on the Essenes and the Septuagint, his well-known work, *Introduction to the Mishnah,* and the results of Geiger's most interesting and suggestive researches on the older and later Halachah, and on the Pharisees and Sadducees, had yet to be written. Rapoport's great treatise,

Erech Millin,[19] had not been published at that time, and Steinschneider was not yet working at his historical sketch of Jewish literature. It was not till six years after Krochmal's death (viz. in 1846) that Landauer's memorable studies on the Jewish mystics were given to the world. Even the bad books of Julius Fürst, such as his *History of the Canon*, and his still worse *History of Jewish Literature in Babylon*, were then unwritten. Neither the most charlatanic *History of the Opinions and Teachings of All the Jewish Sects*, by Peter Beer, the universal provider, nor Jost's most honest but narrow-minded and superficial *History of the Jews*, was of much use to Krochmal. Jost's more scholarly works were not published till long afterwards. Krochmal was thus without the guidance of those authorities to which we are now accustomed to turn for information. Excepting the aid that he derived from the writings of Azariah de Rossi,[20] Krochmal was therefore compelled to prosecute all the necessary research for himself; he had to establish the facts of Jewish history as well as to philosophise upon them. Hence, in the very midst of his philosophical analysis, the author was bound to introduce digressions on historical subjects, in order to justify as well as to form the basis of that analysis. He had to survey the ground and to collect the materials, besides constructing the plan of the edifice and working at its erection. Nevertheless, it is precisely for these historical excursuses that Krochmal has deserved the gratitude of posterity. He it was who taught Jewish scholars how to submit the ancient Rabbinic records to the test of criticism and the way in which they might be utilised for purpose of historical studies; he it was who enabled them to trace the genesis of the tradition, and to watch the inner germination of that vast organism. He even indicated to them how they might continue to connect their own lives with it, how they might derive nourishment from it, and in their turn further its growth.

I may assert with the utmost confidence that there is scarcely a single page in Krochmal's book that did not afterwards give birth to some essay or monograph or even elaborate treatise, though their authors were not always very careful about mentioning the source of their inspiration. Thus Krochmal justly deserves the honourable title assigned to him by one of our greatest historians, who terms him the Father of Jewish Science.

So far, I have been speaking of the importance of Krochmal's treatise and of its significance in the region of Jewish Science. It is necessary, I think, to add a few words with regard to the general tendency of his whole work. I have already alluded to the characteristic modesty of Krochmal; I have pointed out how little he cared for publicity, how dearly he loved retirement. The question accordingly presents itself—What can have been the real and sufficient causes that prevailed upon him to yield to the solicitations of his friends and to write upon what the Talmud would term "matters standing on the heights of the world" ?

The answer to this question may, I think, be found in the title of Krochmal's book, the *Guide of the Perplexed of the Time*. It is indeed a rather unusual coincidence for the title of a Hebrew book to have any connexion with its subject matter. The same merit is possessed by the *Guide of the Perplexed* of Maimonides, the title of which undoubtedly suggested that of Krochmal's treatise. There is, however, one little addition in Krochmal's title that contains a most important lesson for us. I mean the words "of the Time." By these words Krochmal reminds us that, great as are the merits of the immortal work of Maimonides—and it would be difficult to exaggerate its value and importance—still it will no longer suffice for us. For, as Krochmal himself remarks, every time has its own perplexities, and therefore needs its own guide. In order to show that these words are no idle phrase, I shall endeavour to illustrate them by one example at least. In the *Guide of the Perplexed* of Maimonides, Part II, Chapter XXVI, occurs a passage which runs thus: "In the famous chapters known as the 'Chapters of R. Eliezer the Great,' [21] I find R. Eliezer the Great saying something more extraordinary than I have ever seen in the utterances of any believer in the Law of Moses. I refer to the following passage: 'Whence were the heavens created? He (God) took part of the light of His garment, He stretched it like a cloth, and thus the heavens were extending continually, as it is said (Ps. civ. 2): He covereth Himself with light as with a garment, He stretcheth the heavens like a curtain. Whence was the earth created? He took of the snow under the throne of glory, and threw it; according to the words (in Job xxxvii. 6), He said to the snow be thou earth.' These are the words given there (in the 'Chapters of R. Eliezer the Great'), and I, in my surprise, ask, What was the belief of this sage? Did he think it impossible that something be produced from nothing? . . . If the terms 'the light of His garment' and the 'snow of glory' mean something eternal (as matter) they *must* be rejected. . . . In short, it is a passage that greatly confuses the notions of all intelligent and religious persons. I am unable to explain it sufficiently."

So far Maimonides; and we are quite able to conceive his perplexity in dealing with this passage. On one side, Maimonides himself believed that Judaism is a dogmatic religion, and that one of its dogmas is the principle of *Creatio ex nihilo*. On the other side, he found R. Eliezer—one of the greatest authorities of the early part of the second century—apparently denying this dogma. The perplexity was indeed a serious one for Maimonides, but we find no difficulty whatever in extricating ourselves from it. In the first place, there are many who cling to the theory which holds that there are no dogmas in Judaism at all, and to them Maimonides' difficulty would have no relevance. Secondly, those who believe that there are dogmas in Judaism may regard such expressions as those quoted above from the "Chapters of R. Eliezer" in the light of mere poetical metaphors, or may call them fairy tales or legends, or include them in some other section of literature, known under the name of folklore, which is an excuse for every absurdity, the fortunate authors of which are responsible neither to philosophy nor to religion, and sometimes not even to common sense. But there is a third consideration that affords the best solution of the difficulty. The "Chapters of R. Eliezer," despite their pompous title, are not the work of R. Eliezer at all. Criticism has taught us to attach no importance to the heading of a chapter or the title-page of a book. We are now in a position to judge from the tone, style, and contents of the work, that the "Chapters of R. Eliezer" is a later compilation of the eighth century, and that its author could not have been R. Eliezer, the teacher of R. Akiba, in the second century. In this way, these particular difficulties of Maimonides solve themselves for us in a sufficiently easy way. But it is just these solutions that open up new difficulties and perplexities which did not exist for the generation of the great Spanish philosopher. Suppose that we accept the view that Judaism is not a dogmatic religion. But how are we to conceive a religion without dogmas, or, if you prefer the expression, without principles or bases of belief? Or is Judaism, as some platitudinarians think, a mere national institute with some useful dietary and sanitary laws, but with nothing that makes for the sanctification of man, with no guidance to offer us in the great problems of our life, and in the greatest anxieties of the human soul? On the other hand, granted that we may consider certain things as mere legend, how are we to discriminate between these and the things that must be taken seriously? Does it depend on the nature of the subject, or on the position of the book in the canon of Hebrew literature? In the thirteenth century symbolical meanings were given to certain difficult passages in the Talmud; but the process was carried further, and the Biblical narratives were subjected by philosophers to a like treatment. R. Solomon ben Adereth and his colleagues (in the thirteenth century) settled the question by indiscriminately excommunicating all young men who should study philosophy; but this method is scarcely one to be commended for present use.

The third, or the philological solution of difficulties, leads to fresh troubles. A hundred years ago men were in that happy state of mind in which they knew everything. They knew the exact author and date of every Psalm; they knew the author of each and every ancient Midrash; they knew the originator of every law and ordinance; they even knew the writer of the Zohar, and of other mystical books. There were certainly a few who did not know all these things, among them Ibn Ezra, Azariah de Rossi, and the two Delmedigos.[22] But they were merely a miserable historical blunder, men who had no right to be born when they were. But the philological method has swept away all this knowingness as by a deluge from heaven, and men find that they know nothing. True, there linger on a few who still know all these things, but it is they who are now the anachronism. These, and such as these, are the perplexities of our time, to the resolution of which the labours of Krochmal and of a noble band of scholars have been directed in this century.

Have these perplexities, we must ask, and these puzzles been solved by Krochmal and his coadjutors? We may with all certainty answer: They have only pointed out the way, it is for ourselves to proceed by it. It would be unreasonable to expect that difficulties which have been accumulating during the course of thousands of years should be solved by the men of one or two generations. Again, we live in a

century in which excavations and discoveries in other fields
have added at once to our knowledge and to our uncertainty.
Each country, we might almost say, over and above the perplexities that trouble mankind in general, has its own special
difficulties which are entirely unknown to those who dwell
outside its frontiers. I am not disposed to discuss these difficulties in this place. Nor have I the ability to do so. But
of two things I am perfectly certain: the first is, that for a
solution of these difficulties which, in the language of Maimonides, "confuse the notions of all intelligent and religious
persons," the only hope is in true knowledge and not in
ignorance; and secondly, this knowledge can only be obtained
by a combination of the utmost reverence for religion and
the deepest devotion to truth. The poor old Rabbis who have
been so foully decried by their calumniators as hedonists,
and so foolishly praised by sorry apologists as materialistic
optimists, strongly insisted that when a man woos the truth,
his suit can only prosper if he is influenced by the purest
and most single-hearted affection. "A man," says the *Siphré,*
"must not say: 'I will study the Torah in order that I may
attain the title of Rabbi or savant, or that I may become rich
by it, or that I may be rewarded for it in the world to come.'
He must study for love's sake." Such a knowledge, which is
free from all taint of worldliness and of other-worldliness, a
knowledge sought simply and solely for pure love of God,
who is Truth—such a knowledge is in the highest sense
saving knowledge, and Nachman Krochmal was in possession
of it.

NOTES

NOTES

[1] The Hebrew title of the work is דור דור ודורשיו.

[2] That is, vows of an ascetic nature (not vows or oaths enforced by a court of justice), which the tribunal could annul when there was sufficient reason for it.

[3] The ten Rabbis who are named as the bearers of tradition during the period between 170 and 30 B.C. The "pair" in each case is supposed to have consisted of the president and the vice-president of the Sanhedrin for the time being. See, however, Kuenen, *Gesammelte Schriften*, p. 49 seq.

[4] דרשנים גדולים.

[5] הלכות למשה מסיני. They amount, in the whole of Rabbinic literature, to about forty, of which more than ten concern the preparation of the phylacteries, whilst others relate to the libations of water at the Feast of Tabernacles and similar subjects.

[6] This is the time when the school of R. Johanan b. Zaccai began its activity. Others place the Tannaitic age in Hillel's time (30 B.C.). בת קול.

[7] בת קול.

[8] בית דין, lit. "Court of Justice," as above, note 16 to Elijah Wilna, but it means also a sort of permanent Synod, in which of course justice was also administered as a part of religion.

[9] עדיות, "Evidences given by Witnesses." The tractate consists mostly of a number of laws attested by various Rabbis as having come down to them as old traditions.

[10] The family of Hillel, which was supposed to be descended from the house of David, supplied the Jews with patriarchs for many gen-

347

erations. Gamaliel II. flourished about 120 A.C., whilst Simon b. Gamaliel's activity as Patriarch falls about 160 A.C.

11 שמחות, *Semachoth*. It is a euphemistic title, the tractate dealing with the laws relating to funeral ceremonies and mourning.

12 סבוראי, "Elucidators" or "Explainers." The heads of the schools in Babylon during the fifth and sixth centuries were so designated.

13 The Rabbinic Jews of the dispersion add one day to each festival, and thus celebrate the Passover eight days, the Feast of Weeks two days, etc. The custom arose out of the uncertainty about the first day of the month, the prerogative of fixing the New Moon resting with the great *Beth Din* in Palestine, which had not always the means of communicating in time the evidence given before them that the New Moon had been seen by qualified witnesses. The prerogative was abolished in the fourth century, and the calendar fixed for all future time, but the additional day is still kept by the Rabbinic Jews as the "Custom of their Fathers."

14 היכלות, שיעור קומה, "Chambers (of Heaven)" and the "Measure of the Stature," mystical works in which occasionally gross anthropomorphisms are to be found. Their authorship is unknown.

ON THE STUDY OF THE TALMUD

1 Paper read before the Hebrew class at University College, London October 19, 1899.

2 In connexion with this work I should like to call the attention of students to *Das letzte Passahmahl Christi und der Tag seines Todes*, by Professor D. Chwolson (St. Petersburg, 1892) a work which, for the depth of its Rabbinic learning and the critical acumen displayed in it, has hardly its equal. It is, indeed, so far as I know, the first attempt to treat what one may call the Halachic part of the New Testament with the thoroughness and devotion usually bestowed only on doctrinal points.

3 cf. מונה ז״ן, p. 45 הערות.

4 *Lev. Rabbah*, I.

5 See especially the Midrash *Lekach Tob,* ad loc.

6 *Cant. Rabbah,* ad loc.

7 Ibid.

8 *Pesikta Rabbathi* (ed. Friedmann), p. 36, text and notes.

9 *Shibbole Halleket,* 145 a.

10 B. T. *Baba Mezia,* 45 a, and parallel passages.

11 B. T. *Sanhedrin,* 39 a.

[12] Jer. T. *Sukkah,* 55 a.

[13] Mishnah *Yoma,* VIII, 9.

[14] *Cant. Rabbah,* I, and parallel passages.

[15] *Cant. Rabbah,* ibid.

[16] B. T. *Sanhedrin,* 95 a.

[17] B. T. *Chagigah,* 15 a, and parallel passages.

[18] B. T. *Berachoth,* 3 a.

[19] See Löw, *Gesammelte Schriften,* II, p. 58, note I. A good essay on the subject is still a desideratum.

[20] *Num. Rabbah,* XIV, and parallel passages.

[21] *Lev. Rabbah,* XXI.

[22] Jer. T. *Sotah,* 22 a.

[23] *Chapters of R. Eliezer,* XLIV, but see also B. T. *Yoma,* 22 b.

[24] See *Perek R. Meïr.*

[25] B. T. *Chagigah,* 15 a.

[26] *Pesikta* (ed. Buber), p. 162 seq.

[27] B. T. *Baba Mezia,* 59 a.

[28] *Torath Kohanim* (ed. Weiss), 91 b.

[29] See *Pesikta Rabbathi,* 124 b.

[30] B. T. *Sanhedrin,* 34 a.

[31] *Mechilta,* 3 a, 6 a, etc.

[32] *Tanchuma,* מטות.

[33] *Yalkut,* I, 766. See Dr. Taylor's *Sayings of the Jewish Fathers,* 2nd ed., p. 160.

[34] See Jewish Quarterly Review, VI, pp. 419 and 634, for references.

[35] *Yalkut,* ibid; *Genesis Rabbah,* I, and *Cant. Rabbah* VIII.

[36] *Cant. Rabbah,* VII; *Num. Rabbah,* II; *Siphre* (ed. Friedmann), 143 a; and Rashi's Commentary to Cant. V, 9.

[37] B. T. *Chagigah,* II, and the Jerusalem Talmud, ibid.

THE DOGMAS OF JUDAISM

[1] *Jerusalem,* in Mendelssohn's *Sämmtliche Werke* (Vienna, 1838), especially from p. 264 onwards, and a letter by him published in Frankel-Graetz's *Monatsschrift,* 1859, p. 173. For Mendelssohn's position, see Graetz's *Geschichte,* xi. 86 seq., especially p. 88 and note 1; Kayserling, *Leben und Werke* of M., 2d ed., p. 394; Steinheim, *Moses Mendelssohn* (Hamburg, 1840), p. 30 seq.; Holdheim, *Moses Mendelssohn* (Berlin, 1859), p. 18 seq.; Leopold Löw's pamphlet, *Jüdische Dogmen* (Pesth, 1871).

2 See the Commentaries on Maimonides' ספר המצות, especially R. Simeon Duran's זוהר הרקיע; cf. also ancient and modern commentaries on Exod. xx. 2.

3 See *Siphra* (ed. Weiss), pp. 86 b, 93 b.

4 *Baba Bathra,* 14 b; cf. Fürst's *Kanon,* p. 15.

5 See *Sanhedrin,* 38 b, and *Pseudo-Jonathan* to Gen. iv. 8.

6 *Mechilta,* 33 b.

7 אפיקורוס, Lat. Epicurus.

8 See *Mishnah, Sanhedrin,* x. e, § 1, and Talmud, ibid. 90 a and b, and Rabbinowicz's *Variae Lectiones,* ix. p. 247 notes. Besides the ordinary commentaries on the Talmud, account must also be taken of the remarks of Crescas, Duran, Albo, and Abarbanel on the subject. Cf. also Kämpf in the *Monatsschrift* (1863), p. 144 seq.; Oppenheim, ibid. (1864), p. 144; Friedmann in the *Beth Talmud,* i. p. 210 seq. See also Talmudical Dictionaries, *s.v.* אפיקורוס. The explanation I have adopted agrees partly with Friedmann's and partly with Oppenheim's views.

9 *Sayings of the Fathers,* iii. § 9, and iv. § 22.

10 See אדרת אליהו (Jovslow, 1835), p. 48. In my exposition of the dogmas of the Caraites I have mainly followed the late Dr. Frankl's article "Karaiten" in Ersch u. Gruber's *Encyclopädie* (sec. ii, vol. xxxvi. pp. 12-18). See also his *Ein mutazilitischer Kalam* and his *Beiträge zur Literaturgeschichte der Karäer* (Berlin, 1887) on Bashazi. Cf. also Jost's *Geschichte,* ii. c. 13.

11 Kairowan was one of the greatest centres of Jewish learning in North Africa during that period.

12 See, however, Professor D. Kaufmann's note in the *Jewish Quarterly Review,* i. p. 441. From this it would seem that the creed of R. Judah Hallevi may be formulated in the following articles:—The conviction of the existence of God, of His eternity, of His guidance of our fathers, of the Divine Origin of the Law, and of the proof of all this, the pledge or token of its truth, the exodus from Egypt.

13 אמונה רמה, *Emunah Ramah,* pp. 44 and 69; cf. Gutmann, *Monatsschrift,* 1878, p. 304.

14 For the various translations of the Thirteen Articles which were originally composed in Arabic, see Steinschneider, Cat. Bodl. col. 1887. Cf. Rosin, *Ethik des Maimonides,* p. 30; Weiss, *Beth Talmud,* i. p. 330, and *Ben Chananjah,* 1863, p. 942, and 1864, pp. 648 and 697, and Landshut, עמודי העבודה, p. 231.

15 מנחת קנאות. See pp. 1-16.

16 See *Hammaskir,* viii. pp. 63 and 103.

17 See Steinschneider, *Cat. München,* No. 210.

18 See the Collection דברי חכמים, by Ashkenazi, pp. 56 b seq.

[19] See Albo, c. iii. Probably identical with the author mentioned by Duran, 13 b.

[20] ספר נצחון, "Sepher Nizzachon."

[21] See אור ה' (ed. Johannisburg), preface, and pp. 20 a, 44 b, 59 b, and elsewhere. The style of this author is very obscure. Cf. Joel's pamphlet on this author (Breslau, 1874).

[22] See the first pages of the מגן אבות (Leghorn, 1758), and his משפט אוהב, pp. 13 seq.

[23] עקרים, *Ikkarim*, "Fundamentals."

[24] See *Ikkarim*, i. c. 23, and Maimonides' *Commentary on the Mishnah* (end of tractate Maccoth). On Albo compare Schlesinger's Introduction and notes to the *Ikkarim*, Joel's pamphlet, p. 82; Paulus, *Monatsschrift*, 1874, p. 463, and Brüll's *Jahrb.* iv. p. 52.

[25] I know his work from a MS. in the British Museum, Orient. 39.

[26] דרך אמונה, *Derech Emunah*. Cf. Steinschneider, *Monatsschrift*, 1883, p. 79 seq.

[27] See עקידת יצחק, gate 55.

[28] See his יסוד האמונה and מאמר האחדות.

[29] ראש אמנה.

[30] See בחינת הדת, ed. Reggio, p. 28.

[31] See מעשה טוביה (Venice, 1707), 16 a and 23 a. His language is very vague.

[32] See the Collection by Ashkenazi (as above, note 18), p. 29 b.

[33] See his בשמים ראש, p. 331.

[34] See Weiss's admirable monograph on Maimonides, published in the *Beth Talmud*, i.

THE DOCTRINE OF DIVINE RETRIBUTION IN RABBINICAL LITERATURE

[1] *Sabbath*, 55 a.

[2] *Sayings of the Fathers* (ed. C. Taylor), v. 12-15. See also *Sabbath,* 32 seq., and *Mechilta* (ed. Friedman), 95 b. *Arachin*, 16 a.

[3] See *Mechilta*, 25 a, 32 b. *Gen. Rabbah*, ch. 48, and *Tossephta Sotah,* iv. 7, and parallels.

[4] *Taanith*, 21 a.

[5] *Sayings of the Fathers*, iv. 5.

[6] *Baba Bathra*, 9 b.

[7] *Yoma*, 39 a.

[8] *Berachoth*, 33 a.

[9] *Sabbath*, 13 b.

[10] *Berachoth*, 7 a.

11 See *Mechilta*, 68 b, and parallels. *Siphra*, 112 b. *Pessikta* of R. Kahana, 167 b. Cp. *Sanhedrin*, 44 a.

12 *Aboth* de R. Nathan, 40 a, 59 b, and 62 b.

13 *Baba Bathra*, 10 a.

14 *Eccles. Rabbah*, ix. 7.

15 5 a.

16 7 b.

17 See *Mechilta*, 95 b, and parallels.

18 See *Kiddushin*, 40 b. *Mechilta*, 63 b. *Lev. Rabbah*, iv.

19 See *Sabbath*, 54 a.

20 *Exodus Rabbah*, c. 35, and parallels.

21 See *Negaim*, ii. 1.

22 *Exod. Rabbah*, c. 46.

23 *Taanith*, 11 a.

24 See *Berachoth*, 5 a.

25 *Tanchuma*, ‏כי תצא‎, § 2. Cp. *Mechilta*, 72 b.

26 *Siphré*, 73 b, and parallels.

27 *Taanith*, 8 a.

28 *Arachin*, 16 b.

29 *Sayings of the Fathers*, iv. 15.

30 See *Chagigah*, 5 a.

31 *Sabbath*, 55 a.

32 *Menachoth*, 29 b.

33 *Taanith*, 25 a.

34 *Gen. Rabbah*, xxvii.; *Pessikta*, 136 b; *Sanhedrin*, vi. 5; *Berachoth*, 7 a.

35 *Sayings of the Fathers*, i. 3, p. 27, ed. Taylor. See also note 8.

36 *Abodah Zarah*, 19 a; *Siphré*, 79 b.

37 *Berachoth*, 58 b.

38 See *Exod. R.*, 30, and parallels.

39 See ‏ראשית חכמה‎, i. 9.

40 See ‏רמתים צופים‎, 33 b.

41 See *Sabbath*, 55 b, and *Siphra*, 27 a.

SAINTS AND SAINTLINESS

1 Delivered in the Course of Public Lectures of the Jewish Theological Seminary of America, February 9, 1905.

2 *Kethuboth*, 17 a. A fair collection of references to Rabbinic Literature regarding the expressions *Chasid* and *Chesed* is to be found in the *Sefer Chasidim*, Parma, p. 240, note 1.

³ Rabbi Bachye ben Bakodah, חובות הלבבות, ch. 9; ש"פ, by Maimonides, ch. 4 and ch. 6. Cf. Schechter, Jewish Quarterly Review, X, pp. 8-12, quotations given there in the text and notes.

⁴ See R. Moses Chayim Luzzatto, מסילת ישרים, ed. Wilna, p. 48, something of this definition.

⁵ See Midrash to Psalms, 149.

⁶ See Schultz, "Old Testament Theology," II, p. 80.

⁷ See ibid.

⁸ *Baba Kama*, 30 a.

⁹, ¹⁰ See above, p. 9.

¹¹ See *Kuzari*, ed. Sluzki, p. 61; טוא"ח, 113, on חסידי אשכנז.

¹² See *Berachoth*, 30 b and 32 b.

¹³ See *Sotah*, 40 a; T. J. *Berachoth*, 4 d.

¹⁴ T. J. *Berachoth*, 7 d.

¹⁵ T. J. ibid. See the end of the prayer of R. Tanchum.

¹⁶ See *Midrash* to Ps., ch. 76.

¹⁷ *Berachoth*, 3 b.

¹⁸ See Bachye, חיה"ל, ed. Sluzki, 127 a.

¹⁹ See שערי ציון, a liturgical collection very popular in the East.

²⁰ *Abraham Lincoln, Complete Works,* vol. II, p. 661.

²¹ See *Kuzari*, ibid.

²² See *Bezah*, 16 a.

²³ *Kuzari*, 62 b.

²⁴ See *Pesikta Rabbathi*, 117 b.

²⁵ See *Shabbath*, 150 b, and *Pesikta Rabbathi*, 116 b.

²⁶ See *Shabbath*, 12 b.

²⁷ See *Life and Conversations of R. Nachman of Braslaw.*

²⁸ See *Kuzari*, 59 a.

²⁹ *Yebamoth*, 20 a.

³⁰ See his commentary to Leviticus, 19:2.

³¹ See below, p. 216.

³² See *Mishnah Ta'anith*, IV, 3.

³³ See ראשית חכמה by R. Elijah de Vidas, especially the chapters on Holiness and Repentance.

³⁴ See תולדות אדם, by Ezekiel Feivel ben Zeeb, containing the life of that Rabbi.

³⁵ See *Aboth*, V: 4.

³⁶ See *Little Sefer Chasidim* (page 13 a), by Rabbi Moses Cohen ben Eliezer, printed in Warsaw, 1866. Cf. Guedemann, *Geschichte des Erziehungswesens,* etc., III, p. 212.

³⁷ See אורחות צדיקים (Königsberg), p. 41 a.

³⁸ לקוטי תורה, by Rabbi Mordecai of Czernobile, Lemberg, 1867, p. 6 b.

[39] See מדרש פנחס of Rabbi Pinchas, of Korzek, 26 b. To be quoted hereafter as M. P.

[40] See *M. P.* 27 a.

[41] See *Baba Kama*, 30 a.

[42] See שמירת הלשון, Warsaw, 1884, where all the Rabbinic references on this point will be found.

[43] *Makkoth*, 24 a. Cf. also Rashi's commentary.

[44] J. T. *Terumoth*, 46 c.

[45] See *Ecclesiastes Rabbah*, and *Sefer Chasidim*, 44.

[46] שערי הקדושה, Rabbi Chayim Vital, Warsaw, 1876, p. 9 a, to be quoted in this article as Vital.

[47] See Vital, 15 a.

[48] See *M. P.* 21 b.

[49] See Horodetzky, *Hashiloah*, XV, 167.

[50] See *M. P.* 21 b and 24 b.

[51] Vital, 17 a.

[52] Vital, 9 a.

[53] See *Aboth*, IV: 4.

[54] *Derech Erez Zuta*, 10.

[55] *M. P.* 22 a.

[56] See Vital, p. 13 a, who introduces this passage with אמרו, whilst the whole style proves it to be a Midrash. Cf. *Shabbath*, 31 a, but it forms no exact parallel passage.

[57] Guttman, דרך אמונה ומעשה רב, Warsaw, 1898, 7 a.

[58] *Sefer Chasidim*, Parma, 363.

[59] *M. P.* 28 a.

[60] הנהגות of Rabbi *Melech*.

[61] *M. P.* 26 a.

[62] See Horodetzky, *Hashiloah*, XV, 170.

[63] See *Kethuboth*, 50 a. See also commentaries.

[64] *Aboth*, V: 10.

[65] See *Baba Bathra*, 7 b.

[66] See לקוטי אמרים, ed. Wilna, 1896, p. 52 a seq.

[67] Guttman, ibid., p. 11 a.

[68] See below, p. 277, the story of Loria and Useda.

[69] See Chayim Meïr Heilman, בית רבי, Berditczev, 1892, II: 3 a.

[70] See *Little Sefer Chasidim*, 13 a. See also below, p. 238.

[71] See *Sefer Chasidim*, Parma, 477 and 478.

[72] See Kaydanower, ch. 7.

[73] See above, p. 157, and also below, p. 270.

[74] Ps. 16: 8, 9 seq.

[75] See עמק המלך by Naphtali Bacharach, 121 c, to be quoted hereaftei as Bacharach.

[76] See Bachye, חוה"ל, 126 b seq.

[77] See Rabbi Judah Halevi, *Divan,* II, 91 a.

[78] See *Zohar,* ed. Krotoschin, to Num., p. 222 b. Ibid. to Deut., p. 281 a.
Cf. Luzzatto, מסילת ישרים, 29 a. See also *Sefer Chasidim,* Parma,
p. 240, note 1.

[79] See בית רבי, I: 16 a.

THE CHASSIDIM

[1] SUBJOINED IS A LIST OF SELECTED AUTHORITIES ON THE SUBJECT OF THE
CHASSIDIM.—*Historical and Bibliographical Works:* Graetz (xi. including the polemical literature quoted in the Appendix), Jost, Peter
Beer, M. Bodek (סדר הדורות החדש, Lemberg, 1865), A. Walden (החדש
שם הגדולים, Warschau, 1864), Finn (קריה נאמנה, Wilna, 1860), D.
Kahana, (אבן אופל) in the periodical השחר, iv.), Zederbaum (כתר
כהונה, Odessa, 1868). *Essays and Satires:* T. Erter (הצופה, Wien, 1858),
S. Szantó (*Jahrbuch für Israeliten,* p. 108-178, 1867), A. Gottlober
(in his periodical הבוקר אור, iii.), L. Löw (Ben Chananjah, ii.), Ru-
dermann (השחר, vi.), Rapoport (נחלת יהודה, Lemberg, 1873, p. 10),
Fröhlich (המדריך, Warschau, 1876, p. 63 seq.), S. Maimon (*Auto-
biographie,* Berlin, 1792). Compare also the Hebrew novels by P.
Smolensky, L. Gordon, M. Brandstätter, A. Gottlober and B. Horo-
witz (German). *Occasional references* to the liturgy or the system
of the Chassidim in the "Responses" of R. Ezechiel Landau, Moses
Sopher, E. Flekeles and T. Steinhart, and in the works of Israel
Samostsch, Salomon Chelma and Chayim Walosin. Compare also
Zunz (*Gottesdienstliche Vorträge,* p. 477) and L. Löw (*Mannheimer
Album,* Wien, 1874), Senior Sachs (התחיה, i. 61) and B. L. Zeitlin
(חזות קשה, Paris, 1846). The best book on the whole subject is E.
Zweifel's work שלום על ישראל (Zitomyr 1868, three parts), which I
strongly recommend to students. The books written by the Chassidim
would amount to more than 200. They are catalogued by Bodek and
Walden. I shall only draw the attention of the student to the works
of Beer, Salomon Ladier, and Mendel Witipsker on one side, who
developed the theory of the Immanence, and those of Nachman
Braslaw and Melech Liezensker, who, on the other hand, carried the
theory of Zaddikism to its utmost consequences. The student will find
a fair collection of sayings and sentences arranged according to theological subjects in the books דרך חסידים and לשון חכמים (Anon.,
Lemberg, 1876).

[2] הסידים, "pious ones" (Ps. xxxvii. 28, lxx. 2, etc.). The reader is probably acquainted with the term from the Maccabean history (1 Macc.

ii. 42, vii. 13), in which the strict party, opposed to all Hellenistic influence, are called "Assideans" [R.V. "Hasidaeans"], Gr. Ἀσιδαῖοι.

[3] בעל שם, "The Master of the Name," a term usually applied to exorcists, who cast out devils and performed other miracles through adjuration by the name of God (or angels). The unbelieving Rabbis maintained indeed that in his exorcisms Baalshem employed "impure names" (of devils), whilst the Chassidim, on the other hand, declared that their Master never used "names" at all, his miracles being performed by the divine in Baalshem to which all nature owes obedience. Occasionally the Chassidim call him בעל שם טוב (The Man of Good Name), in allusion to Eccles. vii. 1, shortened by some into *Besht*.

[4] בית המדרש—"House of Research" or of "study" (of the Law), but in which also divine service is held thrice a day.

[5] תלמיד חכם—"Disciple of the Wise," the usual title of a scholar or student.

[6] A Jewish sect, so called after their founder Jacob Leibovicz Frank, who was himself one of the apostles of the pseudo-Messiah Shabbethai Tsebi of Smyrna in Turkey. Among his other doctrines he taught also a sort of Trinity, consisting of the Holy Ancient One, the Holy King or the Messiah, and a feminine person in the Godhead, in which he, like his master, represented the Second Person. The sect ultimately abolished the Law, and, after many controversies with the Rabbinic Jews, went over to Catholicism, the dominant religion in Poland, by which they were soon absorbed. Eybeschütz, chief Rabbi of Prague and Hamburg, was suspected by Emden to be a secret adherent of Shabbethai Tsebi, which was tantamount to apostasy from Judaism. Eybeschütz protested. The litigants excommunicated each other, and the Rabbis divided into two camps, taking sides either with Emden or with his antagonist.

[7] The works of Maimonides or Moses b. Maimon (1135-1204) are too many to be enumerated here. The most important are the *Guide of the Perplexed* (מורה נבוכים) and his *Compendium of the Law* (משנה תורה). Judah Hallevi or Abul Hassan flourished in the first half of the twelfth century. He is well known as a poet by his *Divan* and as a deep religious thinker by his *Cusari*. The former contains also many songs of a secular nature. Isaac Alfasi (died 1103) is best known by his Compendium of the Talmud, which was so greatly admired by his contemporaries that they declared it could never have been composed "without the aid of the Holy Spirit." R. Solomon b. Isaac, also called by his initials Rashi (1040-1105), is well known by his commentaries on the Bible and the Talmud.

[8] רבי, רבינו.

[9] ספר, *Sepher*.

[10] The Hebrew word is פלפול, meaning subtle discussion and sharp distinction. The word is closely related to פלפל or פלפלא, which means "pepper" or "seasoning."

[11] מהרם שיף = R. Meir Shiff, whose *novellæ* on the Talmud are of a very subtle kind, and were very popular with the students of this work.

[12] תנאים—אמוראים, "The Repeaters," and "The Interpreters." The sayings and statements of the former are embodied in the Mishnah, a work compiled by R. Judah the Saint about 220 A.C., and covering a period of about 250 years (30 B.C.-220 A.C.). The latter occupied themselves mainly with the interpretation of the Mishnah, and their discussions and controversies are incorporated in the Talmud of Jerusalem and that of Babylon, and extend over the period from 220-500 A.C. The Talmud of Jerusalem is mostly the product of the schools of Palestine. The Talmud of Babylon is a growth of that country. The authorities of this latter Talmud being far away from the place where the first great Rabbis lived and laboured, their traditions are naturally not so historically reliable as those of the Talmud of Jerusalem. The authorities of Palestine were also simpler in their method of interpretation. These again are followed by the Babylonian schools of new interpreters (of the Talmud).

[13] שדין יהודאין, an expression that goes back as far as to the *Zohar*.

[14] זוהר, "Brightness." Cf. Dan. xii. 3,—the authors of "The Brightness" pretending to be the *Maskilim* or "Wise Ones" mentioned in this verse.

[15] שפלות.

[16] שמחה.

[17] התלהבות.

[18] צדיק, pl. צדיקים.

NACHMANIDES

[1] In Steinschneider's *Catalogue of the Bodleian Library*, under the name of Moses Nachmanides, pp. 1947-1965, all the works which are ascribed to this author are put together, and also discussed as to their authenticity. There are only to be added the new edition of the *Derasha* by Jellinek (Vienna, 1872), in which the variants from Schorr's MS. (החלוץ, viii. 162) are already incorporated; a new edition of the ויכוח, and the commentary to Is. lii.-liii. by Steinschneider (Berlin, 1860); a *Sermon* for the New Year, ed. by H. Berliner (*Libanon*, v. 564); and another Sermon at a wedding (?), ed. by Schorr (*Hechaluz*, xii. 3). For the literature on Nachmanides, besides the

references given by Steinschneider, in his *Catalogue,* and the Addenda, p. cxviii. (cf. also the pedigree in the *Catalogue* 2305), see also Graetz, *Geschichte,* vii., pp. 112-143, and p. 147 seq.; Michael, אור החיים No. 1125, and Weiss, דור דור ודורשיו, v. seq.; Perles' *Monatsschrift,* 1860, p. 175; Zomber, *ibid.* 421; and Z. Frankel, *ibid.* 1868, p. 449, and *The Jewish Quarterly Review,* iv. 245 seq. For Nachmanides' disputation we have to add M. Loeb in the *Révue des Études Juives,* xv. 1 seq., and xviii. 52 (about Abner), and Dr. Neubauer's Essay on Jewish Controversy in the *Expositor,* vol. vii. (third series), p. 98 seq., with the references given there. See also his article on the Bahir and the Zohar in *The Jewish Quarterly Review,* iv. 357. With regard to Nachmanides' mystical system see the references to S. Sachs (whose remarks are most suggestive), Krochmal, and Jellinek in Steinschneider, col. 1949 and 1964, Perles' *Monatsschrift,* 1858, p. 83 seq., and Steinschneider in the *Heb. Bibliographie,* i. 34. See also Professor Kaufmann's *Die Geschichte der Attributenlehre,* and the references given in the index under this name. The *Novellæ* by his son R. Nachman, alluded to in the text, are in the University Library, Cambridge (Add. 1187, 2). The קץ הגאולה is extant in the British Museum, MS. Add. 26,894, and the passage quoted by De Rossi is to be found on p. 163 b, but a few words are erased by the censor. As to the poem given at the end of this paper, see Zunz, *Synagogale Poesie,* p. 478; Landshut, *Amude ha-Abodah s.v.,* the references in Sachs' *Religiöse Poesie der Juden,* and Luzzatto in the *Ozar Nechmad,* ii. 27. Compare also Professor Cheyne's *The Origin of the Psalter,* p. 421.

2 New Year's Day, on the first of Tishri. It is in autumn.

3 A famous Rabbi of the fifteenth century, known by his various casuistical and philosophical works.

4 Chiefly known through his controversial writings against the adherents of the pseudo-Messiah Shabbethai Tsebi. He was for some time the Rabbi of the Portuguese congregation in London.

5 The main objections of the opponents of Maimonides were directed against his rationalistic notions of Revelation, and his allegorising interpretation of the Scriptures, which amounted in some places to a denial of miracles. He was also suspected of having denied bodily resurrection. A history of Jewish rationalism is still a desideratum. I am certain that it would prove at least as interesting as Reuter's *Geschichte der religiösen Aufklärung im Mittelalter* (Berlin, 1845-60).

6 רבינו משה.

7 אגדות, "Homilies."

8 קץ הגאולה, "The end of the Redemption," that is the time when the advent of the Messiah is to be expected.

9 This patriarch is famous in Jewish legend for his hospitality. See Beer's *Leben Abrahams,* pp. 37 and 56.

10 This is the quorum necessary to form a congregation (עדה) for the purpose of holding divine service.

11 By *Zobah,* or *Aram Zobah,* the Jews of the Middle Ages usually understood Aleppo. See Benjamin of Tudela's *Itinerary,* i. 88, ii. 124 (London and Berlin, 1840-41).

12 See subsequently where a full translation of the letter is given.

13 הלכות גדולות, a compendium of the Law, dating from the ninth century, by R. Simon Caro.

14 R. Simlai flourished in Palestine in the third century. He is best known as an Agadic teacher and a great controversialist. According to him, 613 commandments were given to Moses on Mount Sinai, of which 365 are prohibitive laws, whilst the remaining 248 are positive injunctions.

15 שער הגמול, "Treatise on Reward (and Punishment)."

16 עולם הבא.

17 Ps. cix. 4; ואני תפלה.

18 אצילת.

19 נפש חיה.

20 ידיעה, "Knowledge," "Foreknowledge," "Omniscience."

21 שכינה, כבוד.

22 סגולה. See Exod. xix. 5

23 חקים.

24 קרבן, קרב.

25 According to a Jewish tradition (the date of which is uncertain) the advent of the Messiah, the Son of David, will be preceded by that of the Messiah, the Son of Joseph. The latter will perish in the battle against Gog and Magog (the Antichrist of Jewish literature), but will soon be brought back to life on the appearance of the former. Cf. G. H. Dalman's *Der leidende und der sterbende Messias der Synagoge* (Berlin, 1881).

26 בראשית, "In the beginning," Gen. i. 1.

27 מאין; Job xxvii. 12.

28 *Chagigah* 14 b. The activity of these four Rabbis falls chiefly in the second century. R. Akiba died as a martyr in the Hadrianic persecution (about 130). Elisha b. Abuyah, the apostate, was usually called אחר, *Acher,* "the other one."

29 The former lived in the twelfth, the latter in the sixteenth, century. They are both known for their hostility to philosophy.

30 Bachya wrote in the eleventh century a famous book called חובות הלבבות, *The Duties of the Heart.*

31 A younger contemporary of Maimonides, who translated the *Guide* from Arabic into Hebrew.

32 ספר המשכל. R. Moses Cordovera, the author of the פרדס, lived in Safed in the sixteenth century. For R. Isaac Loria, the author of the עץ החיים, see above, note 5 to Elijah Wilna.

33 שושן סודות.

34 ספר הבהיר, a forgery by a Provençal Jew of the thirteenth century, who attributed it to a Rabbi of the first century.

35 This hymn is now incorporated in her excellent little book, *Songs of Zion*, pp. 13-15.

36 זהוב, a gold piece. The country and the date of the writer not being certain, it is impossible to determine the value of this coin.

37 The lawfulness of eating this fish (= sturgeon?) was contested for many centuries, and the controversy still continues.

38 פשוט, a smaller coin than the Zehub.

39 שמע, "Hear," the verses from Deut. vi. 4-9, xi. 13-21, and Num. xv. 37-41, recited twice a day by the Jews.

SAFED IN THE SIXTEENTH CENTURY

1 See Schwartz, p. 476; cf. Baedeker, Index. See also Rapoport, Introduction to קורא הדורות of Shalom Cohen (Warsaw, 1838).

2 See Caro I, 1.

3 See Graetz, *Geschichte d. Juden*, 2d ed., IX: 29 seq.; cf. also English Translation, IV:400 seq.

4 אור החיים, ch. V; cf. Kayserling, *Geschichte d. Juden in Portugal*, pp. 42 and 96.

5 See Neubauer's "Mediæval Jewish Chronicles," I:111. Similar sentiments may also be found in R. Isaac Arama's חזות קשה.

6 Ed. Pietrkow (1902), p. 42.

7 See *Responsa* of R. Asher (Rosh), VIII:10.

8 See Epstein, *Revue des Etudes Juives*, XLII, p. 18, and Büchler, XLIV, p. 241 seq.

9 See Graetz, *Geschichte*, VII : 13; cf. Schwarz, 443. Of course, this brief outline has to be completed by the accounts of the travels of Benjamin of Tudela, and R. Pethahiah, and similar works.

10 See Pharchi, כפתר ופרח.

11 See Hebrew Appendix *Ozar Tob* to *Magazin*, I:027; see also Graetz, *Geschichte*, VII : 182; cf. Hebrew periodical *Jerusalem*, edited by Luncz, II, p. 7.

12 See Graetz, *Geschichte*, VII:308-9, and Jerusalem, II, p. 12.

13 See Carmoly, *Itinéraires*, 261, from an unpublished MS. (cod. Paris, 1070); cf. also Pharchi, 284.

14 See *Jerusalem*, VI, p. 337.

[15] See Graetz, *Geschichte,* IX:28; cf. the Hebrew translation, VIII:26, notes 2 and 4. The name points to a Spanish origin; cf. also Azkari, 24 a, and Azulai, *s. n.* The date of Saragossi's settling in Safed cannot be ascertained, but it must have been during the first two decades of the sixteenth century.

[16] See Bertinoro, 209 and 222; cf. Graetz, *Geschichte,* VIII:278, and IX:26, and Rabinowitz, 213; but see also Luncz in *Jerusalem,* I, p. 58. It should, however, be remarked that the travellers are not quite unanimous in their evidence as to the hostility of the Mohammedan population toward the Jews. On the other hand, it seems that matters with regard to taxes deteriorated later in Safed. Cf. Caro I, 1, and *Jerusalem,* V, p. 161.

[17] See Bertinoro, 222.

[18] See An. Jb., 277.

[19] See Shlomel, 42 d; see also Kaydanower, ch. 16, and טהרת הקודש, I, 43 a.

[20] See Sh. J, 16 b; Shlomel, 43 a; see also Responsa of R. Solomon Cohen, II, 38; Responsa להם רב, by R. Abraham Boton, 148; מאמץ כח by R. Moses Almosnino, 16 a.

[21] See in general about Caro, Graetz, *Geschichte,* IX, Index; Rabinowitz, Index; Cassel, *Joseph Karo und das Maggid Mescharim* (Berlin, 1888), and the authorities mentioned in Dr. Louis Ginzberg's article "Caro," J. Encycl. See Neubauer, Catalogue, no. 2578, containing a list of ten eulogies on the death of Joseph Caro, and as to the *untrustworthiness* of the Mentor-Angel, see Rabinowitz, p. 43, note 4.

[22] MM 17 a.

[23] Cassel, ibid., is almost the only writer who doubted the authenticity of this work. His arguments are in every respect weak, whilst there is contemporary evidence to the contrary. See Rabinowitz, 242 seq., Brüll, *Jahrbücher,* IX:150, and Ginzberg, ibid.

[24] See MM 4 a, 13 c, 18 c, 23 d, 33 b, 49 a.

[25] See MM 3 c.

[26] See Horwitz, של"ה (ed. Warsaw), 162 a seq.

[27] See MM 22 c.

[28] See MM 11 c, 12 a, 17 a, 25 c, cf. Graetz, *Geschichte,* IX:340 and 561, but see also Hebrew translation, VII:415, and appendix at the end by Jaffe.

[29] See especially MM, pp. 25 c and 26 a about הרי"ט (ריוסף? טאיטאצק); cf. Kahana, 77, note 1.

[30] See MM 18 c and 28 a.

[31] See MM 4 a, 16 a, 37 a.

[32] See MM 6 b, 34 a, 50 a.

[33] See MM 28 a.

[34] See MM 35 c.

35 See MM 2 b.

36 See MM 30 d, 37 b.

37 See MM 16 a, 18 d, 46 a.

38 See MM 46 d.

39 See MM 3 a, 14 a, 21 c, 24 c, 25 d, 34 d, 44 d.

40 See MM 3 b.

41 See MM 3 d, 21 b, c.

42 See MM 52 b.

43 See MM 29 d.

44 See MM 3 b, 41 d.

45 See MM 3 b.

46 See MM 13 a, 18 c.

47 See MM 8 a, 10 b, 19 d, 23 d, 26 b.

48 See MM 8b, c.

49 See MM 50 d.

50 See MM 4 d, 13 d, 14 a, 19 d, 20 d, 21 a, 27 a, 29 b. About Nicopolis in particular, ibid., 17 b.

51 See MM 25 c.

52 See MM 12 d, 13 a.

53 See MM 23 a.

54 See MM 5 a, 6 b, 8 d, 14 c, 25 b and c, 27 a, b, c, 28 d, 30 a and b, 34 b, 42 c.

55 See MM 3 d, 4 b and c, 8 c, 9 c, 16 d, 19 d, 24 d, 30 c, 46 c, 50 a and d. About the possibility of references to Alkabez, see Rabinowitz, 245, note 1. See also below, note 76.

56 The following remarks about Molko are mostly based on Graetz, *Geschichte,* IX, Index. See also English translation IV, Index, and Vogelstein and Rieger, *Geschichte der Juden in Rom,* II, Index.

57 See Graetz, *Geschichte,* VIII:253 and 562, and references given there, to which Sambari, p. 147, may be added. See, however, Rabinowitz, 152, note 1. His doubts are fully justified, as there is not a single real trace in all the contemporary literature coming from Palestine pointing to Molko's staying in that country.

58 See references given to MM in note 55, especially the one to MM 50 a.

59 See above, note 50. See also Horwitz, של"ה I, 134 b, and Guttman, דדך אמונה ומעשה רב, Warsaw, 1898, 14 b.

60 See Azulai *s. n.;* cf. also Ghirondi, p. 380 seq. See also Alkabez, Introduction to his ברית הלוי (Lemberg, 1863); cf. Brüll, *Jahrbücher,* IX, 150, and Rabinowitz, 245. See also Landshut, עמודי העבודה, *s. n.*

61 See MM 50 d (headed עמום), which is dated in the MSS. of the MM the second Adar רצו (March, 1536), and it is clear from the contents that Caro was still in חוץ לארץ at that period. For the fact that there were about one thousand families in Safed, I have only the authority of Graetz, *Geschichte,* VII:302. See Trani, III, 48.

[62] See Trani, I, 28; Caro II, 16 c. Alsheich, Responsa, no, 27, and cf. Shlomel, 43 a.

[63] See Frumkin, 7.

[64] See Responsa of Berab, no. 22; Bacharach, 109 c; Boton, לחם דר, no. 92, and Vital, 13 b. There are also in the book תקון ישׁשׁכר, by R. Issachar b. Mordecai b. Shushan, references to קהלות הספרדים and קהל האשׁכנזים.

[65] See Trani, III, 48.

[66] See Trani, I, 106; II, 115 and 131; Responsa by Alsheich, no. 27; Responsa by R. Joseph Trani, I, 82.

[67] See Sh. J., 16 b, and Bertinoro, 222.

[68] See Sh. J., 16 b, and Trani, III, 46.

[69] See Berab, no. 22; Trani, I, 171; II, 25; Radbaz, II, 638, and Responsa of R. Moses Galanti, no. 11.

[70] See Chabib, 292 d.

[71] See R. Chayim Alsheich's Preface to the Pentateuch Commentary of R. Moses Alsheich, ed. Venice, 1601, p. 6 a. Cf. Leo Modena's *Briefe* (ed. by Prof. Dr. L. Blau), Letter 147.

[72] See Berliner, periodical *Jerusalem*, II, 68 seq. The Jewish Theological Seminary Library possesses the most important productions of this press.

[73] See Sh. J., 16 b, and Shlomel, 43 a.

[74] See Responsa of R. Isaac de Latas, p. 54; cf. Graetz, *Geschichte*, IX, end.

[75] See above, p. 209.

[76] See MM 19 d; cf. ibid. 4 d. There can be little doubt that the Solomon mentioned there is Solomon Alkabez.

[77] About Berab and the history of the Ordination controversy, see Graetz, *Geschichte*, IX:300 seq.; Rabinowitz, 218 seq.; and the references given there, especially to the אגרת הסמיכה forming an appendix to the Responsa of Chabib. It should never be forgotten that in judging Berab we are entirely dependent on material coming from an opponent, who in the heat of the controversy could with all his meekness not remain impartial to his antagonist, and therefore large deductions should be made from all that is said in the aforementioned appendix of the harshness of Berab's character and of the real motives for his action. Cf. also Frumkin, 38 seq.

[78] See Chabib, 186 d, 198 d, 302 b, and 305 c.

[79] See Chabib, 188 d. Of the four ordained, we have only the names of Caro and Trani. Graetz, *Geschichte* IX:307, note, and Frumkin, 73, note 1, advance hypotheses as to the names of the other two. Yachya in his שׁלשׁלת הקבלה speaks of ten who received the Ordination, but the meaning of the passage is not quite certain.

[80] See MM 29 a; cf. Graetz, ibid. 311. Caro seems to have given up the

matter altogether afterwards, there being not a single reference to the Ordination question, either in his חשן משפט, no. 61, or in his commentary to Maimonides' ה' סנהדרין משנה תורה, IV. Only in his בית יוסף to the חשן משפט, no. 295, there is a faint reference to it. Cf. Azulai's חשן משפט בדבי יוסף to, חשן משפט, 64.

81 See MM 16 d.

82 About Trani, see Fin, הכדמל (octavo edition), II, 586 seq.

83 See Trani, II, 67; cf. also I, 41 and 47.

84 See Trani, III, 48.

85 See e. g. Trani, I, 156, 189, 274, 336; II, 46 and 180; cf. Caro I, 24.

86 See אהבת ציון, Anon., 26 d. Cf. also Caro I, 14, where he speaks of his lack of time, which is given to lecturing to the *Chaberim* both in the morning and in the evening.

87 See Alsheich, Opinion incorporated in Caro I, 73.

88 See Caro I, 92; II, 14 seq. Cf. R. Menahem Azariah of Fano, Preface to the פלח הרמון. Cf. also Azulai; Conforte; Sambari; and Kahana, p. 80 seq.

89 See *Pardes*, Preface.

90 See ברית הלוי, 39 b seq.

91 See SG, pp. 1 a 23 a and b, 24 b; cf. Kahana, p. 80, note 2.

92 With regard to Alkabez see טהרת הקודש, II, 25 b.

93 See אור הישר by Popers, 23 b. See also reference given above, note 60.

94 See Kahana, p. 145, note 6, to which are to be added R. Menahem Azariah of Fano and R. Sabbatai Horwitz, the author of שפע טל.

95 See Preface to the work mentioned in note 88. Cf. *Catalog der hebräischen Handschriften der kgl. Bibliothek in Modena*, S. Jona, p. 10 seq.; cf. also Kaufmann.

96 See the authorities quoted above in note 88; cf. also Bacharach, 7 a and 33 c.

97 Besides the usual authorities, such as Conforte (Index), Sambari (Index), and Azulai, *s. n.*, see also Calimani, and Alsheich's Preface to his Commentary to Proverbs. Cf. Leo Modena's *Briefe*, Letter 98. Most of the biographers give the relation of Loria as stated in the text. Cf. also Vital, 2 b. Rabbi Abraham Chazkuni, however, in his book זאת חוקת התורה, states in the name of Alsheich that he had a direct tradition from Loria regarding a certain mystic point, whilst according to Calimani he was one of the direct recipients of Loria's mystical teachings. See also Steinschneider, *Jerusalem*, III, no. 33 c, to a MS. חזות קשה by Alsheich on the precarious condition of the Jews of Safed. Unfortunately, the MS. was inaccessible to me.

98 See Appendix A 298:17.

99 See Appendix A 297:4; 293:20.

[100] See Conforte (Index), and Azulai, *s. n.* Cf. Bacharach 109 c; Ch. Y. II, 4 a, and IV, 10 b; Kaydanower, 93, and Popers, 7 b.

[101] See Appendix A 294:1;2;295:6, 8; 296:13, 14, 15; 297:2; 298:15.

[102] See Azkari, Preface; cf. Kahana, p. 149.

[103] See Appendix A 297:3.

[104] See ראשית חכמה (ed. Cracow), 174 a.

[105] See Appendix A 294:36; cf. 298:11, 19, 22.

[106] See Azkari, 95 a seq.

[107] See Appendix A 293:25, cf. *Baba Bathra,* 10 a, ש"עא"ח, no. 92, end.

[108] See Appendix A 296:27; 298:16, 27.

[109] See Appendix A 293:22; cf. 294:4.

[110] See Shlomel and Vital, where such legends are scattered over the books, parallels to which are to be found in Bacharach's and Kaydonower's works in various places. Sambari, of whose chronicles the Jewish Theological Seminary Library possesses a good copy, is also replete with such stories. Cf. also נשמת חיים, III, 10, see Kahana, pp. 146, 148, and 150. Yachya in his שה"ק has also any number of such stories.

[111] The legend about Joseph is incorporated in the book לקוטי ש"ם (Livorno, 1790); Kahana, p. 11, note 5.

[112] See Appendix A 293:21; 297:8.

[113] Cf. *Shabbath,* 12 a and b, and the references given there on the margin to the codes of Maimonides and Caro.

[114] See Appendix A 293:19; 295:9, 297:7, 8; 298:13, 20.

[115] See אורחות צדיקים incorporated in the Hebrew book mentioned above in note 111, 69 b.

[116] See Azulai, *s. n.;* Ch. Y., II, 55 b.

[117] The main sources for Loria's biography are the legendary accounts, of which two versions exist. The one is that first published in the *Sammelwerk* נובלות חכמה (see Zedner, 356), and republished any number of times both as appendix to other works as well as by itself under the name of שבחי האר"י. This is the version made use of by almost all writers on the subject. The second version, strongly related to it, but in a somewhat more connected form as well as more precise in its dates, is the ספר הכונות ומעשה ניסים published first in Constantinople in 1720, and then in Safed by R. Samuel Heller in the year 1876. See also אור האמת by Moses Mordecai Lebtob, pp. 214-216, where the first two or three pages of this version are reproduced. Sambari's account of the life of Loria is omitted by Neubauer, but the Jewish Theological Seminary Library possesses a photograph copy of the whole work as preserved in the Paris MS., and a copy of the omissions relating to Safed from the Oxford MS. This account of Sambari is almost identical with the second version. Much

material is also to be found in Bacharach, 6 a, 7 b, 10 b to 14 a, 33 a to 34 a, 77 a, 109 c, 116 b and c, 126 a and d, 138 a, 141 c, 142 a and b, 143 a, 146 b, c, and d, 152 to 154. Bacharach's story is, as is well known, based on Shlomel. Kaydanower has also various legends about Loria (see chs. 2, 5, 7, 9, 12, 16, 22, 31, 34, 46, 48, 77, 80, 87, and 93), which agree on the whole with the second version. Ch. Y. also made use of this version. This version, hardly known to any modern writer except Bloch, in his *Die Kabbalah auf ihrem Höhepunkt und ihre Meister,* (Pressburg, 1905), is extant in various MSS. It is hardly necessary to say that all these legends are greatly exaggerated, and sometimes even written "with a purpose." Cf. Modena, ארי נהם, ch. 25; but on the whole, the legends fairly represent the estimation in which Loria was held by his contemporaries. Cf. also Calimani, Conforte Index, Sambari Index, and Azulai, *s. n.* See further, Graetz, *Geschichte,* IX, Index, and Kahana. The account in the texts is mostly based on the Constantinople edition, to be quoted as MN, the initials of the *Maaseh Nissim* version. Cf. also Dr. Ginzberg's article "Cabala," Jewish Encyclopedia, and the literature given there about the various mystical systems, to which has to be added Bloch as above. The reader who will study the question will find that we are still in want of a good exposition of Loria's Cabbala, its strange and bewildering terminology, and how far it is to be considered a development of Cordovero's system. The best essay on this subject is undoubtedly the just mentioned article by Dr. Ginzberg, and the book of Mieses mentioned by him; but even in these articles we have more of the system of Cordovero as expounded by R. Sabbatai Horwitz than that of Loria as conveyed by his disciple Vital.

[118] See Graetz, *Geschichte,* VIII:211-213. See also ibid., p. 292, note. Cf. Frumkin, pp. 15, 58, 61-68. From the Responsa of R. Samuel de Modena, 2, it is clear that the German-Jewish settlements in the Turkish Empire preceded those of the Spanish Jews. Cf. Solomon Rosanis, דברי ימי ישראל בתוגרמה, p. 163 seq. Graetz's statement in *Geschichte,* IX:24, that the Jewish settlement in Jerusalem counted in the year 1522 fifteen hundred families rests on a mistaken reading of his authority, where Graetz, by some oversight, added the word מאות, which is not to be found in the text. The sense in the Sh. J. is plain enough, that the German community counted fifteen families. Cf. Schwarz, pp. 453 and 457. See also Epstein, משפחת לרויא, pp. 33 and 35. It is interesting to see that our Loria's son was named Solomon Loria, probably after his grandfather.

[119] See MN 2 a. Cf. Azulai, *s. n.,* and Ch. Y., 13 b. According to Conforte (40 b), however, Loria was the pupil of R. David Abi Zimra and the

colleague of R. Bezaleel, a view which is supported by Vital, 9 a, רבך
רדב"ז.

120 See MN 2 a-b. The MS. has the following important additional
matter: ויתן לו הספר ההוא וילך ויתבודד בביתו בחצירו ששה שנים
. . . ולפעמים אומרים לו . . . צריך סיגופים אחרים קשים מהראשונים
וכראותו כן יצא מחצירו והלך כן להתבודד במצרים הישנה סמוך לנהר
נילוס ב' שנים אחרים ובכל ערב שבת הולך לביתו. Sambari has the
following words: במצרים הישנה בכפר אחד שנ' המקייאץ שבצוען מצרים
הנקרא אל"רודא ע"י חמיו שהיה עשיר גדול וזה הכפר היה ברשותו.
See Shlomel's chronology (p. 33 d), which is somewhat different.
It is to be observed that the MS. contains no statement as to
the date of Loria's leaving Egypt, so that it may be fixed with
Graetz, *Geschichte,* IX: 587, not later than 1568. This would allow
ample time for his making the acquaintance of Cordovero, who
died in 1570, and becoming his regular disciple. Kahana's arguments against Graetz (p. 150) are not convincing. We have always
to remember that the tendency was to reduce Loria's residence in
Safed to a minimum, so as to make him entirely independent of
Cordovero.

121 See Shlomel, 33 b, and Preface to the עץ החיים. About the mystical
writings of R. David Abi Zimra, and those of R. Bezaleel, see Azulai,
s. n.

122 See Kahana, p. 203, note 1.

123 See Sambari, 151, and Conforte, 40 b.

124 See MN 1 b. The MS. adds Joseph Ashkenazi.

125 See *Pardes,* 77 a.

126 *Pardes,* 26 a.

127 Introduction to the פלח הרמון, 3 b.

128 See MN 2 b and 3 a. More fully in the MS. 3 a-b. וכובש נביאתו מפני
הרמ"ק . . . וביום שנפטר אמר להם . . . שבימי היו צינורי קדושה
התומים כתבתי דברי בסתום גדול בבחינת ספירות אבל אחרי מותי
יתגלו יותר הצינורות ויפרש האיש ההוא דברי בבחינת פרצופים כדאיתא
בס"פ ד"ץ אידרות. See also Preface to עה"ח. Cf. Graetz, *Geschichte,*
IX: 589. See also Bloch (as above, note 117), p. 35.

129 See above, note 120, and below, note 163, as to the date of Loria's
death.

130 See Shlomel, 44 b, and Bacharach, 6 c. It is to be noticed that Vital
maintained a sceptical attitude toward the relations of Caro's Maggid.
See Kahana, p. 268, text and notes, and Rabinowitz, 243. It is not
impossible that the distrust was mutual.

131 See Shlomel, 34 b seq. See also Preface to עה"ח.

132 See MN 3 a and 5 b. The author of the קול בוכים was a disciple of
Cordovero.

133 See MN 3 a b.

134 See MN 4 a b. The MS. 5 a has that Loria said: לכן עצתי שכל אחד מכם יכתוב לו מה שישמע ממני . . . אמנם לא ניתן רשות לכתוב זולת למה רח"ו. The question whether Loria wrote anything, and how far these so-called traditions in his name are to be relied upon is still a very mooted one. See Kahana, p. 202, text and notes, and references given there. The general impression one receives from the various legendary accounts quoted above is that he declined to write anything, and that he was reluctant to impart any mystical knowledge even by word of mouth.

135 See Azulai, *s. n.* See MN 3 a with regard to Loria's serving on a board.

136 See Modena, ארי נהם, p. 66.

137 See such works as the ספר הכונות in its various editions and arrangements (Zedner, 379), and the נגיד ומצוה by R. Jacob ben Chayim Zemach (Zedner, 299).

138 See *Shabbath*, 10 a.

139 See above, note 137, to which has to be added the פע"ח by Vital.

140 See Shlomel, 141 b. הסגר seems to mean a block of buildings with a synagogue attached to it. According to the Ch. Y., 34 c, it means a College or a Yeshibah. See also Vital, 16 a.

141 See Graetz, *Geschichte*, XI : 587 seq., and references given there. See also כונות (ed. Jessnitz, 1723), 1 a.

142 See above, p. 168.

143 See כונות, 2 d; cf. Kahana, p. 203, note 5.

144 See כונות, 11 c.

145 See כונות, 1 b.

146 See נגיד ומצוה, 45 b.

147 See כונות 6 c. Cf. אורחות צדיקים, 67 a.

148 See Azkari, p. 48. See also the statement of the traveller Samson Bak, *Jerusalem*, II, p. 145.

149 See כונות, 3 a.

150 See ש"ע האר"י הלכות צדקה.

151 See כונות, 1 a.

152 See Ch. Y., IV, 53 a and b.

153 See כונות, 3 b seq., 24 b seq. Bacharach, 11 d.

154 See Shlomel, 39 c, Bacharach, 11 a, and Ch. Y., I, 37 b.

155 See Shlomel, 39, and Bacharach, ibid.

156 See גלגולים (Przemysl, 1875), 86 a and b.

157 See Azulai, *s. n.*, and Kaydanower, ch. 93. Cf. *Pesikta Rabbathi*, 131 b seq., and the Second Esdras, ch. 10, *r. v.*

158 See Azulai, *s. n.*

159 See Shlomel, 39 a, Bacharach, 10 d. Cf. Graetz, *Geschichte*, IX. 588. See also ג"ל, 50 seq.; 61 seq; 87 d seq., about various contemporaries

of Loria. Cf. also Steinschneider, Catalogue Munich, 2d ed., Berlin, 1895, pp. 250-1.

160 See Shlomel, 35 b.

161 See כונות, 1 b, and Ch. Y., I, 48 b, 51 b, and 59 b.

162 See Preface to the עה"ח.

163 The date of Loria's death is given by most bibliographers as the year 1572. Against this we have, however, the evidence of Conforte, 41 a, who fixes it in the year 1573, for which he is attacked by Azulai and others. Sambari, p. 151, fixes it in the year 1574, which is also confirmed by the traveller Samson Bak. See *Jerusalem,* II, p. 146, text and notes.

164 See the statement of R. Moses Galanti, the Younger, in the preface to the book מגן דוד, by R. David Abi Zimra (Amsterdam, 1679).

165 Horwitz is the one who dwells more on the mystical exposition of the ideal man than any of the authors of ספרי מוסר who became popular with the large masses, and a careful reading of the first seventy pages of his של"ה (ed. Warsaw, 8°) will show that it is chiefly the קדושת הגוף and the hope consequent upon it which he is aiming at. Cf. especially page 19 b; 20 a seq.; 28 a seq.; 30 b seq.; 33 a seq.; 47 a seq.; 59 a seq.

166 See *Jerusalem,* II, p. 143, and Frumkin, 117.

167 See Azulai under these names. Cf. also Shlomel, 36 a and 41 d. See also the Responsa of R. Joseph Trani, I, 82. Cf. also Sambari, 161, with regard to the Loria Synagogue.

ELIJAH WILNA

1 גאון, "The Great One." The authorities of the Babylonian schools after the sixth century were also called the Gaonim (גאונים), "[their] Eminences." The title was also given afterwards to great Rabbis distinguished for their learning.

2 R. Joseph Caro (1488-1575) lived in Safed. The title of his code is שלחן ערוך, *Prepared Table.* This is a code of the Oral Law compiled from the Rabbinic literature.

3 קריה נאמנה, containing an account of the Jewish worthies of that city.

4 עלית אליהו.

5 A famous mystic of the sixteenth century, from Safed, who was the more admired the less his pupils understood him.

6 Hai was the last of the authorities called Gaon. With his death (1038) the schools of Babylon fell into decay and soon disappeared.

7 חגיגה, treating of the voluntary offerings brought by the pilgrims to Jerusalem.

8 גמרא, "Perfection or Supplementary Explanations." By this is understood the interpretation given to the Mishnah by the schools in Palestine and Babylon. See above, note 12 to the Chassidim.

9 See Dean Church's *St. Anselm,* from which this story is taken.

10 תוספתא, "Addition" (to the Mishnah), but also containing only the
sayings and discussions of the period of the Tannaim.

11 סדר עולם, "Order of the World," dealing with the Chronology of the
Bible, and dating from about the end of the second century.

12 These "Minor Tractates" include, among others, treatises on proselytes, on the laws concerning funerals, the writing of the Law, and
the like. Others are more of an edifying nature, treating of good
manners, conduct, etc.

13 קבלת גלות.

14 שמונה עשרה, "Eighteen." They are recited thrice a day, and form
the original germ of the prayers, from which a very rich liturgy developed in the course of time.

15 The titles of the old authorities from 70 B.C. to 500 A.C. See above,
note 12 to the Chassidim.

16 נשיא, אב בית דין, "Prince," or "Patriarch," religious head, of the
Jews (not political), and "Father (or president) of the Court of
Justice."

17 זבחים, מנחות, "Sacrifices," "Offerings." They treat of the laws relating to sacrifices and meal-offerings.

18 כלאים, the laws relating to diverse seeds and garments of diverse
sorts. Cf. Deut. xxii. 9-11.

19 מגיד, "Teller," a sort of travelling preacher.

20 לולב, "palm branch." Cf. Lev. xxiii. 40.

21 ישיבה, "High School," or "Academy," in which the Rabbinic literature is studied.

22 ישיבת עץ חיים.

23 סמבטיון, a mythical river which is supposed to stop its course on
Sabbath.

24 בחורים, sing. בחור, "Young man," by which term the Jews usually
understand the *alumni* of their Talmudical schools.

25 Levi b. Gershom (1286-1344) is generally regarded as the greatest successor of Maimonides. Besides his rationalistic commentaries on the
Bible, he wrote various treatises on metaphysics, mathematics, astronomy, medicine, etc.

26 בחינת עולם.

NACHMAN KROCHMAL

[1] R. Johanan b. Zaccai was a contemporary of the Apostles, and died about 110 A.D. He belonged to the peace party in opposition to the Zealots, and obtained permission from the Roman government to establish the school of Jamnia, which, after the destruction of the Temple, became the centre of Jewish religious life. See also p. 188.

[2] R. Saadiah Gaon was born in Egypt in 892, and died as the head of the school of Sura in Babylon in 942. He is known by his translations of and commentaries on the Bible, and many other works, especially his philosophical treatise *Creeds and Opinions*. He was also a great controversialist. Most of his polemical writings are directed against the Caraites (קראים) or "Scripturalists," a Jewish sect founded by Anan in the eighth century. They protested against the Oral Law, and denied Tradition. On the title "Gaon," see note 1 to Elijah Wilna.

[3] מורה נבוכים, *Moreh Nebuchim*, generally considered to be the greatest philosophical work by any Jewish thinker.

[4] R. Abraham Ibn Ezra, who spent some time in London, died about 1161. He is best known by his commentaries on the Bible. He was the first writer who doubted the unity of the book of Isaiah.

[5] תלמיד חבר.

[6] עיר מלאה חכמים וסופרים, meaning "sages" and "scribes," but used by later writers in the sense given in the text.

[7] בכורים, dealing with the laws relating to the firstfruits which were brought to the temple (Ex. xxiii. 19). The processions formed by the pilgrims are very vividly described after the said tractate by Delitzsch in his *Iris*, p. 190 *seq.* (English ed.). See also by the same author, *Jüdisches Handwerkerleben zur Zeit Jesu*, p. 66 seq.

[8] תענית, "Fast," or תעניות, "Fasts."

[9] סדר נזיקין, "Order of Damages," treating of the civil law of the Jews, the procedure of courts of justice, and kindred subjects. This Order also includes the tractate אבות, *Aboth* or "Sayings of the Fathers," which is very important for the study of Rabbinic doctrine and ethics.

[10] סדר טהרות, "Order of Purities," dealing with the laws regarding Levitical purity.

[11] מכילתא, ספרי, (or תורת כהנים), ספרא. These three works form the oldest Rabbinic commentary on Exodus, Leviticus, Numbers, and Deuteronomy. The authorities cited in these commentaries all belong to the period of the Tannaim. See above, note 12 to the Chassidim.

Constituting as they do, to a certain extent, one of the sources used by the *Gemara*, they are naturally indispensable for a scientific study of the Talmud.

12 הצופה, "*Hatsophe*," a spirited satire against the orthodox and especially against the then prevailing belief in the transmigration of souls taught by the mystical schools. The book is written in the purest biblical Hebrew.

13 מורה נבוכי הזמן.

14 מדרש, pl. מדרשים (*Midrashim*), "Research," "Researches," a name usually applied to the homiletical part of the Rabbinic literature. The most important collection of this kind is the *Midrash Rabbah* to the Pentateuch. The usual way of quoting it is *Genesis Rabbah*, *Exodus Rabbah*, and so on.

15 See above, note 12 to the Chassidim.

16 מינים, "Heretics," applied to the first Christians, and more so to certain Gnostic sects.

17 הלכה למשה מסיני, see below, p. 186 and *note*.

18 הגדה or הלכה—אגדה, "rule," "method,"—"narrative." The former deals with the legal side of the Scriptures, and is thus more of a juristic nature; the latter represents a collection of homilies having mostly as their text the historical and exhortatory parts of the Bible, and is thus more of an edifying character. The theological side of Judaism, as well as its ideal aspirations and Messianic hopes, find their expression in the Agadah. The two words are also used as adjectives, as *Halachic* (legalistic, juristic, and obligatory) and *Agadic* (poetic, edifying, and hyperbolic).

19 ערך מלין, a sort of encyclopædia to the Talmud, of which only the first letter appeared.

20 Menahem Azariah de Rossi, an Italian Jew who flourished in the first half of the sixteenth century. His great work, מאור עינים, *Meor Enayim*, "Light of the Eyes," is the first attempt made by a Jew to submit the statements of the Talmud to a critical examination, and to question the value of tradition in its historical records.

21 פרקי דר״ אליעזר.

22 Italian Jews of the fifteenth and seventeenth centuries. The one, Elijah Delmedigo, wrote an Examination of Religion, whilst his grandson, Joseph Solomon Delmedigo, wrote various pamphlets of a deeply sceptical character. See Geiger's Introduction to his *Melo Chofnayim* (Berlin, 1840).

Atheneum Paperbacks

HISTORY—AMERICAN

Atheneum Paperbacks

STUDIES IN AMERICAN NEGRO LIFE

Atheneum Paperbacks

HISTORY

HISTORY—ASIA

Atheneum Paperbacks

THE NEW YORK TIMES BYLINE BOOKS

CHINA *by Harry Schwartz*
RUSSIA *by Harrison E. Salisbury*
THE MIDDLE EAST *by Jay Walz*
AFRICA *by Waldemar A. Nielsen*
LATIN AMERICA *by Tad Szulc*
SOUTHEAST ASIA *by Tillman Durdin*

THE ADAMS PAPERS

TAP THE ADAMS PAPERS: DIARY AND AUTOBIOGRAPHY OF JOHN ADAMS
1,2,3,4   *edited by L. H. Butterfield, 4 vols.*
TAP THE ADAMS PAPERS: ADAMS FAMILY CORRESPONDENCE *edited by*
5,6 *L. H. Butterfield, 2 vols.*
TAP THE ADAMS PAPERS: DIARY OF CHARLES FRANCIS ADAMS *edited by*
7,8 *L. H. Butterfield, 2 vols.*
TAP THE ADAMS PAPERS: LEGAL PAPERS OF JOHN ADAMS *edited by*
9,10,11   *L. H. Butterfield, 3 vols.*

ECONOMICS AND BUSINESS

21   BIG BUSINESS LEADERS IN AMERICA *by W. Lloyd Warner and James Abegglen*
24   PROSPERITY AND DEPRESSION *by Gottfried Haberler*
34   THE DIPLOMACY OF ECONOMIC DEVELOPMENT *by Eugene R. Black*
47   ECONOMIC CONCENTRATION AND THE MONOPOLY PROBLEM *by Edward S. Mason*
78   THE ECONOMICS OF DEFENSE IN THE NUCLEAR AGE *by Charles J. Hitch and Roland N. McKean*
80   FOUNDATIONS OF ECONOMIC ANALYSIS *by Paul Anthony Samuelson*
86   THE CORPORATION IN MODERN SOCIETY *edited by Edward S. Mason*

Atheneum Paperbacks

LAW AND GOVERNMENT

DIPLOMACY AND INTERNATIONAL RELATIONS

Atheneum Paperbacks

Atheneum Paperbacks

Atheneum Paperbacks

THE WORLDS OF NATURE AND MAN

LITERATURE AND THE ARTS